Nurturing Relationships

Cover Art: *People at Sea* (Detail)
Menucha Yankelevitch, 2019, Jerusalem, Israel

Printed in the United States of America
© Copyrighted and published 2024
by the Rohr Jewish Learning Institute
832 Eastern Parkway, Brooklyn, NY 11213

718-221-6900
WWW.MYJLI.COM

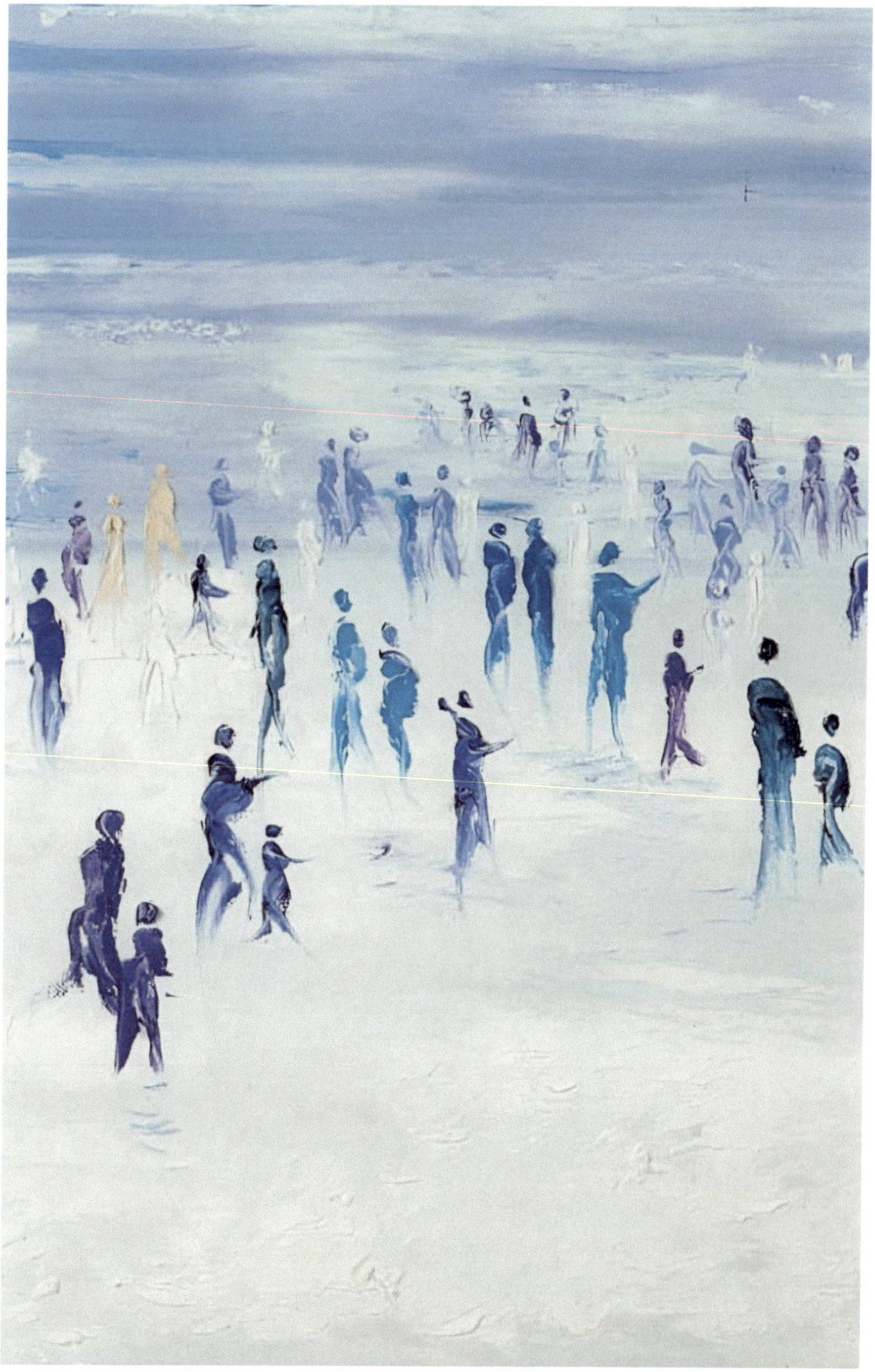

Nurturing Relationships

Jewish Wisdom for Building Deeper,
Richer Connections in All Your Relationships

COURSE
TEXTBOOK

The Rohr Jewish Learning Institute
gratefully acknowledges the pioneering
and ongoing support of

George and Pamela Rohr

Since its inception, the Rohr JLI has been
a beneficiary of the vision, generosity, care,
and concern of the Rohr family.

In the merit of the tens of thousands of hours
of Torah study by JLI students worldwide,
may they be blessed with health, *Yiddishe
nachas* from all their loved ones, and
extraordinary success in all their endeavors.

Citation Types

SCRIPTURE

The icon for Scripture is based on the images of a scroll and a spiral. The scroll is a literal reference; the spiral symbolizes Scripture's role as the singular source from which all subsequent Torah knowledge emanates.

SCRIPTURAL COMMENTARY

Throughout the ages, Jews have scrutinized the Torah's text, generating many commentaries.

TALMUD AND MIDRASH

The Talmud and Midrash record the teachings of the sages—fundamental links in the unbroken chain of the Torah's transmission going back to Mount Sinai.

TALMUDIC COMMENTARY

The layers of Talmudic teaching have been rigorously excavated in each era, resulting in a library of insightful commentaries.

JEWISH MYSTICISM

The mystics explore the inner, esoteric depths. The icon for mystical texts reflects the "*sefirot* tree" commonly present in kabbalistic charts.

CHARACTER AND VIRTUE

Often called *musar*, this literature provides character refinement and personal development strategies.

JEWISH PHILOSOPHY

Jewish philosophic texts shed light on life's big questions and demonstrate the relevance of Jewish teachings even as the sands of societal values continuously shift.

JEWISH LAW AND CUSTOM

The guidance that emerges from Scripture and the Talmud finds practical expression in Jewish law, known as *Halachah* ("the way"), alongside customs adopted by Jewish communities through the generations.

CHASIDUT

Chasidism's advent in the eighteenth century brought major, encouraging changes to Jewish life and outlook. Its teachings are akin to refreshing, life-sustaining waters from a continuously flowing well of the profoundest insights.

LITURGY

The texts of the Jewish prayer book burst with the full spectrum of human emotion, from joy to longing to contrition and to hope. They all share the authentic search for a meaningful encounter with G-d.

PERSPECTIVES

Personal, professional, and academic perspectives, expressed in essays, research papers, diaries, and other works, can often enhance appreciation for Torah ideas and the totality of the Jewish experience.

Contents

Foreword

IT IS NOT GOOD FOR THE HUMAN TO BE ALONE.
—GENESIS 2:18

This iconic quote from the Torah's opening chapters resonates deeply and addresses a truth that transcends time and culture. By their essential nature, humans are social creatures. Whether basking in sunshine or weathering a downpour, we seek the comfort of others by our side. Pain borne in isolation is an unbearable weight, and joy that cannot be shared loses its luster.

Today, a wealth of research into human behavior and emotion supplies support for this ancient insight. It demonstrates the significant degree to which robust relationships enhance quality of life and contribute to improved health, reduced stress, greater happiness, and even longevity—life itself.

Its importance notwithstanding, the adage that necessity is the mother of invention falls woefully short in the case of human relationships. Despite our inherent need for connection, forging and maintaining relationships is far from straightforward. Humans are complex and cast countless hurdles along the paths of interpersonal connection—a tendency exacerbated in today's technology-driven world, in which human bonds often suffer a lack of genuine investment.

Determined to help turn the tide, The Rohr Jewish Learning Institute (JLI) plumbed the Torah's timeless wisdom to collate its guidance on the topic of relationships, with far-reaching and practical application. This course, *Nurturing Relationships: Jewish Wisdom for Building Deeper, Richer Connection in All Your Relationships*, taps this ancient treasure for relatable insights covering the spectrum of adult-to-adult connection: intimate spousal ties, intricate family bonds, and the diversity of relationships with friends, coworkers, and acquaintances.

Nurturing Relationships empowers essential relationship skills that form the foundation of healthy connections: *empathy*, the cornerstone of meaningful connection that facilitates true understanding; *active listening* that leaps beyond hearing and enables deeper relationships; *disagreement management* via respect that is crucial for harmony; *positivity bias* that transforms relationships; *the art of influence* that is central to functioning communication; and *forgiveness and reconciliation* that enable healing and the restoring of bonds.

Nurturing Relationships is timely, essential, and lifesaving. In fact, the skills it offers lead us beyond personal life enhancement and directly contribute to cultivating a more connected, compassionate, and harmonious society.

Endorsements

The JLI's *Nurturing Relationships* course melds ancient spiritual wisdom with contemporary psychology, bolstering the core knowledge and skills needed to navigate interpersonal connection in the modern day. Mental health professionals will undoubtedly benefit from its profoundly deep, yet highly accessible and readily applicable approach.

DAVID H. ROSMARIN, PhD

Associate Professor, Department of Psychiatry, Harvard Medical School

Founder, Center for Anxiety

The evidence is clear that the quality of our relationships with other people has a profound impact on our health and well-being. *Nurturing Relationships* covers several of the processes that we know from research are critical to maintaining and improving relationships. This course will be of interest to anyone who has connections to other people—which should be all of us.

SHELLY L. GABLE, PhD

Professor and Chair, Department of Psychological and Brain Sciences, University of California, S. Barbara

I have been studying and teaching communication in personal relationships for the better part of 30 years. I wholeheartedly endorse this course, which offers an exceptional exploration of the essential skills needed to deepen and enrich human connections. *Nurturing Relationships* provides a powerful framework for fostering empathy, improving communication, resolving conflicts, and cultivating positive interactions. Each lesson addresses critical aspects of relationship-building, from the art of listening and the power of positivity to the significance of forgiveness and influence. Through thoughtful instruction, this course equips participants with the tools to create and maintain meaningful, resilient relationships in every area of life.

HARRY WEGER, JR., PhD

Professor and Associate Director, Nicholson School of Communication and Media, University of Central Florida

JLI and The Wellness Institute have identified a critical issue and designed a course certain to benefit all who engage with it. Our relationships are a critical part of our well-being, and learning the art and science of communication, with both Torah and psychology wisdom, will bring great benefit.

RONA NOVICK, PhD

Dean, Yeshiva University Azrieli Graduate School of Jewish Education

Associate Clinical Professor of Child Psychology, North Shore-LIJ Medical Center

We live in an oddly-fractured social world with rising loneliness that has severe consequences for our health and well-being. *Nurturing Relationships* teaches six key ways to defeat loneliness by winning in relationships. Built on the wisdom of the Jewish faith with contributions from modern psychological science, the course develops empathy, positivity, and forgiveness skills, among others. These are key tools in maintaining and repairing, when needed, our relationships. If you want to protect yourself and others from the pandemic of loneliness, learn how to Nurture Relationships!

LOREN TOUSSAINT, PhD

Professor of Psychology, Luther College

Chair, Templeton World Charity Foundation, Discover Forgiveness Advisory Council

President, Forgiveness Foundation

From a Torah perspective, there is no greater, more-significant concept than relationships. It is G-d's purpose for Creation, and it holds the possibility for us to become greater than ourselves. But relationships are hard. They require effort, insist on care, and demand responsibility. In my years of clinical practice, focusing on children, adolescents, and their parents, I cannot think of a single case where a relationship was not the core of the problem but also the source of eventual improvement. Sustaining relationships does require certain skills—from empathy, to listening, to forgiveness. I am grateful that the *Nurturing Relationships* course explores how to develop these all-important skills. I highly recommend it.

ETHAN EHRENBERG, PhD

Clinical Director of Pediatric Behavioral Health, Premium Health Center, Brooklyn, N.Y.

Genuine, warm, and robust interpersonal relationships are the strongest protective factor in maintaining our resilience and well-being and coping with stresses, particularly during turbulent times.

PROFESSOR DAVID FORBES, PhD

Professorial Fellow, Department of Psychiatry, University of Melbourne

Director, Phoenix Australia— Centre for Posttraumatic Mental Health

Nurturing Relationships is a needed antidote to the poisoning effects of polarization, isolation, and loneliness so many experience. This course will provide the insights and tools to help you and your clients to deepen, renew, and restore interpersonal relationships, a crucial foundation of mental health and well-being. With insights from traditional wisdom and recent research, this training program will provide the skills needed to heal, maintain, and grow your interpersonal connections.

NATHANIEL WADE, PhD

Professor of Psychology, Iowa State University

Coeditor, *The Handbook of Forgiveness*

Continuing Education Credits

FOR MEDICAL PRACTITIONERS

NEW YORK MEDICAL COLLEGE
A MEMBER OF THE TOURO COLLEGE AND UNIVERSITY SYSTEM
School of Medicine

ACCREDITATION STATEMENT

This activity has been planned and implemented in accordance with the accreditation requirements and policies of the **Accreditation Council for Continuing Medical Education (ACCME)** through the joint providership of New York Medical College and the Rohr Jewish Learning Institute. New York Medical College is accredited by the ACCME to provide continuing medical education for physicians.

CREDITS DESIGNATION

New York Medical College designates this live activity for a maximum of **9.0 AMA PRA Category I Credits ™**. Physicians should claim only the credit commensurate with the extent of their participation in the activity.

AMERICAN DISABILITY ACT STATEMENT

New York Medical College fully complies with the legal requirements of the Americans with Disabilities Act. If you require special assistance, please submit your request in writing, thirty (30) days in advance of the activity, to continuingeducation@myjli.com

CONFLICT OF INTEREST DISCLOSURE POLICY

The "**Conflict of Interest Disclosure Policy**" of New York Medical College requires that faculty participating in any CME activity disclose to the audience any relationship(s) with a pharmaceutical product or device company. Any presenter whose disclosed relationships prove to create a conflict of interest, with regard to their contribution to the activity, will not be permitted to present.

New York Medical College also requires that faculty participating in any CME activity disclose to the audience when discussing any unlabeled or investigational use of any commercial product or device not yet approved for use in the United States. New York Medical College and ACCME staff have no conflicts of interest with commercial interests related directly or indirectly to this educational activity.

DISCLOSURE OF COMMERCIAL SUPPORT AND THE UNLABELED USE OF A COMMERCIAL PRODUCT

No member of the planning committee and no member of the faculty for this event has a financial interest or other relationship with any commercial product.

The members of the Planning Committee are:

Edward I. Reichman, M.D.—*Reviewer*
Professor of Emergency Medicine and Epidemiology and Population Health,
Albert Einstein College of Medicine

Sigrid Pechenik, PsyD—*Planner*
Chief Clinical Advisor,
The Wellness Institute

Mindy Wallach—*Course Administrator*
The Rohr Jewish Learning Institute/The Wellness Institute

Disclosure: The members of the Planning Committee present no relevant conflict of interest.

To obtain credit for attending the course (9 credits max.): Medical doctors should complete the registration form at **www.myjli.com/cme at the beginning of the course**. Mental health professionals should inform their instructor that they are seeking credit and provide them with their full professional name, professional credentials, and state(s) they are licensed to practice in.

Continuing Education Credits

FOR PSYCHOLOGISTS AND MENTAL HEALTH PROFESSIONALS

ACCREDITATION STATEMENT

The Wellness Institute is approved by the **American Psychological Association** to sponsor continuing education for psychologists. The Wellness Institute maintains responsibility for this program and its content.

CREDITS PER SESSION: 1.5

BEHAVIORAL LESSON OBJECTIVES FOR PSYCHOLOGISTS

LESSON 1

Discuss the importance of empathy and its role in developing, strengthening, and maintaining successful relationships.

LESSON 2

Describe active listening and explain the positive impact of listening well on our relationships.

LESSON 3

Explain causes of negative escalation of disagreements, and describe a mindset for accord, compromise, and reconciliation.

LESSON 4

Explain the psychology of the Fundamental Attribution Error and how to develop a cognitive bias correction to achieve a "benefit of the doubt" viewpoint.

LESSON 5

Describe empathetic and effective methods of giving (and receiving) constructive criticism.

LESSON 6

Discuss the altruistic and personal benefits of forgiveness and its role in strengthening relationships.

The Wellness Institute is recognized by the **New York State** Education Department's State Board for Psychology as an approved provider of continuing education for **Licensed Psychologists** #PSY-0220; by the New York State Education Department's State Board for Social Work as an approved provider of continuing education for **Licensed Master Social Workers (LMSWs)** and **Licensed Clinical Social Workers (LCSWs)** #SW-0741; by the New York State Education Department's State Board for Mental Health Practitioners as an approved provider of continuing education for **Licensed Mental Health Counselors (LMHCs)** #MHC-0270 and **Licensed Marriage and Family Therapists (LMFTs)** #MFT-0114 in New York

Psychologists, Social Workers, LMFTs, and LPC/LMHCs in many states can satisfy their CE requirements by participating in this course. To verify if your profession is covered, inquire via email continuingeducation@myjli.com. Include your name, credentials, and state(s) you are licensed to practice in.

1

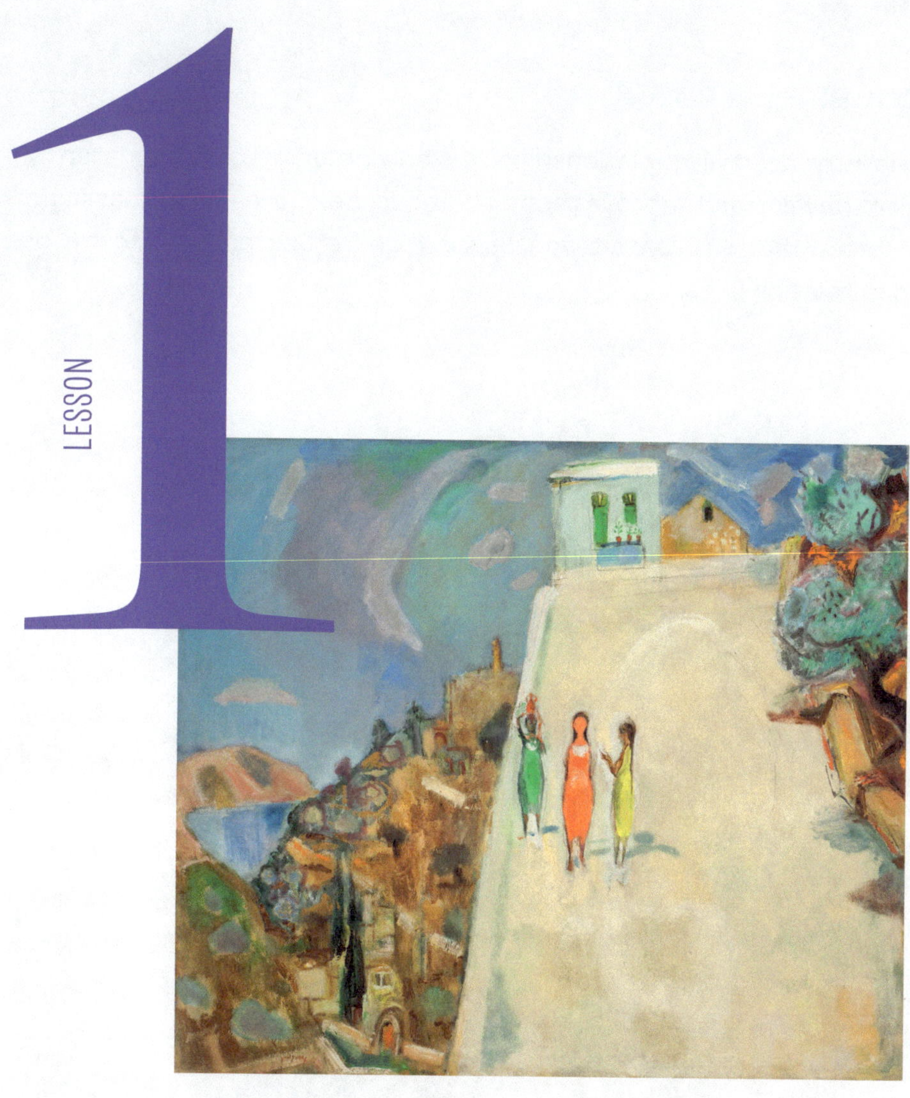

THE ART OF EMPATHY

Empathy is the cornerstone of meaningful connections, allowing us to truly understand and support those around us. How can we cultivate a deeper sense of empathy in our daily interactions?

I. COURSE INTRODUCTION

Life is interlaced with relationships. It is only natural that we constantly seek to develop and improve them. This course explores the remarkable assistance that Judaism's teachings provide for upgrading all forms of human relationships.

THE ARTIST'S FAMILY
Leonid Balaklav, oil on canvas, 2015, Israel

No to Loneliness

Genesis 2:18

וַיֹּאמֶר ה' אֱלֹקִים: לֹא טוֹב הֱיוֹת
הָאָדָם לְבַדּוֹ, אֶעֱשֶׂה לּוֹ עֵזֶר כְּנֶגְדּוֹ.

G-d* said, "It is not good for the human to be alone;
I shall make for him a corresponding counterpart."

*Throughout this book, "G-d" and "L-rd" are written with a hyphen instead of an "o" (both
in our own translations and when quoting others). This is one way we accord reverence to
the sacred Divine name. This also reminds us that, even as we seek G-d, He transcends any
human effort to describe His reality.

JEWISH WEDDING
Issachar Ber Ryback
(Ukraine, 1897–1937), oil
on board, c. 1930, Paris

EXERCISE 1.1

Identify three typical relationship stressors. Try to encapsulate each of these in just a word or two:

1.

2.

3.

TEXT 2

Acquire a Friend

Mishnah, Avot 1:6

יְהוֹשֻׁעַ בֶּן פְּרַחְיָה אוֹמֵר: עֲשֵׂה לְךָ רַב, וּקְנֵה לְךָ חָבֵר, וֶהֱוֵי דָן אֶת כָּל הָאָדָם לְכַף זְכוּת.

Yehoshua ben Perachyah would say, "Appoint a teacher for yourself, acquire a friend for yourself, and judge all people favorably."

**AVOT
(ETHICS OF THE
FATHERS; PIRKEI AVOT)**

A 6-chapter work on Jewish ethics that is studied widely by Jewish communities, especially during the summer. The first 5 chapters are from the Mishnah, tractate Avot. Avot differs from the rest of the Mishnah in that it does not focus on legal subjects; it is a collection of the sages' wisdom on topics related to character development, ethics, healthy living, piety, and the study of Torah.

THE CITY SCENE
H. Weiss, oil on canvas

FIGURE 1.1

Beliefs Predict Participation

Nancy E. Newall, et al., "Causal Beliefs, Social Participation, and Loneliness among Older Adults: A Longitudinal Study," *Journal of Social and Personal Relationships* 26:2–3 (March/May 2009), pp. 273–290

BELIEF

Success depends on effort

ACTION

Investment of time and energy

OUTCOME

More connection

Circles of Support

Judith Snow, *What's Really Worth Doing and How to Do It: A Book for People Who Love Someone Labeled Disabled (Possibly Yourself)* (Toronto: Inclusion Press, 1994)

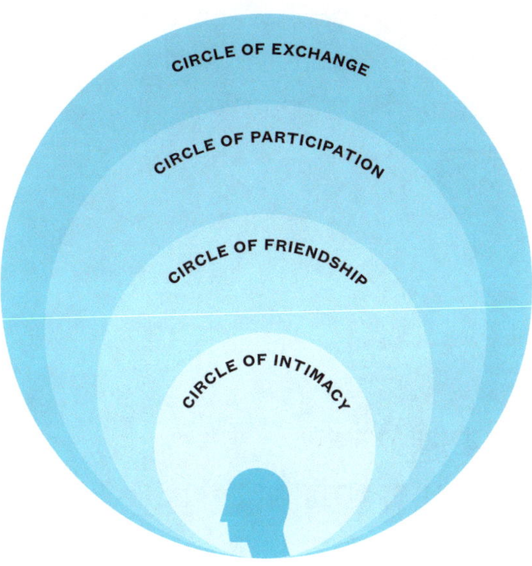

THE CIRCLE OF INTIMACY	The people you know well and spend much time interacting with, often at home. You trust these people with the most personal parts of your life. You can't imagine your life without them.
THE CIRCLE OF FRIENDSHIP	The people who are close to you but not intimately. You share with them your dreams, good news, and troubles.
THE CIRCLE OF PARTICIPATION	The people you interact with frequently: at work, religious services, neighborhood groups, or clubs.
THE CIRCLE OF EXCHANGE	The people paid to be in your life: a doctor, therapist, or hairdresser.

II. SOUL CONNECTION

"Whatever you find hateful when done to you, do not do to your fellow." A foremost Talmudic sage presented this as "the entire Torah." A perplexing statement, perhaps, but a deeper exploration of the two spirits within each person—and their contradictory approaches to relationships—will provide a powerful soul-based understanding of this teaching that revolutionizes how we approach relationships.

TEXT 3A

The Golden Rule

Talmud, Shabbat 31a

אָמַר לוֹ: דַּעֲלָךְ סַנִי לַחֲבֵרָךְ לֹא תַעֲבִיד.

זוֹ הִיא כָּל הַתּוֹרָה כֻּלָּה, וְאִידָךְ פֵּרוּשָׁהּ הוּא, זִיל גְּמֹר.

Hillel told him, "Whatever you find hateful when done to you, do not do to your fellow. This is all of Torah in its entirety; the rest is commentary. Go study the rest!"

BABYLONIAN TALMUD

A literary work of monumental proportions that draws upon the legal, spiritual, intellectual, ethical, and historical traditions of Judaism. The 37 tractates of the Babylonian Talmud contain the teachings of the Jewish sages from the period after the destruction of the 2nd Temple through the 5th century CE. It has served as the primary vehicle for the transmission of the Oral Law and the education of Jews over the centuries; it is the entry point for all subsequent legal, ethical, and theological Jewish scholarship.

ON ONE FOOT
Shoshana Brombacher,
pastel and ink on paper,
2008, Germany

Two Interpretations

Rashi, ad loc.

RABBI SHLOMO YITZCHAKI (RASHI)
1040–1105

"רֵעֲךָ וְרֵעַ אָבִיךָ אַל תַּעֲזֹב" (מִשְׁלֵי כז, י) – זֶה הַקָּדוֹשׁ בָּרוּךְ הוּא. אַל תַּעֲבֹר עַל דְּבָרָיו, שֶׁהֲרֵי עָלֶיךָ שָׂנאוּי שֶׁיַּעֲבֹר חֲבֵרְךָ עַל דְּבָרֶיךָ.

לִישָׁנָא אַחֲרִינָא: חֲבֵרְךָ מַמָּשׁ, כְּגוֹן גְּזֵלָה, גְּנֵבָה, נִיאוּף, וְרֹב הַמִּצְוֹת.

G-d is referred to in the Scriptures as our "fellow," as in the verse, "Do not forsake your Fellow and your father's Fellow" (PROVERBS 27:10). Hillel intended that we should not disregard G-d's wishes, for we hate it when our Fellow ignores our wishes.

An alternate interpretation: Hillel referred quite literally to our fellow humans, indicating the need to avoid robbery, theft, and adultery, and to obey the numerous other interpersonal *mitzvot*.

Most noted biblical and Talmudic commentator. Born in Troyes, France, Rashi studied in the famed *yeshivot* of Mainz and Worms. His commentaries on the Pentateuch and the Talmud, which focus on the straightforward meaning of the text, appear in virtually every edition of the Talmud and Bible.

EXERCISE 1.2

As a rule, Rashi provides a single explanation or interpretation. When he offers two, it is because each interpretation carries a unique disadvantage.

Together with a partner, analyze and discuss the precise wording of Hillel's statement and try to identify the difficulty with each of Rashi's explanations.

**THE DIFFICULTY WITH
THE FIRST EXPLANATION:**

**THE DIFFICULTY WITH
THE SECOND EXPLANATION:**

TEXT 4

Two Conflicting Spirits

Ecclesiastes 3:21

מִי יוֹדֵעַ, רוּחַ בְּנֵי הָאָדָם הָעֹלָה הִיא לְמָעְלָה,
וְרוּחַ הַבְּהֵמָה הַיֹּרֶדֶת הִיא לְמַטָּה לָאָרֶץ.

How many understand that the spirit of
the human ascends on high while the spirit
of the beast descends to the earth?

I AND THE VILLAGE
Marc Chagall, oil on canvas, 1911
(Museum of Modern Art, New York)

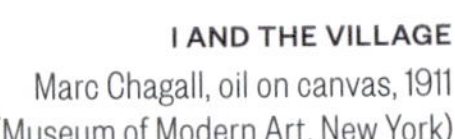

Rabbi Manis Friedman:
Does the natural soul
want to sin, or is it after
something more primal?
myjli.com/relationships

TEXT 5

The Inner Battle

Rabbi Shneur Zalman of Liadi, *Tanya*, *Likutei Amarim*, ch. 9

וּכְמוֹ שְׁנֵי מְלָכִים נִלְחָמִים עַל עִיר אַחַת, שֶׁכָּל אֶחָד רוֹצֶה לְכָבְשָׁהּ וְלִמְלֹךְ עָלֶיהָ, דְּהַיְינוּ לְהַנְהִיג יוֹשְׁבֶיהָ כִּרְצוֹנוֹ, וְשֶׁיִּהְיוּ סָרִים לְמִשְׁמַעְתּוֹ בְּכָל אֲשֶׁר יִגְזוֹר עֲלֵיהֶם.

כָּךְ שְׁתֵּי הַנְּפָשׁוֹת, הָאֱלֹקִית וְהַחִיּוּנִית הַבַּהֲמִית שֶׁמֵּהַקְּלִפָּה, נִלְחָמוֹת זוֹ עִם זוֹ עַל הַגּוּף וְכָל אֵבָרָיו.

Imagine two kings locked in battle, each desperate to gain control over the same city, rule its inhabitants according to his will, and ensure that they obey his every decree.

That same battle rages within each of us, between our two souls. Our G-dly soul and its rival the animalistic soul wage war over our bodies and all its limbs.

TEXT 6

Primary vs. Secondary

Siddur, Morning Blessings

אֱלֹקַי, נְשָׁמָה שֶׁנָּתַתָּ בִּי טְהוֹרָה הִיא.

My G-d, the soul You placed within me is pure.

RABBI SHNEUR ZALMAN OF LIADI (ALTER REBBE) 1745–1812

Chasidic rebbe, Halachic authority, and founder of the Chabad movement. The Alter Rebbe was born in Liozna, Belarus, and was among the principal students of the Magid of Mezeritch. His numerous works include the *Tanya*, an early classic containing the fundamentals of Chabad Chasidism; and *Shulchan Aruch HaRav*, an expanded and reworked code of Jewish law.

SIDDUR

The siddur is the Jewish prayer book. It was originally developed by the sages of the Great Assembly in the 4th century BCE and later reconstructed by Rabban Gamliel after the destruction of the Second Temple. Various authorities continued to add prayers, from then until contemporary times. It includes praise of G-d, requests for personal and national needs, selections from the Bible, and much else. Various Jewish communities have slightly different versions of the siddur.

TEXT 7

Soul Arithmetic

Rabbi Dovber of Lubavitch, cited in *Hayom Yom*, 20 Tevet

אַז אײַנער רעדט מיט דעם אַנדערען בְּעִנְיְנֵי
עֲבוֹדָה און זײ לערנען צוזאַמען, איז דאָס צווײ
נֶפֶשׁ אֱלֹקִית אויף אײן נֶפֶשׁ הַטִּבְעִית.

When two people discuss spiritual growth
and study Torah together, there are two
G-dly souls against one natural soul.

**RABBI DOVBER
OF LUBAVITCH
(MITELER REBBE)
1773–1827**

Rabbi Dovber was the
eldest son of and successor
to Rabbi Shneur Zalman of
Liadi and greatly expanded
upon and developed his
father's groundbreaking
teachings. He was the 1st
Chabad rebbe to live in
the village of Lubavitch.
Dedicated to the welfare
of Russian Jewry, at that
time confined to the Pale of
Settlement, he established
Jewish agricultural colonies.
His most notable works on
Chasidic thought include
*Shaar Hayichud, Torat
Chayim,* and *Imrei Binah.*

THE DOORS OF BINAH
Esther Pam Zibell

TEXT 8

The Baron and the Pike

Rabbi Adin Even-Yisrael (Steinsaltz), *Simple Words*
(New York: Simon & Schuster, 1999), pp. 190–191

There is a Jewish folktale that illustrates how vague the meaning of the word "love" can be, and also demonstrates some of the basic problems in statements such as "I love you."

Once upon a time, a fisherman caught a large pike, and when he pulled the fish out of the water and saw its size, he said, "This is wonderful! I'll take it to the Baron; he loves pike."

The poor fish says to himself, "There's some hope for me yet."

The fisherman brings the fish to the manor house, and the guard says, "What do you have?"

"A pike."

"Great," says the guard. "The Baron loves pike."

The fish feels that there is some corroboration of the facts.

The fisherman enters the palace, and though the fish can hardly breathe, he still has hope: the Baron loves pike. He is brought into the kitchen, and all the cooks exclaim how much the Baron loves pike. The fish is placed on a table, and the

RABBI ADIN EVEN-ISRAEL (STEINSALTZ) 1937–2020

Talmudist, author, and philosopher. Rabbi Steinsaltz is considered one of the foremost Jewish thinkers of the 20th century. A resident of Jerusalem, Rabbi Steinsaltz was the founder of the Israel Institute for Talmudic Publications, a society dedicated to the translation and elucidation of the Talmud, and he authored numerous works about the Talmud and Jewish mysticism. Praised by *Time* magazine as a "once-in-a-millennium scholar," he was awarded the Israel Prize for his contributions to Jewish study.

Baron himself enters and gives instructions, "Cut off the tail, cut off the head, and slit it this way."

With his last breath, the fish cries out in great despair, "Why did you lie? You don't love pike, you love yourself!"

The Soul of the Torah

Rabbi Shneur Zalman of Liadi, *Tanya*, *Likutei Amarim*, ch. 32

וְזֶהוּ שֶׁאָמַר הִלֵּל הַזָּקֵן עַל קִיּוּם מִצְוָה זוֹ:
"זֶהוּ כָּל הַתּוֹרָה כֻּלָּה, וְאִידָךְ פֵּרוּשָׁא הוּא כוּ'".

כִּי יְסוֹד וְשֹׁרֶשׁ כָּל הַתּוֹרָה הוּא לְהַגְבִּיהַּ
וּלְהַעֲלוֹת הַנֶּפֶשׁ עַל הַגּוּף.

This is what Hillel the Elder meant when he stated regarding the mitzvah to love your fellow, "This is the entire Torah; the rest is commentary," etc.

For the foundation and root of the entire Torah is to prioritize and raise the Divine soul over the body.

III. EMBRACING EMPATHY

Torah sources discuss distinct internal experiences upon which modern psychology has bestowed the respective terms *cognitive empathy* and *affective empathy*.

Cognitive empathy is the ability to recognize and understand another person's emotions. Affective empathy (sometimes referred to as emotional empathy) involves having a matching or corresponding emotional reaction to the feelings of another individual.

Joseph and the Chamberlains

TEXT 10A   Genesis 40:5–8

וַיַּחַלְמוּ חֲלוֹם שְׁנֵיהֶם, אִישׁ חֲלֹמוֹ בְּלַיְלָה אֶחָד,
אִישׁ כְּפִתְרוֹן חֲלֹמוֹ, הַמַּשְׁקֶה וְהָאֹפֶה אֲשֶׁר
לְמֶלֶךְ מִצְרַיִם אֲשֶׁר אֲסוּרִים בְּבֵית הַסֹּהַר.

וַיָּבֹא אֲלֵיהֶם יוֹסֵף בַּבֹּקֶר, וַיַּרְא אֹתָם וְהִנָּם זֹעֲפִים.

וַיִּשְׁאַל אֶת סְרִיסֵי פַרְעֹה אֲשֶׁר אִתּוֹ בְמִשְׁמַר
בֵּית אֲדֹנָיו לֵאמֹר, מַדּוּעַ פְּנֵיכֶם רָעִים הַיּוֹם.

וַיֹּאמְרוּ אֵלָיו, חֲלוֹם חָלַמְנוּ וּפֹתֵר אֵין אֹתוֹ, וַיֹּאמֶר
אֲלֵהֶם יוֹסֵף, הֲלוֹא לֵאלֹקִים פִּתְרֹנִים, סַפְּרוּ נָא לִי.

Each of them—the cupbearer and the baker
for the king of Egypt, who were imprisoned
in the dungeon—dreamed a dream; each

one had his dream on the same night, and
each dream had its own meaning.

Joseph came to them in the morning and
saw them—they looked disturbed.

He questioned Pharaoh's chamberlains, who
were with him in the prison of his master's house,
asking, "Why are your faces poorly today?"

They told him, "We dreamed a dream,
and there is no interpreter for it."

Joseph responded to them, "Do interpretations
not belong to G-d? Tell them now to me."

TEXT 10B

Joseph's Daily Empathy

Rabbi Don Yitzchak Abarbanel, ad loc.

וְאָמַר מִלַּת "הַיּוֹם" - כְּלוֹמַר, עִם הֱיוֹתוֹ מִן הַדִּין שֶׁלִּהְיוֹתְכֶם
אֲסוּרִים יִהְיֶה לָכֶם לֵב רַע וּפָנִים נִזְעָמִים, הִנֵּה לְפִי שֶׁרָאִיתִי
שִׁנּוּי לַיּוֹם הַזֶּה עַל שְׁאָר הַיָּמִים שֶׁהֱיִיתֶם אֲסוּרִים, לָכֵן אֶשְׁאָל.

Joseph specified "today." Joseph understood
and expected that individuals suffering
incarceration would be in a foul mood and
look glum. However, he asked because he
noticed a distinction between that specific day
and every prior day of their incarceration.

TEXT 11

Cognitive and Emotive Empathy

Brené Brown, *Atlas of the Heart: Mapping Meaningful Connection and the Language of Human Experience*
(New York: Random House, 2021), pp. 120–121

Empathy, the most powerful tool of compassion, is an emotional skill set that allows us to understand what someone is experiencing and to reflect back that understanding. . . .

Most researchers agree that there are at least two elements to empathy: cognitive empathy and affective empathy.

Cognitive empathy, sometimes called perspective taking or mentalizing, is the ability to recognize and understand another person's emotions.

Affective empathy, often called experience sharing, is one's own emotional attunement with another person's experience.

**BRENÉ BROWN
1965–**

Social worker and author. A native of Texas, Brené Brown received her PhD in social work from the University of Houston, where she currently serves as a professor. She is the author of a number of self-help books and is known for her work on topics of shame, vulnerability, and leadership.

Why do we need a natural soul? Doesn't it just take us away from G-d? **Rabbi Shais Taub** explains.
myjli.com/relationships

Empathy at All Costs

TEXT 12

The Rebbe, Rabbi Menachem Mendel Schneerson,
Torat Menachem 5734:1 (74), pp. 365–366

וְלִכְאוֹרָה: כֵּיוָן שֶׁיּוֹסֵף הָיָה בְּמַצָּב כָּזֶה שֶׁגָּרְמוּ לוֹ עָוֶל הֲכִי גָּדוֹל בְּכָךְ שֶׁמְּכָרוּהוּ לְמִצְרַיִם, וּבְמִצְרַיִם גּוּפָא . . . שָׂמוּ אוֹתוֹ בְּבֵית הַסֹּהַר לְלֹא עָוֹן בְּכַפּוֹ - הֲרֵי מִטֶּבַע הַדְּבָרִים הָיָה צָרִיךְ לִהְיוֹת מְאוּכְזָב וּמְמוּרְמָר, "בְּרוֹגֶז עַל הָעוֹלָם". . . וְאַף עַל פִּי כֵן, בִּרְאוֹתוֹ בְּבֵית הַסֹּהַר אֶת סָרִיסֵי פַרְעֹה, שַׂר הַמַּשְׁקִים וְשַׂר הָאוֹפִים, שֶׁ"הִנָּם זֹעֲפִים" - פָּנָה אֲלֵיהֶם וְשָׁאַל אוֹתָם: "מַדּוּעַ פְּנֵיכֶם רָעִים הַיּוֹם"? . . .

וְהַהַסְבָּרָה בָּזֶה: יוֹסֵף הָיָה מִזַּרְעוֹ שֶׁל אַבְרָהָם "אֲשֶׁר יְצַוֶּה אֶת בָּנָיו וְאֶת בֵּיתוֹ אַחֲרָיו לַעֲשׂוֹת צְדָקָה וּמִשְׁפָּט" (בְּרֵאשִׁית יח, יט) . . . וְלָכֵן בִּרְאוֹתוֹ בְּרִיָּה שֶׁל הַקָּדוֹשׁ בָּרוּךְ הוּא בְּמַעֲמָד וּמַצָּב שֶׁאֵינוֹ בְּשִׂמְחָה - תְּמוּרַת זֶה שֶׁצָּרִיךְ לִהְיוֹת בְּשִׂמְחָה מִצַּד עֶצֶם הֱיוֹתוֹ בְּרִיָּה שֶׁל הַקָּדוֹשׁ בָּרוּךְ הוּא, שֶׁזּוֹהִי תַּכְלִית הַשְּׁלֵמוּת - הִנֵּה כֵּיוָן שֶׁהוּא רָאָה זֹאת, הֲרֵי זוֹ הוֹכָחָה שֶׁזֶּהוּ עִנְיָן הַשַּׁיָּיךְ אֵלָיו, וְלָכֵן מִיָּד הִשְׁתַּדֵּל לְנַסּוֹת לַעֲזוֹר.

Joseph had been made to suffer the greatest injustices. He was sold as a slave in Egypt and . . . then jailed without guilt. One might have expected him to be embittered, angry at the world. . . . Nevertheless, when he noticed that Pharaoh's chief cupbearer and baker looked unusually distraught, he approached them and inquired, "Why are your faces poorly today?" . . .

RABBI MENACHEM MENDEL SCHNEERSON 1902–1994

The towering Jewish leader of the 20th century, known as "the Lubavitcher Rebbe," or simply as "the Rebbe." Born in southern Ukraine, the Rebbe escaped Nazi-occupied Europe, arriving in the U.S. in June 1941. The Rebbe inspired and guided the revival of traditional Judaism after the European devastation, impacting virtually every Jewish community the world over. The Rebbe often emphasized that the performance of just one additional good deed could usher in the era of Mashiach. The Rebbe's scholarly talks and writings have been printed in more than 200 volumes.

Joseph descended from Abraham, regarding whom
G-d proclaimed that "he would command his children
and his household after him to keep G-d's ways by
doing righteousness and justice" (GENESIS 18:19).
. . . Consequently, upon seeing one of G-d's creatures
in a mood quite the contrary of joyful (after all, the
mere recognition that a person is a creation of the
Holy One should be sufficient cause for joy), Joseph
took the fact that the matter had caught his attention
as evidence that the matter was relevant to him.
Therefore, he immediately sought to be of assistance.

**JOSEPH'S BROTHERS
THROW HIM INTO THE PIT**
Yoram Raanan, Israel

Understand the Needy

Midrash Tehilim 41

"אַשְׁרֵי מַשְׂכִּיל אֶל דָּל" (תְּהִלִים מא, ב): . . .

מַהוּ "מַשְׂכִּיל"? שֶׁמִּסְתַּכֵּל וְחוֹשֵׁב עָלָיו הֵיאַךְ לְהַחֲיוֹתוֹ.

כֵּיצַד? אִם הָיָה אָדָם גָּדוֹל וְיוֹרֵד מִנְכָסָיו, הוּא הוֹלֵךְ אֶצְלוֹ וְאוֹמֵר לוֹ: שָׁמַעְתִּי שֶׁיְּרוּשָׁה בָּאָה לְךָ בְּמָקוֹם פְּלוֹנִי, וְשֶׁחַיָּב לְךָ אִישׁ פְּלוֹנִי כָּךְ וְכָךְ, אִם רְצוֹנְךָ טוֹל מִמֶּנִּי, וְלִכְשֶׁתַּגִּיעַ לְיָדְךָ אוֹתָהּ הַיְרֻשָׁה, אוֹ כְּשֶׁיְּפָרַע לְךָ אִישׁ פְּלוֹנִי חוֹבְךָ, אַתָּה פּוֹרֵעַ לִי.

זֶהוּ "מַשְׂכִּיל אֶל דָּל".

“Praised be one who understands those who are in need” (PSALMS 41:2). . . .

What does “understand” mean in this context? It refers to one who carefully considers and reflects on a strategy to sustain the person in need.

For example, when a wealthy person faces a drastic downturn, the understanding benefactor visits the formerly wealthy person and says, “I heard that an inheritance will be coming your way in such-and-such a location and that so-and-so owes you money. If you wish, accept this sum from me, and when that inheritance comes to you, or when that debtor repays the debt, you can pay me back.”

This person *understands* those who are in need.

MIDRASH TEHILIM

A rabbinic commentary on the book of Psalms. Midrash is the designation of a particular genre of rabbinic literature usually forming a running commentary on specific books of the Bible. This particular Midrash provides textual exegeses and develops and illustrates the principles of the book of Psalms.

TEXT 14A

Two Methods for Anxiety

Talmud, Yoma 75a

רַבִּי אַמִי וְרַבִּי אַסִי:

חַד אָמַר: יַשְׁחֶנָּה מִדַּעְתּוֹ.

וְחַד אָמַר: יְשִׂיחֶנָּה לַאֲחֵרִים.

Rabbis Ami and Asi each suggested a method for handling anxiety:

One said, "Cast it from the mind."

The other said, "Speak it over with others."

ECHOES OF EMPATHY
Edith Torres, acrylic on canvas, 2023, Texas

TEXT 14B

"Others" Qualified

Rabbi Menachem Mendel of Lubavitch,
cited in *Hayom Yom,* 25 Sivan

"לַאֲחֵרִים" רַק בְּגוּף.

אֲבָל מְאוּחָדִים אִתּוֹ עִמּוֹ.

שֶׁמַּרְגִּישִׁים אֶת עִנְיָנוֹ.

They are "others" only in the bodily sense.

However, they are wholly united with you.

For they feel your reality.

**RABBI MENACHEM
MENDEL OF LUBAVITCH
(*TZEMACH TZEDEK*)
1789-1866**

Chasidic rebbe and noted
author. The *Tzemach
Tzedek* was the 3rd
leader of the Chabad
Chasidic movement
and a noted authority
on Jewish law. His
numerous works include
Halachic responsa,
Chasidic discourses, and
kabbalistic writings.
Active in the communal
affairs of Russian
Jewry, he worked to
alleviate the plight of
the cantonists, Jewish
children kidnapped
to serve in the czar's
army. He passed away
in Lubavitch, leaving 7
sons and 2 daughters.

TEXT 15

A Tale of Emotional Empathy

Rabbi Yehudah ben Shmuel Hachasid, *Sefer Chasidim* 434

מַעֲשֶׂה בְּאָדָם אֶחָד שֶׁהָיָה נוֹהֵג בְּעַצְמוֹ כְּשֶׁהָיָה אָדָם אָבֵל,
הָיָה חוֹזֵר לְבֵיתוֹ בְּלֹא מִנְעָלִים לְהִצְטַעֵר עִם הָאָבֵל.

וְהָיָה אוֹתוֹ יוֹם שָׂמֵחַ בּוֹ יוֹם שֶׁנִּקְבְּצוּ כָּל הַקְּהִילוֹת
לְאוֹתוֹ הָעִיר, וְיוֹם ט' בְּאָב הָיָה. וְהָלְכוּ הַכֹּל יְחֵפִים.

וְהֶרְאָה הַקָּדוֹשׁ בָּרוּךְ הוּא שֶׁהַטּוֹב וְהַיָּשָׁר בְּעֵינָיו
עָשָׂה, אַף עַל פִּי שֶׁלֹּא הוּצְרַךְ לַעֲשׂוֹת.

**RABBI YEHUDAH BEN
SHMUEL HACHASID
1140-1217**

Mystic and ethicist. Born
in Speyer, Germany, he was
a rabbi, mystic, and one of
the initiators of Chasidei
Ashkenaz, a Jewish German
moralist movement
that stressed piety and
asceticism. Rabbi Yehudah
settled in Regensburg in
1195. He is best known
for his work *Sefer
Chasidim,* on the ethics
of day-to-day concerns.

There was an incident concerning a man with a unique custom: whenever a member of his community would return [from the burying] of a loved one, this fellow accompanied the mourner home without shoes—to share in the pain of the mourner [who wasn't wearing shoes, as the prescribed expression of intense mourning].

When he passed away, it happened to be an occasion for which Jewish communities from the surrounding areas gathered in his city—for the day of his passing was the <u>ninth of Av</u> [the annual day of mourning for the destruction of the Temple, when Jews refrain from wearing leather footwear]. And so it happened that *everyone* was without shoes on the day of his death.

With this, G-d publicly demonstrated that he had acted appropriately and admirably, though he had no obligation to act that way.

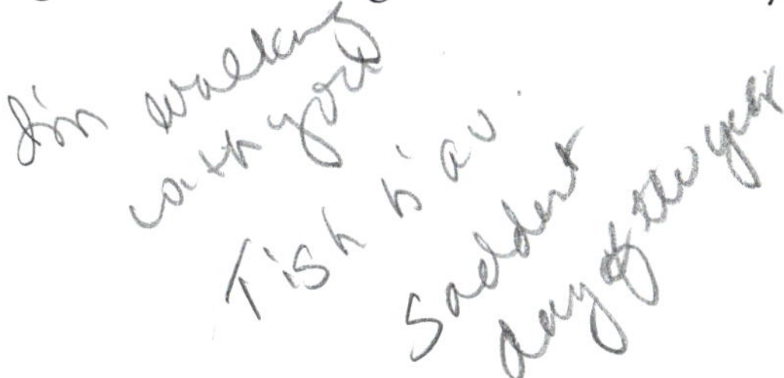

What characteristic made Moses the greatest Jewish leader who ever lived? Discover the answer with **Rabbi Moshe Bryski**. myjli.com/relationships

IV. PRACTICING EMPATHY

Harmonizing soul consciousness with tangible recommendations serves as a potent formula to introduce more empathy into our relationships.

FIGURE 1.3

Empathy Misses

Brené Brown, *Atlas of the Heart: Mapping Meaningful Connection and the Language of Human Experience* (New York: Random House, 2021), pp. 126–127

	EXAMPLES
SYMPATHY VS. EMPATHY	I feel sorry for you.
JUDGMENT	You *should* feel shame.
DISAPPOINTMENT	You've let me down.
DISCHARGING DISCOMFORT WITH BLAME	This feels terrible. Who can we blame? You?
MINIMIZE/AVOID	Let's make this go away.
COMPARING/COMPETING	If you think that's bad!
SPEAKING TRUTH TO POWER	Don't upset people or make them uncomfortable.
ADVICE GIVING/PROBLEM SOLVING	I can fix this and I can fix you.

V. CONCLUSION

For the above insights to be valuable, they require grounding in our personal realities.

EXERCISE 1.3

1. **Consider some of your recent interactions. Identify an individual who displayed a high level of empathy and record what it was in particular that demonstrated this:**

2. **Consider two individuals with whom you have a relationship (family, friends, coworkers, etc.). Identify the types of practical behaviors you might engage in for the sake of infusing greater empathy into the relationship:**

    Relationship 1:

    Relationship 2:

KEY POINTS

1   At times, we are tempted to attribute relationship success to something beyond our control. However, the Mishnah directs us to *acquire* a friend, implying that meaningful relationships do not simply *happen to us*; we can and must *make them happen*.

2   We each have two souls within ourselves. Our self-oriented soul is naturally apathetic to others, while our G-dly soul naturally desires to connect with others, sensing itself and others as part of a larger whole.

3   The apathetic animal soul has a firmer grip on the average person's consciousness. Engaging in relationships and friendships requires *transcending* the animal self, allowing the G-dly soul to shine.

4   To be in a genuine relationship with another implies being in touch with the Divine soul. As such, human connection is not a mere physical or emotional need but an authentic spiritual experience.

5 The factors that led us into a relationship are not critical; it is common for relationships to begin with self-interest in mind. What *is* critical is to grow and advance past a self-serving mindset.

6 Cognitive and emotional empathy are crucial for our relationships. Cognitive empathy is the ability to recognize and understand another person's emotions and to communicate this with the other. Affective empathy is experiencing a matching or corresponding emotional reaction to the emotions of another individual.

7 It can be challenging to unleash empathy consistently, especially when preoccupied. The more in tune we are with our G-dly soul, the easier time we will have in connecting through empathy.

Empathy Explored:
The Science and Significance
of Understanding Others

Empathy is a fundamental feature of human connection. Despite its importance, empathy is often misunderstood and underappreciated. This selection of expert insights explores several dimensions of empathy, ranging from its definition and benefits to the challenges and factors influencing its development. These insights provide us with a more robust appreciation for the role of empathy in our relationships and, when applied, facilitate deeper and more meaningful connections with the people that surround us.

Positive Empathy

Empathy is defined as the psychological process of sharing and understanding another person's emotions. Despite this neutral definition, empathy is often associated with how we relate to people who are *suffering* rather than how we relate to those who are having *positive* experiences. This creates a disparity between empathy's formal definition and its common use. This is yet another expression of negativity bias.

See Paul Rozin and Edward B. Royzman, "Negativity Bias, Negativity Dominance, and Contagion," *Personality and Social Psychology Review* 5:4 (2001), pp. 308–309

Enticing Greater Empathy

In one study, participants were randomly divided into groups. The participants of one group were told that they would be receiving monetary payments according to how accurately they inferred the thoughts and feelings of others, while the other group was not provided with an incentive. Empathic accuracy in the paid group was significantly higher than in the unpaid group, with men and women performing equally well, suggesting "that greater empathic accuracy can be achieved by virtually anyone who is given the proper motivation."

See Kristi J. K. Klein and Sara D. Hodges, "Gender Differences, Motivation, and Empathic Accuracy: When It Pays to Understand," *Personality and Social Psychology Bulletin*, 27:6 (2001), pp. 720–730

The Mindset Effect

We fail at empathy when we find it difficult or distressing to relate to others. What might compel us to try harder to empathize in tough situations? Multiple studies found that individuals who believe empathy can be developed (a malleable mindset) invest greater effort into being empathetic in challenging scenarios, compared to individuals who believe that personal empathy levels are a fixed feature of personality and cannot be changed. The data suggests "that people's mindsets powerfully affect whether they exert effort to empathize when it is needed most."

See Karina Schumann, et al., "Addressing the Empathy Deficit: Beliefs about the Malleability of Empathy Predict Effortful Responses When Empathy Is Challenging," *Journal of Personality and Social Psychology*, 107:3 (2014), pp. 475–493

Benefiting Relationships

Greater empathic accuracy appears to help close relationships when:

» Perceivers use it to identify their partner's current need for support and how to provide the particular type and amount of instrumental support that the partner currently desires;

» Perceivers use it preemptively to anticipate and avoid conflicts with the partner and to solve small problems before they turn into larger ones;

» Perceivers use it to "stay on the same page" with the partner, applying the same interpretive frame to the current situation and tracking the changes in the frames that the partner applies;

» Perceivers use it to put the partner's "bad behavior" into perspective, to recognize the partner's mixed motives, to identify mutually acceptable ways to resolve conflicts with the partner, and to depart from immediate self-interest for the good of the partner and the relationship; and

» Perceivers use it to effectively align and coordinate their own goals with the partner's goals.

William Ickes and Sara D. Hodges, "Empathic Accuracy in Close Relationships," in J. A. Simpson and L. Campbell (eds.), *The Oxford Handbook of Close Relationships* (Oxford, U.K.: Oxford University Press, 2013), pp. 365–366

Empathy Erosion

A 2011 meta-analysis revealed a decline in empathic concern and perspective taking among American college students, noting a significant decrease from 2000 to 2010. Compared to the 1970s and 1980s, college students were less likely to agree with statements such as "I often have tender, concerned feelings for people less fortunate than me" and "I sometimes try to understand my friends better by imagining how things look from their perspective." The authors speculate that "one likely contributor to declining empathy is the rising prominence of personal technology and media use in everyday life" as well as "shrinking family sizes over time." These reduce opportunities for siblings to develop empathy-related skills through daily interactions, thereby diminishing opportunities for empathy development.

See Sara H. Konrath, et al., "Changes in Dispositional Empathy in American College Students over Time: A Meta-Analysis," *Personality and Social Psychology Review*, 15:2 (2011), pp. 180–198

Validation Matters

A 2019 study examined the role of mothers' responses to their adolescents' conversations in influencing the degree to which the adolescents would disclose additional information. The study investigated different types of responses: negative (such as contempt, criticism, sadness), positive (such as humor, affection), interest (open-ended questions, positive nonverbal attention), validation (direct expressions of understanding), and neutral. The findings revealed that adolescents were more likely to engage in frequent disclosure when their mothers responded with validation and interest, compared to positive, negative, or neutral reactions. "Parental communication of validation and interest are particularly important in promoting adolescent disclosure in the context of parent-adolescent conversations."

See Janice Disla, et al., "The Effect of Mothers' Emotion-Related Responses to Adolescent Disclosures and Adolescent Perspective Taking on the Timing of Future Disclosures," *Social Development* 28:3 (2019), pp. 657–673

Modes of Relationships in the Life of Joseph: A Time Line

YEAR: 2205 AGE: 6

YEAR: 2216 AGE: 17

YEAR: 2217 AGE: 18

Self-Sacrifice

Joseph shields his mother Rachel from Esau's evil intentions (Genesis 33:7; Rashi ad loc.).

Judging others negatively; talebearing and defamation

Joseph discerns certain negative behaviors in his brothers and reports them to their father (Genesis 37:2).

Insensitivity

Joseph shares his dreams—which predict his future greatness and leadership—with his brothers, fueling their jealousy and animosity (Genesis 37:5–11).

Failure to repair the relationship

The brothers throw Joseph into a pit and subsequently sell him into slavery. Joseph pleads with them for mercy, but they remain unmoved (Genesis 37:23–28, 42:21).

Charisma; Haughtiness and self-centeredness

Joseph revels in his success as the chief manager of Potiphar's affairs (Genesis 39:2–6; Rashi, ad loc.).

Loyalty; Integrity

Potiphar's wife becomes obsessed with Joseph's beauty and aggressively pursues him. Joseph rejects her advances (Genesis 39:7–12).

YEAR: 2227 AGE: 28

Empathy

Joseph notices the dejected mood of his fellow prisoners, asks them what is troubling them, and interprets their dreams for them (Genesis 40:6–19).

YEAR: 2229 AGE: 30

Humility

When summoned to interpret Pharaoh's dreams, Joseph attributes his wisdom and abilities to G-d (Genesis 41:16).

Solution-oriented (not just "doing my job")

After interpreting Pharaoh's dreams, Joseph also offers his advice on how to prepare for the seven years of famine, which the dreams predict (Genesis 41:33–36).

YEAR: 2237 AGE: 38

Restraint

When the brothers come to Egypt, Joseph conceals his identity from them in order to move them through the process of repairing their broken relationship (Genesis 42:7–44:34).

YEAR: 2238 AGE: 39

Generosity

Joseph supports his brothers and their families throughout the years of famine (Genesis 47:12).

Forgiveness

Joseph repeatedly reassures his brothers that he bears no grudge against them and that he views all that he experienced to have been ordained from Above for a higher purpose (Genesis 45:5–7, 50:19–21).

Vulnerability

When Joseph finally reveals his identity to his brothers, he weeps openly. He embraces and comforts them, allowing them to recover from their overwhelming feelings of shame (Genesis 45:1–15).

YEAR: 2238–2255 AGE: 39–56

Discretion

For the entire seventeen years that Jacob lived in Egypt, Joseph never told him what his brothers did to him (Ramban, Genesis 45:27; *Daat Zekeinim Mibaalei HaTosafot*, ad loc., 48:1).

YEAR: 2309 AGE: 110

Self-Sacrifice

When Jacob passed away, he had Joseph promise to take his body out of Egypt to be buried in the Holy Land. But Joseph chose to remain in exile with his people to keep alive the promise that "G-d will remember you, and He will take you up from this land . . . and you will take my bones up with you" (Genesis 50:24–26).

Psychology References

Ameli M, Dattilio, F. (2013) Enhancing cognitive behavior therapy with logotherapy: Techniques for clinical practice. *Psychotherapy (Chicago, Ill.)*, *50*(3). 387–91. doi.org/10.1037/a0033394.

Brown SL, Brown RM. (2015) Connecting prosocial behavior to improved physical health: Contributions from the neurobiology of parenting. *Neuroscience and Biobehavioral Reviews*, Volume 55, 1–17. ISSN 0149-7634, doi.org/10.1016/j.neubiorev.2015.04.004.

Moccia L, et al. (2018) The experience of pleasure: A perspective between neuroscience and psychoanalysis. *Frontiers in Human Neuroscience*, *12*:359. doi:10.3389/fnhum.2018.00359.

Nelson-Coffey S, et al. (2016) Do unto others or treat yourself? The effects of prosocial and self-focused behavior on psychological flourishing. *Emotion.* *16*(6), 850–861. doi.org/10.1037/emo0000178.

Stavrova O, Ehlebracht D. (2015) A longitudinal analysis of romantic relationship formation: The effect of prosocial behavior. *Social Psychological and Personality Science 6*(5), 521–27. doi.org/10.1177/1948550614568867.

APPENDIX A—RELATIONSHIPS AND LONGEVITY

TEXT 16

The Story of Roseto

Malcolm Gladwell, *Outliers: The Story of Success*
(New York: Little, Brown and Company, 2008), p. 10

When Bruhn and Wolf first presented their findings to the medical community, you can imagine the kind of skepticism they faced. They went to conferences where their peers were presenting long rows of data arrayed in complex charts and referring to this kind of gene or that kind of physiological process, and they themselves were talking instead about the mysterious and magical benefits of people stopping to talk to one another on the street and having three generations under one roof.

Living a long life, the conventional wisdom at the time said, depended to a great extent on who we were—that is, our genes. It depended on the decisions we made—on what we chose to eat, and how much we chose to exercise, and how effectively we were treated by the medical system. No one was used to thinking about health in terms of *community*.

**MALCOLM GLADWELL
1963–**

British-Canadian journalist and writer. Gladwell was born in England and grew up in rural Ontario. He was a reporter and editor for *The Washington Post* and is now a staff writer at *The New Yorker.* His 4 books have all been on the *New York Times* bestseller list.

TEXT 17

Traits of Longevity

Rabbi Yisrael Alnaqua, *Menorat Hama'or*, ch. 20

וְכָל מִי שֶׁהוּא זָהִיר בְּדֶרֶךְ אֶרֶץ וּמְעוֹרָב
עִם הַבְּרִיּוֹת, זוֹכֶה וַיַאֲרִיךְ יָמִים.

כִּדְגַרְסִינַן . . . (מְגִלָה כח, א) שָׁאֲלוּ תַּלְמִידָיו אֶת
רַבִּי נְחוּנְיָא בֶּן הַקָנָה: בַּמָה הֶאֱרַכְתָּ יָמִים?

אָמַר לָהֶם:

מִיָמַי לֹא נִתְכַּבַּדְתִּי בִּקְלוֹן חֲבֵרִי.

וְלֹא עָלְתָה עַל מִטָתִי קִלְלַת חֲבֵרִי.

וַתְרָן בְּמָמוֹנִי הָיִיתִי.

RABBI YISRAEL ALNAQUA
D. 1391

Ethicist. A resident of
Spain, Rabbi Yisrael
Alnaqua studied under
Rabbi Asher (Rosh) in
Toledo. He is the author
of *Menorat Hama'or*,
a guide on ethics and
piety. He was killed
during the 1391 wave
of pogroms in Spain.

Those who are particular about respecting others
and integrating with them will merit longevity.

As the Talmud (MEGILAH 28A) states: . . . Rabbi
Nechunia ben Hakanah was asked by his disciples,
"By what virtue have you reached old age?"

He replied:

"Never in life did I seek respect through
the degradation of my fellow.

"Nor have I ever gone to bed harboring
animosity toward another.

"And I have been openhanded with my money."

APPENDIX B—RELATIONSHIPS AND EMOTIONAL WELL-BEING

TEXT 18

The Benefits of Connection

Sonja Lyubomirsky, *The Myths of Happiness*
(New York: Penguin Books, 2014), p. 63

Most of the time, social support won't make a problem disappear, but it can go a long way in helping us address the problem, mitigate it and lighten our emotional reaction to it.

In a clever study that supports this claim, researchers recruited volunteers who happened to be passing the base of a hill and were either alone or with a friend. Incredibly, those who were accompanied by a friend—especially a friend they were close to and knew a long time—judged the hill to be *less steep* than those who were alone.

Serving as a metaphor for the challenges of life . . . companions and confidants can make us feel that our problems and stresses are less steep as well.

SONJA LYUBOMIRSKY, PHD

Leading expert in positive psychology. Dr. Lyubomirsky is professor of psychology at the University of California, Riverside. Originally from Russia, she received her PhD in social/personality psychology from Stanford University. Her research on the possibility of permanently increasing happiness has been honored with various grants, including a million-dollar grant from the National Institute of Mental Health. She has authored *The How of Happiness* and *The Myths of Happiness*.

TEXT 19

Two Are Better
Ecclesiastes 4:9–10

טוֹבִים הַשְּׁנַיִם מִן הָאֶחָד

אֲשֶׁר יֵשׁ לָהֶם שָׂכָר טוֹב בַּעֲמָלָם.

כִּי אִם יִפֹּלוּ הָאֶחָד יָקִים אֶת חֲבֵרוֹ,

וְאִילוֹ הָאֶחָד שֶׁיִּפּוֹל

וְאֵין שֵׁנִי לַהֲקִימוֹ.

Two are better than one,

Because they have good reward for their toil.

For if they fall, one will lift the other;

But woe to those who fall

And have no second one to lift them up.

TEXT 20

Introverts Included

Ed Diener and Robert Biswas-Diener, *Happiness: Unlocking the Mysteries of Psychological Wealth* (Malden, Mass.: Blackwell Publishing, 2011), pp. 50–52

Throughout the day, we signaled the research participants with random alarms, after which they would complete a short mood survey and indicate the type of situation they were in: Were they alone, or with other people?

Initially, we suspected that introverts would be happier when they were alone and that extroverts would be happier when they were in a social setting. . . .

Flying in the face of our prediction, both extroverts and introverts had more positive emotions when they were with other people.

**ED DIENER, PHD
1946–2021**

Psychologist. Born in Glendale, California, Ed Diener received his PhD in psychology from the University of Washington and was a longtime professor at the University of Illinois. Nicknamed "Dr. Happiness," he was an influential researcher on happiness, exploring the influences on well-being and methods of measuring it.

**ROBERT BISWAS-DIENER, PHD
1972–**

Positive psychologist. Biswas-Diener is the son of Edward Diener and is an instructor at Portland State University. Biswas-Diener's research focuses on income and happiness, culture and happiness, and positive psychology. Biswas-Diener's research has led him to India, Greenland, Israel, Kenya, and Spain, and he has been called the "Indiana Jones of positive psychology." He sits on the editorial boards of the *Journal of Happiness Studies* and the *Journal of Positive Psychology*.

APPENDIX C—TWO TYPES OF LOVE

TEXT 21

Who Can Love?

Rabbi Shneur Zalman of Liadi, *Tanya*, *Likutei Amarim*, ch. 32

וְהִנֵּה עַל יְדֵי קִיּוּם הַדְּבָרִים הַנִּזְכָּרִים לְעֵיל, לִהְיוֹת גּוּפוֹ נִבְזֶה
וְנִמְאָס בְּעֵינָיו, רַק שִׂמְחָתוֹ תִּהְיֶה שִׂמְחַת הַנֶּפֶשׁ לְבַדָּהּ, הֲרֵי זוֹ
דֶּרֶךְ יְשָׁרָה וְקַלָּה לָבֹא לִידֵי קִיּוּם מִצְוַת "וְאָהַבְתָּ לְרֵעֲךָ כָּמוֹךָ"
(וַיִּקְרָא יט, יח) לְכָל נֶפֶשׁ מִיִּשְׂרָאֵל, לְמִגָּדוֹל וְעַד קָטָן . . .

בְּשֶׁגַּם שֶׁכֻּלָּן מַתְאִימוֹת וְאָב אֶחָד לְכֻלָּנָה, וְלָכֵן
נִקְרְאוּ כָּל יִשְׂרָאֵל אַחִים מַמָּשׁ, מִצַּד שֹׁרֶשׁ
נַפְשָׁם בַּה' אֶחָד. רַק שֶׁהַגּוּפִים מְחֻלָּקִים.

וְלָכֵן הָעוֹשִׂים גּוּפָם עִקָּר וְנַפְשָׁם טְפֵלָה, אִי אֶפְשָׁר לִהְיוֹת
אַהֲבָה וְאַחֲוָה אֲמִתִּית בֵּינֵיהֶם, אֶלָּא הַתְּלוּיָה בְּדָבָר לְבַדָּהּ.

Acting on the suggestion mentioned above—
to view one's bodily desires with scorn and
contempt and to find joy in the joy of the soul
alone—is a direct and easy way to fulfill the
commandment, "Love your fellow as yourself"
(LEVITICUS 19:18), toward every soul of
Israel, from the greatest to the smallest. . . .

For all souls are equal, and all have a single Father,
to the point that all of us are referred to as actual
siblings due to the source of our souls: the One
G-d. It is only our bodies that separate us.

Consequently, those who prioritize their bodies while considering their souls less significant cannot experience true love and brotherhood; they can only experience love contingent on nonessential factors.

APPENDIX D—GROWING INTO ESSENTIAL LOVE

Two Types of Love

TEXT 22A   Mishnah, Avot 5:16

כָּל אַהֲבָה שֶׁהִיא תְלוּיָה בְדָבָר, בָּטֵל דָּבָר, בְּטֵלָה אַהֲבָה.

וְשֶׁאֵינָהּ תְּלוּיָה בְדָבָר, אֵינָהּ בְּטֵלָה לְעוֹלָם.

אֵיזוֹ הִיא אַהֲבָה שֶׁהִיא תְלוּיָה בְדָבָר? זוֹ אַהֲבַת אַמְנוֹן וְתָמָר.

וְשֶׁאֵינָהּ תְּלוּיָה בְדָבָר? זוֹ אַהֲבַת דָּוִד וִיהוֹנָתָן.

Any love that is dependent on something, when the thing ceases, the love also ceases.

But a love that is not dependent on anything never ceases.

What kind of love is dependent on something? The love of Amnon for Tamar.

What kind of love is not dependent on something? The love of David and Jonathan.

Origins Don't Matter

The Rebbe, Rabbi Menachem Mendel Schneerson,
Torat Menachem 5733:3 (72), pp. 220–221

לְשׁוֹן הַמִּשְׁנָה - שֶׁהוּא "דָּבָר קָצָר וְכוֹלֵל עִנְיָנִים רַבִּים" הוּא:
"אַהֲבָה שֶׁהִיא תְּלוּיָה בְדָבָר", וְלֹא אַהֲבָה שֶׁבָּאָה מִדָּבָר.

כִּי, גַּם כַּאֲשֶׁר הָאַהֲבָה בָּאָה מִדָּבָר מְסֻיָּים, אֵין הֶכְרֵחַ
שֶׁתִּשָּׁאֵר תָּמִיד תְּלוּיָה בַּדָּבָר שֶׁמִּמֶּנוּ בָּאָה, אֶלָּא יָכוֹל
לִהְיוֹת שֶׁלְאַחֲרֵי שֶׁבָּאָה מִדָּבָר זֶה, נַעֲשֵׂית מְצִיאוּת בִּפְנֵי
עַצְמָהּ, וְשׁוּב אֵינָהּ תְּלוּיָה בַּדָּבָר שֶׁמִּמֶּנוּ בָּאָה . . .

וְזֶהוּ פֵּרוּשׁ מַאֲמַר הַמִּשְׁנָה . . . שֶׁאַהֲבָה "שֶׁאֵינָהּ תְּלוּיָה
בְדָבָר", גַּם אִם הִיא בָּאָה מִדָּבָר מְסֻיָּים, אֲבָל עַכְשָׁיו
אֵינָהּ תְּלוּיָה בּוֹ, הִנֵּה גַּם כַּאֲשֶׁר בָּטֵל הַדָּבָר שֶׁמִּמֶּנוּ בָּאָה
הָאַהֲבָה, נִשְׁאֶרֶת הָאַהֲבָה וְ"אֵינָהּ בְּטֵלָה לְעוֹלָם".

וְעַל זֶה מְבִיאָה הַמִּשְׁנָה . . . אַהֲבַת דָּוִד וִיהוֹנָתָן -
הִנֵּה בַּתְּחִלָּה הָיְתָה זוֹ אַהֲבָה שֶׁבָּאָה מִדָּבָר מְסֻיָּים וְדָבָר
חִיצוֹנִי . . . אֶלָּא שֶׁאַחַר כָּךְ נַעֲשֵׂית אַהֲבָה עַצְמִית שֶׁאֵינָהּ
תְּלוּיָה בְדָבָר, כְּמוֹ שֶׁכָּתוּב: "וְנֶפֶשׁ יְהוֹנָתָן נִקְשְׁרָה בְּנֶפֶשׁ
דָּוִד . . . בְּאַהֲבָתוֹ אוֹתוֹ כְּנַפְשׁוֹ" (שְׁמוּאֵל א, יח, א-ג).

The Mishnah's style is a brevity that contains
numerous implications. In this case, it specifies
love that's *dependent* on an external factor—as
opposed to love that *arises* from an external factor.

That is because love may originate from a
particular benefit, but it need not remain

dependent on that benefit. It could blossom into a love that is no longer dependent on the original cause that coaxed it into existence. . . .

This is the meaning of the Mishnah. . . . Love that is "not *dependent* on something"—even if it *originated* due to a specific benefit but is no longer dependent on it—this love "never ceases." The original cause of the love may no longer exist, but the love remains.

That is why the Mishnah cites the case of . . . the love between David and Jonathan. Their mutual love originated due to external factors . . . but it developed into an essential love that was independent of all external factors. As it is described in the verse, "The *soul* of Jonathan was attached to the *soul* of David. . . . He loved him as his own *soul*" (I SAMUEL 18:1–3).

APPENDIX E—ABRAHAM'S EMPATHY

TEXT 23A

Abraham and the Guests

Genesis 18:1–2

וַיֵּרָא אֵלָיו ה' בְּאֵלֹנֵי מַמְרֵא וְהוּא יֹשֵׁב
פֶּתַח הָאֹהֶל כְּחֹם הַיּוֹם.

וַיִּשָּׂא עֵינָיו וַיַּרְא, וְהִנֵּה שְׁלֹשָׁה אֲנָשִׁים נִצָּבִים עָלָיו,
וַיַּרְא וַיָּרָץ לִקְרָאתָם מִפֶּתַח הָאֹהֶל וַיִּשְׁתַּחוּ אָרְצָה.

G-d appeared to him in the plains of
Mamre while he was sitting at the tent
entrance when the day was hot.

He lifted his eyes and saw, and behold, three
men were standing beside him. He saw and
ran toward them from the tent's entrance,
prostrating himself to the ground.

Abraham's Cognitive Empathy

TEXT 23B

Rashi, Genesis 18:2

מַהוּ "וַיַּרְא" "וַיַּרְא" שְׁתֵּי פְּעָמִים?

הָרִאשׁוֹן כְּמַשְׁמָעוֹ.

וְהַשֵּׁנִי לְשׁוֹן הֲבָנָה - נִסְתַּכֵּל שֶׁהָיוּ נִצָּבִים בְּמָקוֹם אֶחָד וְהֵבִין שֶׁלֹּא הָיוּ רוֹצִים לְהַטְרִיחוֹ.

Why is "he saw" written twice in this passage?

The first is literal: he *noticed* the three individuals.

The second refers to discernment: he observed that they were standing in one spot and *discerned* that they did not wish to burden him.

APPENDIX F—WHEN TO SHARE

Selective Sharing

TEXT 24

Rabbi Yehudah ben Shmuel Hachasid, *Sefer Chasidim* 627

כְּתִיב: "לֵב יוֹדֵעַ מָרַת נַפְשׁוֹ" (מִשְׁלֵי יד, י).
פְּשִׁיטָא שֶׁהַלֵּב יוֹדֵעַ!

אֶלָּא מַגִּיד שֶׁפְּעָמִים שֶׁאֵין לוֹ לְאָדָם לְהַגִּיד צַעֲרוֹ לַאֲחֵרִים אֶלָּא יִתְפּוֹשׂ בְּלִבּוֹ. כְּגוֹן שֶׁאָדָם יוֹדֵעַ שֶׁאוֹתָם שֶׁבָּאִים אֶצְלוֹ אֵין חוֹשְׁשִׁים בְּצַעֲרוֹ - אִם כֵּן לָמָה

יַגִּיד לָהֶם? אֲבָל יַגִּיד לְמִי שֶׁיֵּשׁ לוֹ חֵלֶק בְּצַעֲרוֹ. וְעַל זֶה נֶאֱמַר "דְּאָגָה בְלֶב אִישׁ - יַשְׁחֶנָּה לַאֲחֵרִים".

"וּבְשִׂמְחָתוֹ לֹא יִתְעָרַב זָר" (מִשְׁלֵי יד, י) - שֶׁאֵין לוֹ חֵלֶק בְּאוֹתָהּ שִׂמְחָה. כְּלוֹמַר, מִי שֶׁאֵינוֹ שָׂמֵחַ וְאֵינוֹ חוֹשֵׁשׁ בְּשִׂמְחָתוֹ לֹא יְסַפֵּר לוֹ שִׂמְחָתוֹ.

It is stated, "The heart knows its own bitterness, and no stranger shares its joy" (PROVERBS 14:10). Is it not obvious that one's heart is aware of its own troubles?

Rather, this verse teaches us that, at times, we should keep our pain within our hearts instead of expressing it to others. When is that? When we know they are not concerned enough about our troubles to feel our pain. In that case, there is no point in sharing it with them. Instead, we should confide in someone who will actively share in our sorrow. It is specifically regarding such a confidant that our sages advised us to ease our worries by discussing them with someone.

"No stranger shares its joy" refers to those who do not actively participate in our joy. If we know that specific individuals will not be happy for our joy and will not care about it, we should not tell them about it.

APPENDIX G—JOSEPH'S EMOTIONAL EMPATHY

TEXT 25

Joseph and Benjamin

Rashi, Genesis 45:14

"וַיִּפֹּל עַל צַוְּארֵי בִנְיָמִן אָחִיו וַיֵּבְךְּ" (בְּרֵאשִׁית מה, יד): עַל שְׁנֵי מִקְדָּשׁוֹת שֶׁעֲתִידִין לִהְיוֹת בְּחֶלְקוֹ שֶׁל בִּנְיָמִין וְסוֹפָן לֶחָרֵב.

"וּבִנְיָמִן בָּכָה עַל צַוָּארָיו" (שָׁם): עַל מִשְׁכַּן שִׁילֹה שֶׁעֲתִיד לִהְיוֹת בְּחֶלְקוֹ שֶׁל יוֹסֵף וְסוֹפוֹ לֶחָרֵב.

"Joseph fell on his brother Benjamin's neck and wept" (GENESIS 45:14)—for the two Temples, destined to stand in Benjamin's territory, which would ultimately be destroyed.

"Benjamin wept on his neck" (IBID.)— for the Tabernacle at Shiloh, destined to be located in Joseph's territory, which would ultimately be destroyed.

APPENDIX H—POSITIVE EMPATHY

TEXT 26

Moses and Aaron

Exodus 4:14

הֲלֹא אַהֲרֹן אָחִיךָ הַלֵּוִי, יָדַעְתִּי כִּי דַבֵּר יְדַבֵּר הוּא,
וְגַם הִנֵּה הוּא יֹצֵא לִקְרָאתֶךָ, וְרָאֲךָ וְשָׂמַח בְּלִבּוֹ.

What about your brother, Aaron the
Levite? I know he will surely speak; behold,
he is going out toward you, and when he
sees you, he will rejoice in his heart.

TEXT 27

The Ultimate Romantic Wish

Midrash, *Shir Hashirim Rabah* 8:1

"מִי יִתֶּנְךָ כְּאָח לִי" (שִׁיר הַשִּׁירִים ח, א):

בְּאֵי זֶה אָח?

כְּקַיִן לְהֶבֶל? קַיִן הָרַג לְהֶבֶל, שֶׁנֶּאֱמַר:
"וַיָּקָם קַיִן אֶל הֶבֶל אָחִיו וַיַּהַרְגֵהוּ" (בְּרֵאשִׁית ד, ח).

אֶלָּא כְּיִשְׁמָעֵאל לְיִצְחָק? יִשְׁמָעֵאל שׂוֹנֵא לְיִצְחָק.

אֶלָּא כְּעֵשָׂו לְיַעֲקֹב? הֲרֵי נֶאֱמַר:
"וַיִּשְׂטֹם עֵשָׂו אֶת יַעֲקֹב" (שָׁם כז, מא).

SHIR HASHIRIM RABAH

A midrashic text and
exegetical commentary
on the book of Song of
Songs. This Midrash
explicates this biblical
book based on the
principle that its verses
convey an allegory
of the relationship
between G-d and the
people of Israel. It was
compiled and edited
in the Land of Israel
during the 6th century.

אֶלָּא כְּאַחֵי יוֹסֵף לְיוֹסֵף? שׂוֹנְאִין הָיוּ אוֹתוֹ,
שֶׁנֶּאֱמַר: "וַיְקַנְאוּ בוֹ אֶחָיו" (שָׁם לז, יא) ...

הֱוֵי אוֹמֵר כְּיוֹסֵף לְבִנְיָמִין, שֶׁאֲהָבוֹ בְּלִבּוֹ ...

מֹשֶׁה וְאַהֲרֹן, שֶׁנֶּאֱמַר: "וַיֵּלֶךְ וַיִּפְגְּשֵׁהוּ בְּהַר
הָאֱלֹקִים וַיִּשַּׁק לוֹ" (שְׁמוֹת ד, כז).

"If only you were to me like a brother!"
(SONG OF SONGS 8:1).

Like *which* brother?

Like Cain toward Abel? Cain murdered Abel!
As it is stated, "Cain rose up against Abel
and killed him" (GENESIS 4:8).

Like Ishmael toward Isaac?
Ishmael harbors hatred for Isaac!

Like Esau toward Jacob? But it is stated,
"Esau loathed Jacob" (GENESIS 27:41)!

Like Joseph's brothers toward Joseph?
They hated him! As it is stated, "His brothers
envied him" (GENESIS 37:11)....

We must conclude that it is like Joseph toward
Benjamin, for he loved him with his heart....

And like Moses and Aaron. As it says, "Aaron
went and met Moses on the mount of G-d,
and he kissed him" (EXODUS 4:27).

LESSON

2

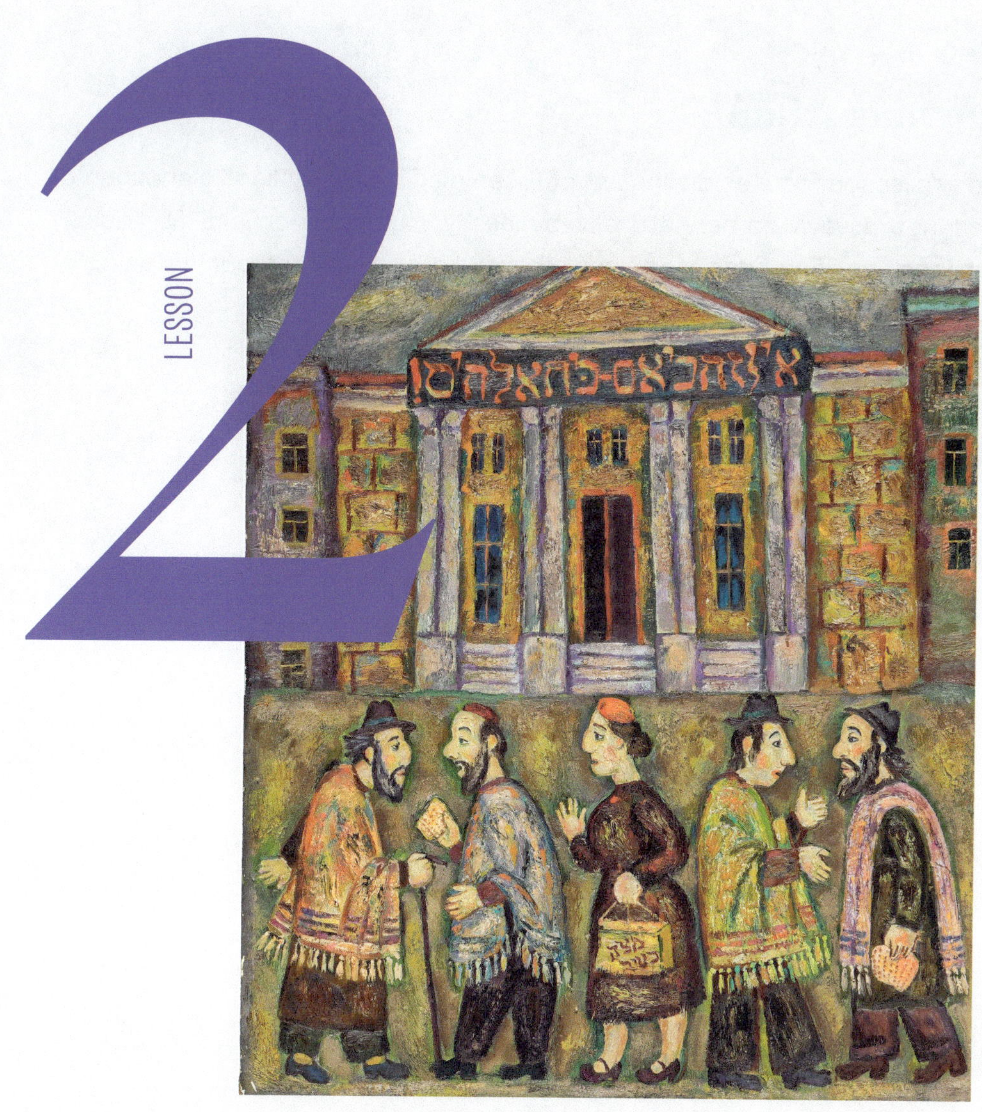

MOSCOW SYNAGOGUE
Grisha Bruskin,
oil on canvas, 1969, Moscow

THE ART OF LISTENING

Effective listening involves opening our hearts and minds to truly absorb and understand the messages being conveyed. How can we become more attentive and responsive listeners?

I. INTRODUCTION

Today's lesson focuses on the art of listening. To truly listen to another does not always come naturally or easily, but it is crucial for our relationships. The first step toward growth is to assess our listening skills.

EXERCISE 2.1

Michael P. Nichols, *The Lost Art of Listening: How Learning to Listen Can Improve Relationships* (New York: Guilford Press, 2009), pp. 67–69

MICHAEL P. NICHOLS

Psychologist and author. Michael P. Nichols is a practicing family therapist and a professor of psychology at the College of William and Mary. He is the author of a number of popular books on the topic of family therapy.

When someone is talking to you, do you:

A—Almost never

B—Sometimes

C—Often

D—Almost always

QUESTION	ANSWER	SCORE
1. Make people feel that you're interested in them and what they have to say?		
2. Think about what you want to say while others are talking?		
3. Acknowledge what the speaker says before offering your own point of view?		
4. Jump in before the other person has finished speaking?		

QUESTION	ANSWER	SCORE
5. Allow people to complain without arguing with them?		
6. Offer advice before you're asked?		
7. Concentrate on figuring out what other people are trying to say, not just respond to the words they use?		
8. Share similar experiences of your own rather than inviting the speaker to elaborate on his or her experience?		
9. Get other people to tell you a lot about themselves?		
10. Assume you know what someone is going to say before he or she is finished?		
11. Restate messages or instructions to make sure you understood correctly?		
12. Make judgments about who is worth listening to and who isn't?		
13. Make a concerted effort to focus on the speaker and understand what he or she is trying to say?		
14. Tune out when someone starts to ramble on, rather than trying to get involved and make the conversation more interesting?		

QUESTION	ANSWER	SCORE
15. Accept criticism without getting defensive?		
16. Think of listening as instinctive, rather than as a skill that requires making an effort?		
17. Make an active effort to get other people to say what they think and feel about things?		
18. Pretend to be listening when you're not?		
19. Respect what other people have to say?		
20. Feel that listening to other people complain is annoying?		
21. Make effective use of questions to invite people to say what's on their minds?		
22. Make distracting comments when other people are talking?		
23. Think other people consider you to be a good listener?		
24. Tell people that you know how they feel?		
25. Not lose your cool when somebody gets angry at you?		

Scoring

Write down your score on the right-hand side of each question.

First score all the odd-numbered questions:

A = 1   B = 2   C = 3   D = 4

Then score your even-numbered questions:

A = 4   B = 3   C = 2   D = 1

Then total the number of points:

85–96	Excellent
73–84	Above average
61–72	Average
49–60	Below average
25–48	Poor

II. WHY LISTEN?

Listening is vital to *provide* to others, *know* them, and *connect* with them.

Below are two classic texts that highlight these functions: A paragraph in the *Haggadah* reminds us that only through listening carefully to what others say can we *provide* them the help they need and *know* their individual characteristics. A poetic verse in King Solomon's Song of Songs highlights the concept of listening to *connect*.

THREE OLDER JEWISH MEN HAVING A CHAT OUTDOORS
Unknown artist, oil on fiberboard, Bohemia, c. 1800s (United States Holocaust Memorial Museum, Katz Ehrenthal Collection, Washington, D.C.)

FIGURE 2.1

The Children's Questions

EXODUS 12:26–27	When your children say to you, "What is this service to you?" you shall say . . .
EXODUS 13:8	You shall tell your child on that day, saying . . .
EXODUS 13:14	In the future, when your child asks you, "What is this?" you shall say . . .
DEUTERONOMY 6:20	In the future, when your child asks you, "What are these testimonies, statutes, and ordinances that our G-d has commanded you?" you shall say . . .

TEXT 1

The Four Children

Passover *Haggadah*

כְּנֶגֶד אַרְבָּעָה בָנִים דִּבְּרָה תוֹרָה: אֶחָד חָכָם,
וְאֶחָד רָשָׁע, וְאֶחָד תָּם, וְאֶחָד שֶׁאֵינוֹ יוֹדֵעַ לִשְׁאוֹל.

The Torah discusses four children:
one is wise, one is wayward, one is simple,
and one does not know how to ask.

PASSOVER *HAGGADAH*

The Passover *Haggadah* was compiled during the Talmudic era. It incorporates verses from the Torah and Talmudic exegesis to tell the story of the Exodus. The *Haggadah*, which also establishes the structure of the *seder*, has been printed in thousands of editions and has spawned thousands of commentaries, making it one of the most popular books in the history of literature.

EXERCISE 2.2

Identify the corresponding verse for each child based on the language used in Figure 2.1. Circle your selected choice.

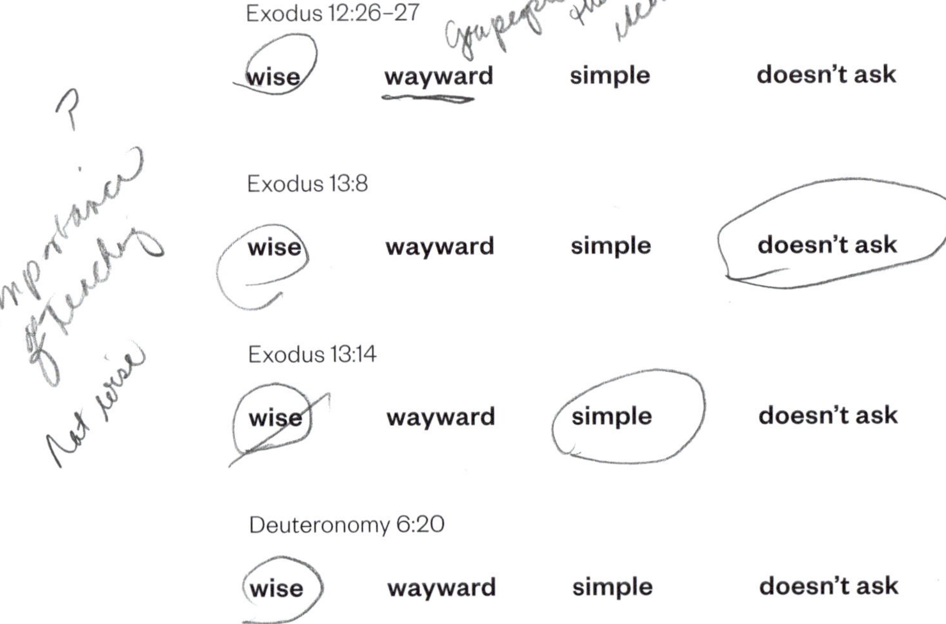

Understandings That Motivate Listening

FIGURE 2.2

1. Listen to provide.

2.

3.

TEXT 2

Speech Mirrors Character

Rabbi Yosef Yitzchak Schneersohn, *Sefer Hamaamarim* 5700, p. 44

דְּכָל אֶחָד מֵאַרְבָּעָה סוּגִים שׁוֹאֵל כְּפִי מָה שֶׁהוּא.

שֶׁזֶּהוּ פֵּירוּשׁ וּבִיאוּר הַפִּיסְקָא "חָכָם מַה הוּא אוֹמֵר": דְּמָה שֶׁהוּא בְּעֶצֶם מַהוּתוֹ הִנֵּה כֵן הוּא אוֹמֵר וּמְגַלֶּה בְּעַצְמוֹ.

וְכֵן כֻּלָּם.

The four types of children inquire according to their respective natures.

This is the deeper interpretation of the statement, "The one who is wise, what is he saying?" If you want to know "what *is* he," analyze his "saying."

The same applies to all four types of children.

FIGURE 2.3

Understandings That Motivate Listening

1. Listen to provide.

2. **Listen to know.**

3.

RABBI YOSEF YITZCHAK SCHNEERSOHN (RAYATZ, FRIERDIKER REBBE, PREVIOUS REBBE) 1880–1950

Chasidic rebbe, prolific writer, and Jewish activist. Rabbi Yosef Yitzchak, the 6th leader of the Chabad movement, actively promoted Jewish religious practice in Soviet Russia and was arrested for these activities. After his release from prison and exile, he settled in Warsaw, Poland, from where he fled Nazi occupation and arrived in New York in 1940. Settling in Brooklyn, Rabbi Schneersohn worked to revitalize American Jewish life. His son-in-law Rabbi Menachem Mendel Schneerson succeeded him as the leader of the Chabad movement.

Learn the art of truly listening to your child, with **Rabbi Daniel Schonbuch, LMFT.** **myjli.com/relationships**

TEXT 3

A Desire of Love

Song of Songs 2:14

הַרְאִינִי אֶת מַרְאַיִךְ, הַשְׁמִיעִינִי אֶת קוֹלֵךְ,
כִּי קוֹלֵךְ עָרֵב וּמַרְאֵיךְ נָאוֶה.

Show me your appearance, let me listen
to your voice; for your voice is pleasant
and your appearance is comely.

SONG OF SONGS

Biblical book. Written by
King Solomon (849–797
BCE), Song of Songs
is part of the Writings
(Ketuvim) section of the
Bible. This book depicts
the love between G-d
and the Jewish people,
employing the metaphor
of the love between a
bride and groom.

FIGURE 2.4

Understandings That Motivate Listening

1. Listen to provide.

2. Listen to know.

3. **Listen to connect.**

III. A MYSTICAL TAKE ON LISTENING

As explained in Lesson One, Jewish mysticism reveals that we each contain two souls: a Divine soul and an impulsive, animalistic soul. Each soul bears a different attitude toward listening. The G-dly soul has a purpose-oriented mindset, viewing apparently random occurrences as meaningful events. This perspective influences its motivation to listen.

QUESTION
Samuel Bak, oil on canvas,
1995, Massachusetts

TEXT 4

The Immersive Prayer

Rabbi Yosef Yitzchak Schneersohn,
Sefer Hasichot 5702, pp. 84–85

אַז ר' הֶלֵל פְלֶעגְט אַרוֹיסְפָארְן אִין וֶועג, פְלֶעגְט עֶר
מִיטְנֶעמֶען . . . זַיין תַּלְמִיד ר' שָׁלוֹם הוּמֶענֶער . . .

פָארְנַאכְט־צוּ, זַיינֶען זֵיי אָנְגֶעקוּמֶען אִין אַ אַכְסַנְיָא אִין
מַאלָארָאסְיָא. ר' שָׁלוֹם הָאט זִיךְ גֶעשְׁטֶעלְט דַאוֶונֶען
מַעֲרִיב אוּן הָאט מַאֲרִיךְ גֶעוֶוען אִין דַאוֶונֶען בִּיז עֶס אִיז
גֶעוָוארְן טָאג. אִיז וִוי קֶען מֶען זִיךְ דָאס לֵייגְן שְׁלָאפְן?
הָאט ר' שָׁלוֹם זִיךְ גְלַייךְ מֵכִין גֶעוֶוען צוּם דַאוֶונֶען
בְּעֶרֶךְ אַ שָׁעָה אַדֶער מֶעהר, אוּן הָאט זִיךְ גֶעשְׁטֶעלְט
דַאוֶונֶען שַׁחֲרִית, אוּן הָאט אַזוֹי גֶעדַאוֶונֶענְט אַ גַאנְצֶען
טָאג. בִּיז אַז עֶר אִיז צוּגֶעקוּמֶען צוּ קְרִיאַת שְׁמַע, שְׁמַע
יִשְׂרָאֵל ה' אֱלֹקֵינוּ וְגוֹ' אִיז שׁוֹין גֶעוֶוען מִנְחָה צַייט.

דֶער בַּעַל הָאַכְסַנְיָא, אַ דָארְפְס־מַאן, אִיז גֶעקוּמֶען דַאוֶונֶען
מִנְחָה. עֶרְשְׁט עֶר דֶערְזֶעהְט וִוי ר' שָׁלוֹם הַאלְט עֶרְשְׁט
אִין מִיטְן דַאוֶונֶען שַׁחֲרִית. רוּפְט עֶר זִיךְ אָפּ: "וָואס אִיז
דָאס מִיט דֶעם אִידְן? נֶעכְטְן הָאט עֶר אָפְּגֶעדַאוֶונֶענְט
אַ גַאנְצֶע נַאכְט מַעֲרִיב בִּיז טָאג, אוּן הַיינְט אַ גַאנְצֶען
טָאג אַז עֶר דַאוֶונֶענְט. בַּא מִיר אִיז אַנְדֶערְשׁ. אִיךְ קֶען
גְלַייךְ זָאגְן שְׁמַע יִשְׂרָאֵל אוּן עֶר אִיז אַזוֹי פִיל מַאֲרִיךְ.
עֶס אִיז גָאר פָּשׁוּט, בַּיי אִיהם אִיז אַ פְרָאסְטֶע קָאפּ!"

ר' שָׁלוֹם הָאט שׁוֹין גֶעהַאט גֶעעֶנְדִיגְט דֶעם דַאוֶונֶען אוּן
הָאט זִיךְ צוּגֶעהֶערְט וָואס דֶער דָארְפְסְמַאן זָאגְט.

הָאט נָאכְדֶעם גֶעזָאגְט ר' הִלֵּל, אַז דְרַיי יָאהר
חֲסִידוּת וָואס ר' שָׁלוֹם הָאט בַּיי אִים גֶעלֶערְנְט
הָאט נִיט גֶע'פּוֹעֶל'ט אַזוֹי פִּיעל וְוִי דִי וֶוערְטֶער
פוּן דֶעם דָארְפְּס-מַאן הָאט גֶע'פּוֹעֶל'ט.

Whenever Rabbi Hillel of Paritch traveled, he would take along . . . his student, Shalom Huminer. . . .

One evening, they arrived at an inn somewhere in Ukraine. Shalom began his evening prayers, and he spent so much time in profound meditation and prayer that dawn had arrived by the time he was done. But how can one go to sleep after such a powerful spiritual experience? Instead, Shalom launched into his preparations for the morning prayers, which took him at least another hour. He then recited the morning prayers, which took the entire day. He reached the recitation of the *Shema—Shema Yisrael Hashem Elokeinu Hashem Echad—* when it was already time for the afternoon prayer!

The innkeeper who hosted them was a simple villager. He had left in the morning and returned now to recite his afternoon prayers. He entered his inn and discovered Shalom, who had just concluded his morning devotions. He cried out, "What is with this Jew? Last night, he spent the entire night praying, and now he has prayed the entire day! I'm not like that; I can simply say,

'*Shema Yisrael,*' but this fellow takes so long!
Obviously, he must be an illiterate ignoramus!"

Shalom heard the villager's outburst,
having just completed his prayers.

His teacher, Rabbi Hillel, subsequently remarked,
"These words of the simple villager had a profound
effect on Shalom [in terms of motivation to
self-refinement]. In fact, it affected him more
than my three years of studying with him!"

QUESTION

**What underlying beliefs prompted Shalom to be deeply
impacted by the words he heard?**

TEXT 5

Personal Divine Providence

The Rebbe, Rabbi Menachem Mendel Schneerson, *Reshimot* 44

"כָּל מַה שֶּׁבָּרָא הַקָּדוֹשׁ בָּרוּךְ הוּא בְּעוֹלָמוֹ,
לֹא בָּרָא דָּבָר אֶחָד לְבַטָּלָה" (שַׁבָּת עז, ב) ...

וְכֵן הוּא גַם כֵּן בְּכָל הַמְאוֹרָעוֹת וְהַמִּקְרִים שֶׁבָּעוֹלָם.
שֶׁאֵין דָּבָר אֶחָד לְבַטָּלָה. כִּי הַכֹּל בְּהַשְׁגָּחָה פְּרָטִית ...

וְכָל מַה שֶּׁאֵינוֹ נוֹגֵעַ לוֹ בַּעֲבוֹדָתוֹ אֶת הַשֵּׁם יִתְבָּרֵךְ,
אֵינוֹ יוֹדֵעַ עַל דָּבָר זֶה, כִּי אֵין דָּבָר וִידִיעָה לְבַטָּלָה.

The Talmud teaches that "of all that G-d created
in His world, not a single thing was created
without purpose" (SHABBAT 77B). . . .

This principle extends to all events and occurrences,
none of which is purposeless, for all that transpires
is directed by Personal Divine Providence. . . .

Similarly, awareness of specific information
is not purposeless. We are not made aware of
anything irrelevant to our service of G-d.

Rabbi David Aaron: Every
challenge is an opportunity
myjli.com/relationships

FIGURE 2.5

Understandings That Motivate Listening

1. Listen to provide.

2. Listen to know.

3. Listen to connect.

4. **Listen to align.**

SELF DISCOVERY
Alex Levin, oil on canvas,
2020, Israel

IV. TO MASTER LISTENING: A GUIDE

The Jewish sages conveyed numerous teachings about listening in the context of Torah study. One notable statement calls for us to approach study—and, by extension, all forms of listening—with "a child's mindset." The sages also enumerated behaviors that create an environment conducive to listening.

TEXT 6

The Child's Mindset

Mishnah, Avot 4:20

אֱלִישָׁע בֶּן אֲבוּיָה אוֹמֵר:

הַלּוֹמֵד תּוֹרָה יֶלֶד לְמָה הוּא דוֹמֶה? לִדְיוֹ כְּתוּבָה עַל נְיָר חָדָשׁ.

וְהַלּוֹמֵד תּוֹרָה זָקֵן לְמָה הוּא דוֹמֶה? לִדְיוֹ כְּתוּבָה עַל נְיָר מָחוּק.

Elisha the son of Avuyah would say:

"Learning Torah as a child is comparable to ink inscribed on fresh paper.

"Learning Torah as an older person is comparable to ink inscribed on erased paper."

**AVOT
(ETHICS OF THE
FATHERS; PIRKEI AVOT)**

A 6-chapter work on Jewish ethics that is studied widely by Jewish communities, especially during the summer. The first 5 chapters are from the Mishnah, tractate Avot. Avot differs from the rest of the Mishnah in that it does not focus on legal subjects; it is a collection of the sages' wisdom on topics related to character development, ethics, healthy living, piety, and the study of Torah.

CHILDREN IN *CHEDER*
Saul Raskin (1878–1966), etching on paper

Active Listening

Rabbi Shalom Dovber Schneersohn, *Sefer Hamaamarim* 5679, pp. 604–605

TEXT 7

וּכְתַלְמִיד הַיּוֹשֵׁב לִפְנֵי רַבּוֹ, הִנֵּה לְבַד זֹאת שֶׁצָּרִיךְ לְפַנּוֹת דַּעְתּוֹ וּמַחֲשַׁבְתּוֹ מֵעִנְיָנִים אֲחֵרִים, וּלְהַפְשִׁיט אֶת עַצְמוֹ מִכָּל מַחְשְׁבוֹתָיו הָעַצְמִיִּים, דִּכְשֶׁאֵינוֹ מַפְשִׁיט אֶת עַצְמוֹ מִמַּחְשְׁבוֹתָיו לֹא יְקַבֵּל כְּלָל אֶת הַשֵּׂכֶל הַנִּשְׁפָּע לוֹ, כִּי אִם צָרִיךְ לְהַפְשִׁיט אֶת עַצְמוֹ כַּנִּזְכָּר לְעֵיל.

אָמְנָם צָרִיךְ גַּם כֵּן לְהַנִּיחַ שִׂכְלוֹ, שֶׁבְּעֵת שֶׁשּׁוֹמֵעַ אֶת הַשֵּׂכֶל מֵהָרַב לֹא יְשַׁמֵּשׁ בְּשִׂכְלוֹ לְהָבִין הַדְּבָרִים לְעַצְמוֹ, דְּאָז אֵינוֹ בִּבְחִינַת מְקַבֵּל, וְלֹא יְקַבֵּל אֲמִיתַּת הַשֵּׂכֶל שֶׁהָרַב מַשְׁפִּיעַ לוֹ, רַק צָרִיךְ לְהַנִּיחַ שִׂכְלוֹ לְגַמְרֵי וְרַק לִשְׁמֹעַ וְלִקְלֹט הַשֵּׂכֶל שֶׁשּׁוֹמֵעַ מֵהַמַּשְׁפִּיעַ, וַאֲזַי הוּא מְקַבֵּל אֶת הַשֵּׂכֶל כִּדְבָעֵי . . .

וְהַיְינוּ דְּהַכְּלִי לְקַבָּלָה הִיא בְּחִינַת בִּיטוּל דַּוְקָא.

RABBI SHALOM DOVBER SCHNEERSOHN (RASHAB) 1860–1920

Chasidic rebbe. Rabbi Shalom Dovber became the 5th leader of the Chabad movement upon the passing of his father, Rabbi Shmuel Schneersohn. He established the Lubavitch network of *yeshivot* called Tomchei Temimim. He authored many volumes of Chasidic discourses and is renowned for his lucid and thorough explanations of kabbalistic concepts.

When students study with their mentor, they must divest their minds and thoughts from other matters, stripping themselves of all personal thoughts. Failure to detach themselves from personal thoughts will obstruct their ability to absorb the communicated ideas.

Additionally, when listening to the teacher's delivery, students must not employ their own intellect to understand the spoken concepts. If they do, then at that moment, they will not be in a state of receptivity, and they will not truly receive the concepts imparted by the teacher. Instead, they must set aside their own minds, only listening to and absorbing the ideas from the teacher. That is when they truly receive the communicated ideas. . . .

In other words, to be in a state of reception means to be in a state of *bitul* (self-surrender).

TEXT 8

Habits of Successful Listeners

Mishnah, Avot 5:7

שִׁבְעָה דְבָרִים בְּגוֹלָם וְשִׁבְעָה בְחָכָם.

חָכָם:

אֵינוֹ מְדַבֵּר לִפְנֵי מִי שֶׁגָּדוֹל מִמֶּנּוּ בְּחָכְמָה וּבְמִנְיָן.

וְאֵינוֹ נִכְנָס לְתוֹךְ דִּבְרֵי חֲבֵרוֹ.

וְאֵינוֹ נִבְהָל לְהָשִׁיב.

שׁוֹאֵל כְּעִנְיָן וּמֵשִׁיב כַּהֲלָכָה.

וְאוֹמֵר עַל רִאשׁוֹן רִאשׁוֹן וְעַל אַחֲרוֹן אַחֲרוֹן.

וְעַל מַה שֶּׁלֹּא שָׁמַע, אוֹמֵר "לֹא שָׁמַעְתִּי".

וּמוֹדֶה עַל הָאֱמֶת.

וְחִלּוּפֵיהֶן בְּגוֹלָם.

Seven traits are present in a *golem* (immature person) and seven in a *chacham* (wise person).

Wise people:

1. do not speak in front of one who is greater than they in wisdom or number;

2. do not interrupt the words of another;

3. do not hasten to respond;

4. ask to the point and answer as is proper;

5. respond to the first point first and the last point last;

6. declare, "I have not heard," when they did not hear; and

7. concede to the truth.

The opposites of these traits are to be found in the *golem*.

Listening Behaviors

1. Avoid interrupting.

2. Avoid responding impulsively.

3. Avoid unilaterally changing the subject.

4. Ask clarifying questions.

5. Maintain the order of the points.

6. Acknowledge new information.

7. Be honest about not understanding.

**TWO WOMEN IN BUSY
CONVERSATION**
Gerard Johan Staller
(1880–1956), Amsterdam

V. CONCLUSION

The human anatomy carries an important reminder regarding the superiority of listening, subtly implying that we should consider this topic in a personal way.

EXERCISE 2.3

1. Which items featured in Figure 2.6 are you already good at?

2. Regarding which of those items could you use some improvement?

3. Of the room-for-improvement items, which one do you consider most critical for good listening?

TEXT 9

Speak Less, Hear More

Rabbi Yosef Nachmias, Avot 3:19

שֶׁאָדָם אֶחָד רָאָה אָדָם מְדַבֵּר יוֹתֵר
מִמָּה שֶׁהָיָה שׁוֹמֵעַ. אָמַר לוֹ:

שְׁפוֹט בֵּין אָזְנֶךָ לְפִיךָ. שֶׁלְּכָךְ בָּרָא לְךָ הַקָּדוֹשׁ בָּרוּךְ הוּא
שְׁתֵּי אָזְנַיִם וּפֶה אֶחָד: לִשְׁמוֹעַ כִּפְלַיִם מִמָּה שֶׁאַתָּה מְדַבֵּר.

A person once observed that a colleague tended to
speak far more than he listened, so he told the fellow:

"Notice the difference between your ears and
your mouth. G-d created you with *two* ears
but just a single mouth—implying that we
should listen twice as much as we speak."

**RABBI YOSEF NACHMIAS
14TH CENTURY**

Bible commentator and
ethicist. Little is known
about the life of Rabbi
Yosef Nachmias, other
than his being a student
of Rabbi Asher (The
Rosh) in Toledo during
the 14th century. He
wrote commentaries
to a number of biblical
books and is best known
for his commentary
to *Pirkei Avot*.

A BUSINESS SECRET
Isidor Kaufmann
(Austria/Hungary,
1853–1921), oil on panel

Rabbi Simon Jacobson
reflects on the art of
listening.
myjli.com/relationships

KEY POINTS

1   *Hearing* is the perception of sound, whereas *listening* requires opening the mind and heart to absorb an articulated message. Hearing is effortless; listening is a challenging art to master.

2   Listening is crucial for relationships. We need to listen to *provide* properly to those around us, to *know* them meaningfully, and to *connect* with them profoundly.

3   *Providing* for others, *knowing* others, and *connecting* with others are not inherent to the makeup of the animal soul. Listening becomes more natural when we are in tune with our *best selves*, giving the G-dly soul—*a natural listener*—a stronger voice in our lives.

4   Jewish mysticism emphasizes the importance of living with a mission mindset, discovering how every experience, including the words we hear, relates to our greater purpose. This awareness motivates us to listen to align with what G-d expects of us in the moment.

5   To listen means to adopt a "child's mindset"—quieting the mind not only from thoughts *unrelated* to the subject but also from reflection and judgment about the articulated message. After the speaker concludes, the second step of good listening is carefully analyzing the message to "read between the lines."

6   The Mishnah advocates several communication habits that create an environment conducive to good listening.

Divine Providence

The Talmud (Shabbat 77b) states, "Of everything that G-d created in His world, He did not create anything without purpose." There are two ways in which we can view the purposefulness of everything. We can speak of a *general* purpose for each type of creation: for example, trees form an integral part of the environment that supports life on Earth. But Rabbi Yisrael Baal Shem Tov (1698–1760) clarified and enriched this concept by espousing the doctrine of *Hashgachah Peratit*, or "Particular Divine Providence," positing that each individual creation, and each event that occurs, is purposeful. If a particular leaf on a particular tree is moved by a particular gust of wind in a particular direction, this has been specifically ordained by G-d to serve a particular function within the Divine purpose of Creation. Moreover, when something happens, in addition to the fact that this event was directed from Above, the fact that I witnessed it or heard about it was also directed from Above. After all, the event could have happened without my being aware of its occurrence.

The Chasidic tradition includes numerous stories that illustrate this sensibility. Represented here are three such anecdotes.

A Pushcart Prophet

Rabbi Israel Baal Shem Tov was teaching his disciples when they were disturbed by a knock on the shutter. A peasant, hauling a cart of tools, peered through the window. "Need any fixing?" he cried. "Any shaky tables, broken chairs? A loose brick in the hearth, perhaps?"

"No, no," came the impatient reply from within, where all were eager to get on with the interrupted lesson. "Everything is in perfect condition. There's no need for any repairs."

"Nothing to repair?" called the peasant. "That simply cannot be! Look well, and you're sure to find something that needs fixing."

The Baal Shem Tov turned to his students: "Think of the words we just heard—how profoundly relevant they are to each of us! Is everything really in perfect condition? At times it might seem so. But when a person truly searches their heart and evaluates their life, are they not sure to find something that requires repair?"

www.Chabad.org/53343

Two Sides of the Mouth

One day, the Chasidic master Rabbi Yaakov Yitzchak of Peshischa (ca. 1766–1813, known as the "Holy Jew of Peshischa") instructed his disciple, Rabbi Bunim (ca. 1765–1827), to embark on a journey. Rabbi Yaakov Yitzchak did not tell his disciple where to go, nor did he ask. Taking a number of his compatriots with him, they allowed Divine Providence to direct their wagon where it may, confident that the destination and purpose of their trip would be revealed in due time.

After traveling for several hours, they stopped at a wayside inn to eat and rest. Now this group of pious Jews naturally insisted on the highest standards of *kashrut*; when they learned that their host planned to serve them meat in their meal, they asked to see the *shochet* of the house, interrogated him as to his knowledge and piety, and examined his knife for any possible blemishes.

As they spoke and ate, a voice emerged from behind the oven, where an old beggar was resting amidst his bundles. "Dear Jews," the voice called out, "are you as careful with what comes out of your mouth as you are with what enters into it?"

The party of Chasidim concluded their meal in silence, climbed onto their wagon and turned back home. They now understood the purpose for which their master had dispatched them on their journey that morning.

Sipurei Chasidim, Toldot

A Question of Will

Rabbi Leib (1725–1811, known as the "Shpoler Zeide") shunned the role of leader and rebbe (Chasidic master), preferring to find his place as one among the many disciples of Rabbi Dov Ber of Mezeritch (d. 1772).

Once, when Rabbi Leib was making his way on foot to Mezeritch, he came upon a heavily laden wagon that had become stuck in the mud. The wagon driver called out to him for assistance, but the physically frail Rabbi Leib demurred. "I'm sorry," he said, "I wish I could help you. But I am not capable of lifting such a heavy load."

"You are capable, you are capable!" responded the wagon driver. "You just don't want to!"

For the rest of his journey to Mezeritch, Rabbi Leib knew no rest. He felt that the wagon driver's words must be a message from Above and that they came to address his inner reluctance to assume the task that had been ordained for him. When he arrived in Mezeritch, Rabbi Dov Ber said to him: "My master, Rabbi Israel Baal Shem Tov, once said to me, concerning you, that 'he can drag a burdened soul out of its spiritual mud.' You can and you must be a rebbe."

Igrot Kodesh HaRayatz 9, p. 98

Lessons in Listening, from the Torah

The Torah's narratives are rich with life lessons. The following five biblical anecdotes are analyzed to reveal timeless insights into the importance of active listening and refraining from interjecting. Each narrative provides another angle of observation into this principle, yielding a distinct lesson that applies to our lives.

Abraham and G-d

GENESIS   18:20–33

G-d informs Abraham that the city of Sodom's extreme evil warrants its destruction. Abraham boldly pleads for the city, asking that it be spared considering that fifty of its residents may be innocent. G-d responds that Sodom lacks fifty such individuals. Abraham keeps repeating his request, reducing the numbers each time: forty-five, forty, thirty, twenty, and finally, ten. Each time, G-d informs him that Sodom lacks that number of innocent individuals.

▶ **ANALYSIS**
Avot DeRabbi Natan, ch. 37

G-d knew what Abraham intended to request and that Abraham operated under a mistaken assumption that the city included a minority of innocents. When Abraham issued his initial proposal, G-d could have cut the conversation short with the reply, "There are no innocents in Sodom." Nevertheless, G-d patiently permitted Abraham to present each possibility and negated each in turn. Only after Abraham exhausted his options did the conversation formally end.

▶ **LISTENING LESSON**

We tend to interject when we know what others plan to say, especially if they are mistaken and we desire to set the record straight. Even in such instances, we should take our cue from G-d's conduct with Abraham and allow others to conclude their thoughts.

Aaron and Moses

LEVITICUS

10:16–20

The momentous day of the Tabernacle's inauguration is also the start of a new month—warranting the offering of a monthly animal sacrifice. Moses directs Aaron and his sons (the Kohanim, priests) to present parts of this sacrifice to G-d on the altar and to eat the rest of the meat. Instead, Aaron and his sons burn their portions. Moses confronts them and elaborates as to why this kind of sacrifice merits consumption. Aaron responds that two of his sons met a sudden death that day, and it was inappropriate for him to eat the sacred meat. Moses is pleased with Aaron's response.

THE TEMPLE'S VESSELS
A Torah codex manuscript, Perpignan, 1299 (National Library of France, MS Hebrew 7)

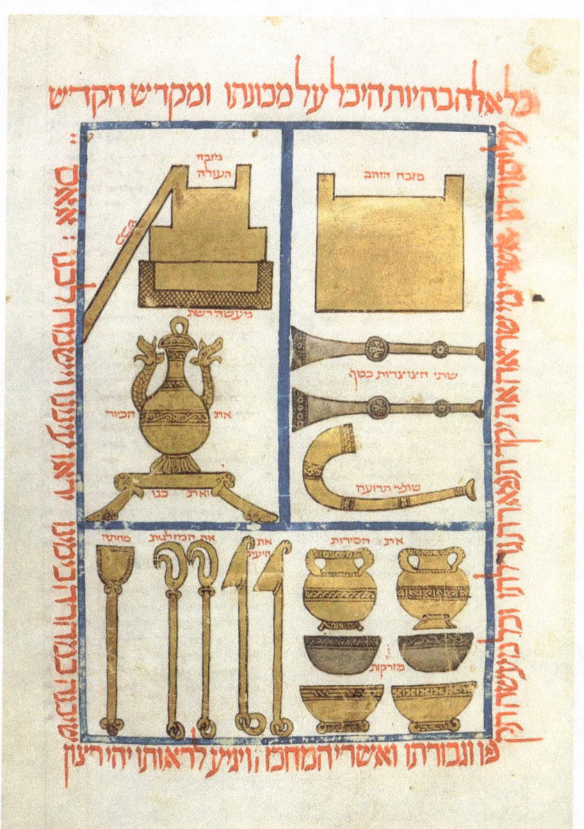

▶ **ANALYSIS**

Avot DeRabbi Natan, ch. 37

As soon as Moses protested that this kind of sacrifice merited consumption, Aaron could have easily interjected to clarify that he had not misunderstood the requirements of this sacrifice—but rather, the fact that he had entered a state of grieving led him to burn the meat. Despite that, he allowed Moses to complete his entire presentation before offering a response.

▶ **LISTENING LESSON**

We tend to become less patient and prone to interjecting when experiencing grief or troubling emotions. We learn from Aaron that even under emotionally trying circumstances, there is a need to retain dignity in communication by truly listening.

Miriam, Aaron, and the Almighty

NUMBERS   12:1–9

Aaron and Miriam discuss Moses's marital status, questioning his separation from his wife to exclusively focus on transmitting the words of G-d to the people. G-d reprimands them for this, explaining that the decision was G-d's, not Moses's, and that Moses's uniquely intense form of prophecy demands this extraordinary step.

▶ **ANALYSIS**

Sifrei, Numbers 12:5

The Torah reports that G-d began His reprimand with the phrase "Hear My words." Our sages interpret this to mean that Aaron and Miriam attempted to interject, leading G-d to direct them to remain silent until He finished His message, even though G-d would not have been discombobulated in the slightest by an interjection.

▶ **LISTENING LESSON**

We might allow ourselves the luxury of interjecting when we are certain that the other party will not be confused or taken aback by the interruption. G-d's directive to Miriam and Aaron reminds us to avoid cutting off another party even when such a certainty exists.

MIRIAM'S SONG
The Golden Haggadah, Catalonia, c. 1320 (British Library, MS 27210)

Moses and Korah

NUMBERS 16:1–11

Korah instigates a rebellion against Moses, publicly and derogatorily accusing him of nepotism in several of his appointments to positions of prominence and responsibility. Ultimately, Korah and his rebels meet a bitter end: G-d causes the earth beneath them to open, and they and their derogatory claims simultaneously vanish.

▶ **ANALYSIS**
Rabbi Yitzchak Abarbanel, *Nachalat Avot* 5:7

Moses listened to Korah's claims without interjecting; he only offered a rebuttal once Korah had concluded his rebellious diatribe.

▶ **LISTENING LESSON**

When we feel attacked and our integrity is called into question, we tend to stop listening and respond impulsively. Moses's conduct under pressure inspires us to avoid interjecting even in such unpleasant cases.

The Two Tribes and Moses

NUMBERS 32:1–33

As the Israelites approach the Jordan River, the tribes of Reuben and Gad notice that the lands on the eastern side of the river are perfect for their giant herds. Their leaders approach Moses, requesting to settle there instead of crossing the Jordan into the future Land of Israel with the rest of the Israelites. Moses is deeply upset. He criticizes them at length for forsaking their brethren, suggesting that their proposal would weaken their brethren's resolve in conquering the Land. In response, the tribal leaders promise to lead the nation in its battles for the Land before returning to settle the territory under discussion, whereupon Moses agrees to their proposal.

▶ **ANALYSIS**
Rabbi Eliyahu of Vilna, Mishnah, Avot 5:7

The tribal leaders waited patiently for Moses to conclude his sharp and lengthy critique—ten complete verses—despite realizing that he would be extremely gratified to hear that they were willing to first cross the Jordan to join the battles.

▶ **LISTENING LESSON**

We tend to interject for the sake of damage control when someone is upset with us and a quick clarification can readily demonstrate that it was a misunderstanding. The conduct of the tribal leaders reminds us to exercise patience in listening regardless.

Psychology References

Bodie GD, et al. (2015) The role of "active listening" in informal helping conversations: Impact on perceptions of listener helpfulness, sensitivity, and supportiveness and discloser emotional improvement. *Western Journal of Communication, 79*(2), 151–173. doi.org/10.1080/10570314.2014.943429.

Jonsdottir IJ, Kristinsson K. (2020) Supervisors' active-empathetic listening as an important antecedent of work engagement. *International Journal of Environmental Research and Public Health, 17*(21):7976. doi.org/10.3390/ijerph17217976. PMID: 33142984; PMCID: PMC7662981.

Kuhn R, et al. (2018) The power of listening: Lending an ear to the partner during dyadic coping conversations. *Journal of the Division of Family Psychology of the American Psychological Association (Division 43), 32*(6), 762–772. doi.org/10.1037/fam0000421.

Manusov V, et al. (2018) Conditions and consequences of listening well for interpersonal relationships: Modeling active-empathic listening, social-emotional skills, trait mindfulness, and relational quality. *International Journal of Listening, 34*(2), 110–126. doi.org/10.1080/10904018.2018.1507745.

Tennant K, et al. (2024) Active Listening [Updated 2023 Sep 13]. In: *StatPearls [Internet]*. Treasure Island (FL): StatPearls Publishing. Available from: www.ncbi.nlm.nih.gov/books/NBK442015/.

Weger H, et al. (2014) The relative effectiveness of active listening in initial interactions. *International Journal of Listening, 28*(1), 13–31. doi.org/10.1080/10904018.2013.813234.

APPENDIX A—TO LEARN FROM EVERYONE

TEXT 10

True Wisdom

Mishnah, Avot 4:1

בֶּן זוֹמָא אוֹמֵר: אֵיזֶהוּ חָכָם? הַלּוֹמֵד מִכָּל אָדָם.

Ben Zoma would say: "Who is wise?
One who learns from every person."

TEXT 11

The Student Mindset

Rabbi Shmuel de Uceda, *Midrash Shmuel,* Avot, ad loc.

מַה מָּתוֹק מִדְּבַשׁ מַה שֶּׁמָּצִינוּ בְּדִבְרֵי רַבּוֹתֵינוּ זִכְרוֹנָם
לִבְרָכָה שֶׁמְּכַנִּים אֶת הַחֲכָמִים בְּשֵׁם "תַּלְמִידֵי חֲכָמִים",
לְהוֹדִיעֵנוּ הָעִנְיָן הַנִּפְלָא הַזֶּה: כִּי מֵעוֹלָם לֹא יִצְדַּק שֶׁיִּקָּרֵא
שֵׁם חָכָם לְבַד מִבְּלִי שֶׁיִּצְטָרֵף אֵלָיו שֵׁם תַּלְמִיד.
כִּי אִם אֵינוֹ חוֹשֵׁב שֶׁהוּא תַּלְמִיד, אֵינוֹ חָכָם, כִּי אִי אֶפְשָׁר
לְהַפְרִיד שֵׁם חָכָם מִשֵּׁם תַּלְמִיד. וְאַף אִם שֵׁם תַּלְמִיד
יִפָּרֵד מִשֵּׁם חָכָם - כִּי יֵשׁ תַּלְמִיד שֶׁאֵינוֹ חָכָם, וְהוּא
בִּתְחִילַת לִימוּדוֹ, כִּי אָז לֹא יִצְדַּק עָלָיו שֵׁם חָכָם - עִם
כָּל זֶה שֵׁם חָכָם אִי אֶפְשָׁר שֶׁיִּפָּרֵד מִשֵּׁם תַּלְמִיד.

How special that our sages label wise scholars as
talmidei chachamim [which translates as "wise
students"]! It is not appropriate to grant the term
"wise" (*chacham*) to an individual unless we attach

RABBI SHMUEL DE UCEDA
C. 1545–1604

Author and kabbalist.
His name, Uceda,
originates from the
town of that name in
the archbishopric of
Toledo. Rabbi Shmuel
was born in Safed, where
he was a pupil of the
Arizal and Rabbi Chaim
Vital, with whom he
studied kabbalah. He
grew to become a rabbi
and teacher in Safed and
later in Constantinople.
He wrote commentaries
to some biblical books
but is most noted for
his *Midrash Shmuel*
commentary on *Ethics
of the Fathers.*

the word "student" (*talmid*) as well, for those who fail to consider themselves as students are not wise. True, the reverse is possible: an individual can be a student without being wise—such as a student in the early stages of study, who has yet to accumulate much wisdom. But it is impossible to be wise without simultaneously being a student.

APPENDIX B—THE POWER TO ABSORB

TEXT 12

Suspend Your Agenda

Michael P. Nichols, *The Lost Art of Listening: How Learning to Listen Can Improve Relationships* (New York: Guilford Press, 2009), pp. 75–77

The act of listening requires a submersion of the self and immersion in the other. This isn't always easy. We may be interested but too concerned with instructing or reforming the other person to be truly open to his point of view. Parents have trouble hearing their children as long as they can't suspend the urge to set them straight. Even therapists, presumably exemplars of understanding, are often too busy trying to change people to really listen to them. (Unfortunately, most people aren't eager to be changed by someone who doesn't understand them.) . . .

MICHAEL P. NICHOLS

Psychologist and author. Michael P. Nichols is a practicing family therapist and Professor of Psychology at the College of William and Mary. He is the author of a number of popular books on the topic of family therapy.

Suspending the self does not of course mean losing
the self—though that seems to be precisely what
some people are afraid of. Otherwise, why do they
insist on relentlessly repeating their own arguments,
when a simple acknowledgment of what the other
person says would be the first step toward mutual
understanding? It's as though saying "I understand
what you're trying to say" meant "You're right
and I'm wrong." Or that to give someone who's
angry at you a fair hearing and then say "I see why
you're upset with me" meant "I surrender." . . .

To really listen you have to suspend your
own agenda, forget about what you want to
say, and concentrate on being a receptive
vehicle for the other person. . . . Genuine
listening means suspending memory, desire,
and judgment—and, for a few moments
at least, existing for the other person.

TEXT 13

Awareness of a Lack

Dr. Yaakov Brawer, "In Pursuit of Ignorance,"
www.chabad.org/2940

Essential ignorance is achieved when a person becomes truthfully and sincerely cognizant that he lacks understanding. In contrast to passive ignorance, essential ignorance represents a relatively advanced state of self-comprehension. In Chassidic parlance it is described by the term *bittul* (self-negation).

Essential ignorance is not a lack of awareness, but rather the awareness of a lack, and as such, it renders the mind an empty vessel prepared to receive. Without *bittul*, the mind cannot function as a true vessel to admit wisdom because its standards of admission are distorted by bias, emotional needs, background, and habit. Essential ignorance motivates individuals to pursue truth regardless of the cost or the consequences.

DR. YAAKOV BRAWER

Scientist and professor. Dr. Yaakov Brawer is professor emeritus on the faculty of medicine at McGill University in Montreal. He lectures on neuroendocrinology and Chasidism. He has authored two books on Chasidic philosophy, *Something from Nothing* and *Eyes That See*.

The Mental Power of *Yesod*

TEXT 14

Rabbi Shneur Zalman of Liadi, *Maamarei Admur Hazaken*
5562:2, pp. 395–396

שֶׁאָנוּ רוֹאִים שֶׁיֵּשׁ מִי שֶׁיָּכוֹל לְקַלוֹט הַרְבֵּה מְאֹד בְּמוֹחוֹ, לֹא יִפְסוֹק מִלְּקַבֵּל וְלֹא יִלְאֶה לְעוֹלָם. וְיֵשׁ מִי שֶׁאֵינוֹ יָכוֹל כָּל כָּךְ לְקַבֵּל שֶׁפַע שֶׁכֶל הַרְבֵּה בְּפַעַם אַחַת, וְיִלְאֶה כֹּחַ שִׂכְלוֹ לְקַבֵּל כוּ'.

וְלֹא תִהְיֶה הַסִּבָּה מִצַּד הַחִסָּרוֹן שֶׁל הַמְקַבֵּל שֶׁלֹּא יִהְיֶה חָכָם כָּל כָּךְ - אַדְרַבָּה, יוּכַל לִהְיוֹת שֶׁחָכָם גָּדוֹל וּבַר הֲבָנָה גָּדוֹל לֹא יוּכַל לְקַלוֹט הַרְבֵּה בְּפַעַם אַחַת, וּבְמָה שֶׁמְּקַבֵּל וּמֵבִין הוּא חָכָם מוּפְלָג וְחָרִיף כוּ'. וְיֵשׁ קָטָן הֵימֶנּוּ שֶׁיּוּכַל הַרְבֵּה יוֹתֵר לְקַלוֹט בְּתוֹכוֹ בְּפַעַם אַחַת, וְאֵינוֹ חָרִיף כָּל כָּךְ בְּמָה שֶׁכְּבָר קִיבֵּל כוּ'.

אַךְ הַסִּבָּה הוּא שֶׁיֵּשׁ כֹּחַ מְיוּחָד בַּשֵּׂכֶל, וְהוּא הַנִּקְרָא יְסוֹד, שֶׁמְּקַבֵּל כָּל שֶׁפַע. וְעִיקַר עִנְיַן כֹּחַ זֶה הוּא שֶׁיּוּכַל לְצַמְצֵם עַצְמוּתוֹ וּלְהַפְשִׁיט כָּל מַחְשְׁבוֹתָיו הָעַצְמִיִּים, וְלִיתֵּן כָּל מוֹחוֹ רַק לִשְׁמֹעַ וְלִקַלוֹט הַשֵּׂכֶל שֶׁשּׁוֹמֵעַ מֵהַמַּשְׁפִּיעַ שֶׁלּוֹ. וְכָל מִי שֶׁיֵּשׁ בּוֹ יוֹתֵר כֹּחַ צִמְצוּם וְסִילוּק עַצְמוּתוֹ, פָּנוּי הוּא יוֹתֵר לְקַבֵּל כָּל שֶׁפַע, אֲפִילוּ הַרְבֵּה מְאֹד, כִּי "כְּלִי רֵיקָן מַחְזִיק" (בְּרָכוֹת מ, א).

We observe that some individuals can mentally absorb a great deal of information; they never cease to absorb and never tire of absorbing. On the other hand, others struggle to take in a substantial amount of information at once.

The limitation is not due to a lack of intelligence; on the contrary, highly intelligent people may be unable to absorb a large *quantity* at once, even as they excel in processing with clarity and sharpness that which they do absorb. Conversely, less intelligent individuals might rapidly absorb significant data, but their comprehension may be inferior.

The reason for this phenomenon is that the mind contains a specific power known as *yesod* [lit., "foundation"; often translated as "attachment"], responsible for the reception of ideas. The essence of this power lies in its ability to contract our personal presence, in the sense of divesting ourselves of all personal thoughts, to devote our entire mental capacity to hearing and absorbing the information from the person delivering it. The greater extent to which we can contract ourselves, the more open we are to receiving intellectual information, even a vast quantity—for as the Talmud points out, "an *empty* container is able to retain" (BERACHOT 40A).

APPENDIX C—KING SOLOMON LISTENED

TEXT 15

Solomon's Wisdom
I Kings 3:22–23

וַתֹּאמֶר הָאִשָּׁה הָאַחֶרֶת: לֹא, כִּי בְּנִי הַחַי וּבְנֵךְ הַמֵּת. וְזֹאת אֹמֶרֶת, לֹא, כִּי בְּנֵךְ הַמֵּת וּבְנִי הֶחָי. וַתְּדַבֵּרְנָה לִפְנֵי הַמֶּלֶךְ.

וַיֹּאמֶר הַמֶּלֶךְ: זֹאת אֹמֶרֶת, זֶה בְּנִי הַחַי, וּבְנֵךְ הַמֵּת. וְזֹאת אֹמֶרֶת, לֹא, כִּי בְּנֵךְ הַמֵּת וּבְנִי הֶחָי.

The second woman argued, "Not so! My son is the living one, and your son is the dead one." However, the first woman insisted, "Not so! Your son is the dead one, and my son is the living one." Thus they argued before the king.

The king said, "This one says, 'My son is the living one, and your son is the dead one,' and the other says, 'Not so! Your son is the dead one, and my son is the living one.'"

QUESTION

There is a linguistic distinction between the statements of these two mothers. Can you identify it? What might be the implication?

KINGS

Biblical book. The book of Kings, part of the Prophets section of the Hebrew Bible, relates the history of the Israelites and their kings and prophets, from the final days of King David in 837 BCE until the destruction of the first Temple in 423 BCE. Written by the prophet Jeremiah, Kings is a single work that was later split into 2 parts.

Judicial Procedure

TEXT 16

Rabbi Yehoshua Falk Hakohen Katz, *Me'irat Einayim,*
Choshen Mishpat 17:15

וּסְבָרָא הִיא, כְּדֵי שֶׁיְּהֵא נוֹחַ דַּעַת בַּעֲלֵי דִין, וְלֹא יַעֲלֶה עַל
לִבָּם שֶׁמָּא הַדַּיָּינִים יִשְׂאוּ וְיִתְּנוּ בַּדִּין וְלֹא הֵבִינוּ טַעֲנָתָן ...

וְעוֹד, שֶׁמָּא בֶּאֱמֶת הַדַּיָּינִים לֹא עָמְדוּ הֵיטֵב
עַל דִּבְרֵי טַעֲנוֹתָן, וּבְשַׁנּוֹתָן לִפְנֵי הַבַּעֲלֵי דִין
יְעוֹרְרוּ אוֹתָן לוֹמַר כֹּה וָכֹה הָיוּ טַעֲנוֹתֵיהֶם.

The judges need to restate the arguments to
put the litigants' minds at ease, so that they
do not worry that the judges are deliberating
the case without having adequately
understood their respective claims. . . .

Moreover, it is possible that the judges
misunderstood the arguments. If this
occurred, then when the judges restate the
arguments, the litigants have the opportunity
to correct the misunderstanding.

**RABBI YEHOSHUA FALK
HAKOHEN KATZ**
1555–1614

Polish rabbi, Talmudist,
and authority on
Jewish law. Rabbi Falk
is best known for his
Perishah and *Derishah*
commentaries on the
Arbaah Turim, as
well as *Sefer Me'irat
Einayim* on the Shulchan
Aruch. Rabbi Falk was
a pupil of Rabbi Moshe
Isserlis and served as
head of the yeshiva in
Lemberg as well as on the
Council of Four Lands,
a central body of Jewish
authority in Poland.

APPENDIX D—DON'T INTERRUPT!

TEXT 17

Let the Speaker Finish

Orchot Tzadikim, Shaar Hashetikah

אִם אָדָם אוֹמֵר לְךָ דָּבָר שֶׁיָּדַעְתָּ כְּבָר, שְׁתוֹק עַד שֶׁיִּגְמוֹר הַדָּבָר, כִּי אוּלַי יְחַדֵּשׁ לְךָ בּוֹ דָּבָר שֶׁלֹּא יָדַעְתָּ מִתְּחִלָּה.

גַּם יֵשׁ לוֹ הֲנָאָה שֶׁיֹּאמַר לְךָ דָּבָר, וַאֲפִילוּ אִם יוֹדֵעַ אַתָּה שֶׁלֹּא יְחַדֵּשׁ לְךָ, שְׁתוֹק עַד שֶׁיִּגְמוֹר.

If someone tells you something you already know, remain silent until the speaker has finished, for you may discover a new detail of which you were not previously aware.

Even if you anticipate no fresh information, remaining silent allows the speaker the pleasure of relating something to you.

**ORCHOT TZADIKIM
C. 14TH CENTURY**

A classic work on Jewish ethics. The identity of the author of *Orchot Tzadikim* (*The Ways of the Righteous*) is unknown, but it is believed to have been written by a French scholar, probably in the 14th century. Drawing much material from earlier ethicists Rabbi Shlomo ibn Gabirol, Maimonides, and Rabbi Bachya ibn Pakudah, *Orchot Tzadikim* focuses on character refinement and on explaining the core values of Jewish religious life.

Divine Patience

Avot DeRabbi Natan, ch. 37

וְאֵינוֹ נִכְנָס לְתוֹךְ דִּבְרֵי חֲבֵרוֹ . . . כַּיּוֹצֵא בּוֹ בְּאַבְרָהָם אָבִינוּ, כְּשֶׁהָיָה מִתְפַּלֵּל עַל אַנְשֵׁי סְדוֹם, אָמַר לוֹ הַקָּדוֹשׁ בָּרוּךְ הוּא: "אִם אֶמְצָא בִסְדוֹם חֲמִשִּׁים צַדִּיקִים וְנָשָׂאתִי לְכָל הַמָּקוֹם בַּעֲבוּרָם" (בְּרֵאשִׁית יח, כו). גָּלוּי וְיָדוּעַ לִפְנֵי מִי שֶׁאָמַר וְהָיָה הָעוֹלָם שֶׁאֵלּוּ הָיוּ מְצוּיִין בִּסְדוֹם ג' אוֹ ה' צַדִּיקִים, לֹא גָרַם בָּהּ עָוֹן. אֶלָּא הִמְתִּין הַקָּדוֹשׁ בָּרוּךְ הוּא אֶת אַבְרָהָם עַד שֶׁסִּיֵּם דְּבָרָיו, וְאַחַר כָּךְ הֱשִׁיבוֹ.

Wise people do not interrupt the words of another. . . . We observe this virtue when Abraham prayed for the people of Sodom. G-d told him, "If I find fifty righteous people in Sodom, I will spare the entire place for their sake" (GENESIS 18:26). It was indeed revealed and known to G-d that Sodom did not harbor even three or five righteous individuals; for if they existed, Sodom would not have been such a sinful city. Nevertheless, G-d waited for Abraham to finish speaking, and only then did He respond to him.

AVOT DERABBI NATAN

A commentary on, and an elaboration of, the Mishnaic tractate Avot, bearing the name of Rabbi Natan, one of the sages of the Mishnah. The work exists in two very different versions, one of which appears in many editions of the Talmud.

THE ART OF DISAGREEING

Disagreements are inevitable, but they don't have to lead to discord and resentment. How can we navigate conflicts with grace while maintaining harmony in our relationships?

I. INTRODUCTION

Navigating disagreements successfully is crucial for our relationships. This lesson explores Judaism's empowering framework for achieving that prized but elusive goal.

OLD COUPLE WITH SAMOVAR
Gaina Rozin, oil on canvas,
1970, Russia

FIGURE 3.1

Examples of Disagreements

CIRCLE OF INTIMACY

- Spouses disagree over spending habits, budgeting priorities, or savings goals.

- Spouses disagree over the division of labor and household chores.

- Spouses disagree about their diet and eating habits.

- Parents disagree about disciplinary approaches, educational philosophies, or screen time rules.

- Siblings disagree over the best way to care for their aging parents.

CIRCLE OF PARTICIPATION

- Members of a synagogue disagree over leadership roles and governance structure.

- Members of an association disagree over the decision-making process and the allocation of resources.

- Coworkers or partners disagree on whether to minimize risks or adopt a more ambitious strategy.

- Neighbors disagree over social issues, the role of government, and the economy.

EXERCISE 3.1   From the above lists (Figure 3.1), select an item that parallels your personal experience. Consider what that experience taught you. What might be three essential dos and don'ts for maintaining harmony in a relationship despite disagreements?

DOS	DON'TS

II. DEBUNKING MISCONCEPTIONS

There are several common misconceptions regarding disagreements: (a) viewing a disagreement as an unexpected and unhealthy crisis, (b) believing that love is the solution, or (c) presuming that a disagreement must always be raised in direct conversation for the sake of working it through.

UNTITLED
Boris Deutsch (1892–1978),
watercolor and ink, California

TANCHUMA

A Midrashic work bearing the name of Rabbi Tanchuma, a 4th-century Talmudic sage quoted often in this work. "Midrash" is the designation of a particular genre of rabbinic literature usually forming a running commentary on specific books of the Bible. *Tanchuma* provides textual exegeses, expounds upon the biblical narrative, and develops and illustrates moral principles. *Tanchuma* is unique in that many of its sections commence with a Halachic discussion, which subsequently leads into nonhalachic teachings.

Unique Minds

TEXT 1A

Midrash, *Tanchuma*, *Pinchas* 10

כְּשֵׁם שֶׁאֵין פַּרְצוּפֵיהֶן שֶׁל אָדָם שָׁוִין זֶה
לָזֶה, כָּךְ אֵין דַּעְתָּם שָׁוִין זֶה לָזֶה.

Just as human faces are not identical,
so their minds are not alike.

Mindful Tolerance

TEXT 1B

Rabbi Menachem Mendel Morgenstern,
Emet Ve'emunah (Jerusalem, 2005), no. 629, p. 448

בְּתַנְחוּמָא פָּרָשַׁת פִּנְחָס: כְּשֵׁם שֶׁאֵין פַּרְצוּפֵיהֶן שֶׁל
אָדָם שָׁוִין זֶה לָזֶה, כָּךְ אֵין דַּעְתָּם שָׁוִין זֶה לָזֶה.

כְּשֵׁם שֶׁהִנְךָ יָכוֹל לִסְבּוֹל שֶׁפַּרְצוּפוֹ שֶׁל
אָדָם אַחֵר אֵינוֹ דּוֹמֶה לְשֶׁלְךָ, כָּךְ תִּסְבּוֹל אִם
דֵּעוֹתָיו שֶׁל אַחֵר אֵינָן דּוֹמוֹת לְדֵעוֹתֶיךָ.

The Midrash teaches, "Just as human faces are
not identical, so their minds are not alike."

Just as you tolerate others despite their *looking*
different from you, so must you tolerate
others who *think* differently from you.

RABBI MENACHEM MENDEL MORGENSTERN 1787–1859

Chasidic rabbi and leader. Born near Lublin, Poland, Rabbi Menachem Mendel went on to succeed the Chozeh (Seer) of Lublin and Rabbi Simchah Bunim of Peshischa as a Chasidic rebbe in Kotsk. His teachings, some of which are gathered in *Ohel Torah* and *Emet Ve'emunah*, are well-known in the Chasidic world for their sharpness.

TEXT 2A

Student Discord

Talmud, Yevamot 62b

שְׁנֵים עָשָׂר אֶלֶף זוּגִים תַּלְמִידִים הָיוּ לוֹ
לְרַבִּי עֲקִיבָא . . . שֶׁלֹּא נָהֲגוּ כָּבוֹד זֶה לָזֶה.

Rabbi Akiva had twelve thousand pairs of students. . . . They did not behave toward each other with respect.

BABYLONIAN TALMUD

A literary work of monumental proportions that draws upon the legal, spiritual, intellectual, ethical, and historical traditions of Judaism. The 37 tractates of the Babylonian Talmud contain the teachings of the Jewish sages from the period after the destruction of the 2nd Temple through the 5th century CE. It has served as the primary vehicle for the transmission of the Oral Law and the education of Jews over the centuries; it is the entry point for all subsequent legal, ethical, and theological Jewish scholarship.

REBBE AKIVA LEARNING THE ALEPH BEIS
Ilan Block, acrylic on canvas, 2023, New Jersey

Love as Impetus

TEXT 2B

The Rebbe, Rabbi Menachem Mendel Schneerson,
Likutei Sichot 32, pp. 149–150

אָמְרוּ חֲכָמֵינוּ זִכְרוֹנָם לִבְרָכָה שֶׁאֵין דֵּעוֹתֵיהֶם שֶׁל בְּנֵי
אָדָם שָׁווֹת. וְכַמּוּבָן שֶׁכֵּן הוּא בְּנוֹגֵעַ לְכ״ד אֶלֶף תַּלְמִידֵי רַבִּי
עֲקִיבָא, שֶׁכָּל אֶחָד וְאֶחָד מֵהֶם הִשִּׂיג תּוֹרַת רַבִּי עֲקִיבָא לְפִי
דַרְכּוֹ וְדַעְתּוֹ, וּבִשְׁיקוּל הַדַּעַת שֶׁלּוֹ מַסְקָנָתוֹ שֶׁבְּוַדַּאי כְּפִי
שֶׁהִשִּׂיג הוּא כֵּן הוּא הַפֵּירוּשׁ הָאֲמִיתִּי בְּדִבְרֵי רַבִּי עֲקִיבָא.

וְלָכֵן כַּאֲשֶׁר שָׁמַע שֶׁחֲבֵירוֹ לוֹמֵד אֶת דִּבְרֵי רַבּוֹ בְּאוֹפֶן
שׁוֹנֶה - וּבִלְתִּי נָכוֹן לְפִי דַעְתּוֹ - לֹא הָיָה יָכוֹל לִנְהוֹג בּוֹ
כָּבוֹד וְהַעֲרָכָה . . . מִצַּד הוֹרָאָתוֹ הַיְסוֹדִית הַנִּזְכֶּרֶת לְעֵיל
שֶׁל רַבִּי עֲקִיבָא שֶׁאָמַר: "וְאָהַבְתָּ לְרֵעֲךָ כָּמוֹךָ - זֶה כְּלָל
גָּדוֹל בַּתּוֹרָה" (סִפְרָא, קְדוֹשִׁים ד). לוּלֵא הוֹרָאָה זוֹ, יִתָּכֵן
שֶׁלֹּא יִהְיֶה אִיכְפַּת לָהֶם כָּל כָּךְ מָה שֶׁיֵּשׁ תַּלְמִיד שֶׁאֵינוֹ
מַשִּׂיג תּוֹרַת רַבָּם לַאֲמִיתָּהּ; אֲבָל מִכֵּיוָן שֶׁרַבִּי עֲקִיבָא
רַבָּם לִימְּדָם עַל דְּבַר מַעֲלַת קִיּוּם מִצְוַת "וְאָהַבְתָּ לְרֵעֲךָ
כָּמוֹךָ" . . . כָּל אֶחָד וְאֶחָד מֵהֶם הִשְׁתַּדֵּל לְהַשְׁפִּיעַ עַל
כָּל שֶׁבִּגְדֶר "רֵעֲךָ", וּבִפְרָט תַּלְמִידֵי רַבּוֹ, שֶׁגַּם הֵם יַשִּׂיגוּ
תּוֹרַת רַבָּם בְּאוֹתָהּ הַדֶּרֶךְ הָאֲמִיתִּית (לְפִי דַעְתּוֹ).

וְאֵלֶּה שֶׁלֹּא קִיבְּלוּ זֶה - לֹא הָיָה יָכוֹל לִנְהוֹג בָּהֶם כָּבוֹד
(וּבִפְרָט כָּבוֹד כְּפִי הַדָּרוּשׁ מִתַּלְמִידֵי רַבִּי עֲקִיבָא).

RABBI MENACHEM MENDEL SCHNEERSON 1902-1994

The towering Jewish leader of the 20th century, known as "the Lubavitcher Rebbe," or simply as "the Rebbe." Born in southern Ukraine, the Rebbe escaped Nazi-occupied Europe, arriving in the U.S. in June 1941. The Rebbe inspired and guided the revival of traditional Judaism after the European devastation, impacting virtually every Jewish community the world over. The Rebbe often emphasized that the performance of just one additional good deed could usher in the era of Mashiach. The Rebbe's scholarly talks and writings have been printed in more than 200 volumes.

Our sages note that each human mind varies from all others. This was also the case with the twenty-four thousand students of Rabbi Akiva: they all grasped their master's teachings according to their individual paths and understandings, each assuming that their own interpretation was the true meaning of Rabbi Akiva's words.

When they realized that their colleagues understood their master's words differently, in a manner that they regarded as incorrect, they became disinclined to treat the others with esteem, . . . *specifically because* of the fundamental teaching of Rabbi Akiva: "Love your neighbor as yourself—this is the Torah's major principle" (*SIFRA*, *KEDOSHIM* 4). Without this mandate, they might not have cared so much if a colleague failed to grasp what they considered to be the true meaning of their master's Torah. However, since their teacher Rabbi Akiva taught them about the importance of fulfilling the commandment to "love your neighbor *as yourself*" . . . each student endeavored to influence all those included in the definition of "neighbor," especially their fellow students, so that they would similarly grasp their master's Torah in the "true" way.

They could not respect a colleague who did not accept this "true" way (at least not to the extent expected of Rabbi Akiva's students).

TEXT 3

The Unifying Force

Rabbi Shmuel Lew, "The Unifying Force," *Here's My Story*
(Jewish Educational Media), January 11, 2014

On the day after Simchas Torah in 1974 . . .
the Rebbe asked me if recently I had heard
from a certain person, a communal figure in
England. I said that, as a matter of fact, I had.
I added that I had heard that this person had
very strongly criticized the Rebbe. . . .

The Rebbe told me the reason for this person's
harsh statements was that somebody had
misinformed him about what the Rebbe had
said about him in a public talk. As a result, this
person believed that the Rebbe had attacked
him personally. But, said the Rebbe, "I do not
speak about personalities; I speak about ideas."

As the Rebbe was saying this . . . I decided, within a
split second, that as soon as I returned to England,
I would make an appointment with this communal
figure and straighten things out. As I was thinking it,
at that very moment, the Rebbe said, "It's not a good
idea for you to tell him that I told you about this."

Now, unfortunately, I'm a little bit of a wise guy, so I
immediately figured out a way around it. I thought,
"I won't do it, but I'll get somebody else to do it." I
was desperate to clear things up, so that this person
shouldn't have a negative feeling about the Rebbe.

**RABBI SHMUEL LEW
1940–**

Educator. Born in
Brooklyn, Rabbi
Shmuel Lew studied at
the Central Lubavitch
Yeshivah in New
York. He has served
as a Chabad rabbi in
London since 1965
and is the principal of
the local Lubavitch
Senior Girls' School.

But again, as I was thinking this—this was within a split second—the Rebbe said, "And it's not a good idea for you to ask somebody else to go speak with him. . . . The point is that there are 613 commandments in the Torah. . . . If this person will not work with us on this one *mitzvah*, let him work with us on the other 612."

He then explained to me about how to become close with this person and how to befriend him. He described how positive this man and his family were, and how they could be forces for good.

And, to me, this became a directive for life in general: Look for the unifying force. Always look for that which you have in common with the other person and build on that.

How to Disagree

1. **DON'T PANIC**

   Disagreements are an expected reality of any relationship. Far from indicating problems, they are a sign of maturity.

2. **MORE RESPECT**

   Love alone is insufficient to navigate differences effectively. Integrating a robust foundation of respect is crucial.

3. **LEAVE IT ALONE**

   Not every disagreement demands resolution. It is possible to cultivate a strong connection by focusing on other shared interests and goals.

III. CONFLICT AS A CATALYST

The Torah teaches that disagreements, handled properly, can be a relationship *enhancer*. This approach is embedded in the Torah's narrative of Creation and is apparent in the story of two leading Talmudic sages.

THE THIRD DAY OF CREATION
Ofra Friedland, oil on canvas, Israel

Not Good

Midrash, *Bereishit Rabah* 4:6

לָמָה אֵין כְּתִיב בַּשֵּׁנִי "כִּי טוֹב"? . . .

רַבִּי חֲנִינָא אוֹמֵר: שֶׁבּוֹ נִבְרֵאת מַחֲלוֹקֶת, שֶׁנֶּאֱמַר: "וִיהִי מַבְדִּיל בֵּין מַיִם לָמָיִם" (בְּרֵאשִׁית א, ו).

אָמַר רַבִּי טַבְיוּמֵי: אִם מַחֲלוֹקֶת שֶׁהִיא לְתִקּוּנוֹ שֶׁל עוֹלָם וּלְיִשּׁוּבוֹ אֵין בָּהּ "כִּי טוֹב", מַחֲלוֹקֶת שֶׁהִיא לְעִרְבּוּבוֹ עַל אַחַת כַּמָּה וְכַמָּה.

Why doesn't the Torah report "it was good" on the second day? . . .

Rabbi Chanina taught: Division was created on that day, as it is stated, "Let there be a separation between water and water" (GENESIS 1:6).

Rabbi Tavyomei taught: If G-d declined to declare an act of division necessary for the planet's betterment as "good," how much more so regarding division [among people] that inflicts disturbance on the world!

BEREISHIT RABAH

An early rabbinic commentary on the book of Genesis. This Midrash bears the name of Rabbi Oshiya Rabah (Rabbi Oshiya "the Great"), whose teaching opens this work. This Midrash provides textual exegeses and stories, expounds upon the biblical narrative, and develops and illustrates moral principles. Produced by the sages of the Talmud in the Land of Israel, its use of Aramaic closely resembles that of the Jerusalem Talmud. It was first printed in Constantinople in 1512 together with 4 other Midrashic works on the other 4 books of the Pentateuch.

Between Two and Three

Rabbi Yehudah Loew, *Derech Chayim* 3:3

שְׁנַיִם הֵם רִיבּוּי וְלֹא יִתְאַחֲדוּ. וּשְׁלֹשָׁה יֵשׁ לָהֶם
הִתְאַחֲדוּת כְּאִלוּ הֵם דָּבָר אֶחָד . . . וְזֶה תּוּכַל לְהָבִין
בְּצוּרָה: כַּאֲשֶׁר תַּנִּיחַ שְׁנֵי קַוִּים זֶה אֵצֶל זֶה, אֵין זֶה
נִרְאֶה כְּאֶחָד כְּלָל, בַּעֲבוּר שֶׁלֹּא יִתְאַחֲדוּ הַקַּוִּים, כְּמוֹ
זֶה ∧, הֲרֵי אֵין כָּאן דָּבָר אֶחָד. אֲבָל כַּאֲשֶׁר אַתָּה מֵנִיחַ
שְׁלֹשָׁה כְּמוֹ זֶה △, הֲרֵי הַקַּוִּים הֵם מִתְאַחֲדִים.

The number two symbolizes a plurality that cannot
unite. The number three, by contrast, symbolizes
unity. . . . We observe this when depicting it:
Two adjacent lines, like this: ∧, cannot unite,
and do not appear as one entity. However, with
three lines, like this: △, the lines can unite.

**RABBI YEHUDAH LOEW
(MAHARAL OF PRAGUE)
1525–1609**

Talmudist and philosopher.
Maharal rose to prominence
as leader of the famed
Jewish community of
Prague. He is the author of
more than a dozen works
of original philosophic
thought, including *Tiferet
Yisrael* and *Netzach Yisrael*.
He also authored *Gur
Aryeh,* a supercommentary
to Rashi's biblical
commentary; and a
commentary on the
nonlegal passages of
the Talmud. He is
buried in the Old Jewish
Cemetery of Prague.

IN UNITY
Yaeli Vogel, acrylic on
canvas, New York

FIGURE 3.3

From Singularity to Harmony

	STATUS	EXPLANATION	SYMBOL	DESIGNATION
DAY 1	Uniformity	Existence was imbued with a Divine consciousness.			Defined as good.
DAY 2	Division	The physical world obtained a sense of separation from its Divine source.	∧	Not defined as good.
DAY 3	Harmony	The stage was set for the human to harness the physical for spiritual objectives, introducing reconciliation.	△	Defined as *doubly* good.

FIGURE 3.4

Lessons from the Creation Narrative

1. **Conflict is woven into the fabric of Creation.**

2. **Conflict is a negative phenomenon.**

3. **If navigated properly, conflict can give rise to reconciliation.**

4. **Reconciliation can introduce greater value than the prior uniformity.**

Rabbi Shais Taub
addresses why many Jewish practices are rooted in arguments.
myjli.com/relationships

QUESTION

Are there positive outcomes that can be produced by a disagreement? If so, what are they?

TEXT 6

Yearning for Challenge

Talmud, Bava Metzi'a 84a

נָח נַפְשֵׁיה דְרַבִּי שִׁמְעוֹן בֶּן לָקִישׁ, וַהֲוָה קָא
מִצְטַעֵר רַבִּי יוֹחָנָן בַּתְרֵיה טוּבָא.

אָמְרוּ רַבָּנָן: מַאן לֵיזִיל לְיַתְבֵיה לְדַעְתֵּיה?
נֵיזִיל רַבִּי אֶלְעָזָר בֶּן פְּדָת דִמְחַדְדִין שְׁמַעְתָּתֵיה.

אָזַל יָתִיב קַמֵּיה. כָּל מִילְתָא דַהֲוָה אָמַר רַבִּי
יוֹחָנָן אָמַר לֵיה: תַּנְיָא דִמְסַיְיעָא לָךְ.

אָמַר: אַתְּ כְּבַר לָקִישָׁא? בַּר לָקִישָׁא, כִּי הֲוָה אֲמִינָא מִילְתָא,
הֲוָה מַקְשֵׁי לִי עֶשְׂרִין וְאַרְבַּע קוּשְׁיָיתָא, וּמְפָרְקִינָא לֵיה
עֶשְׂרִין וְאַרְבָּעָה פְּרוּקֵי, וּמִמֵּילָא רָוְוחָא שְׁמַעְתָּא. וְאַתְּ
אָמְרַתְּ תַּנְיָא דִמְסַיֵּיע לָךְ? אָטוּ לֹא יָדַעְנָא דְשַׁפִּיר קָאמִינָא?

הֲוָה קָא אָזִיל וְקָרַע מָאנֵיה וְקָא בָּכֵי וְאָמַר:
הֵיכָא אַתְּ בַּר לָקִישָׁא? הֵיכָא אַתְּ בַּר לָקִישָׁא?

When Reish Lakish passed away,
Rabbi Yochanan grieved terribly.

The sages told each other, "Who should visit
him to provide comfort? Let Rabbi Elazar
ben Pedat go, for he is a brilliant scholar."

Rabbi Elazar ben Pedat went and sat before Rabbi
Yochanan. To each idea that Rabbi Yochanan
taught, Rabbi Elazar ben Pedat responded, "I know
of an earlier teaching that supports your opinion."

Rabbi Yochanan exclaimed, "Are you supposed
to be like Reish Lakish? In my discussions
with Reish Lakish, whenever I would share a
viewpoint, he would raise twenty-four *objections*
and I would be forced to deliver twenty-four
responses! As a result of our intense give-and-
take, the entire subject was crystallized. You,
however, constantly tell me, 'There is an earlier
teaching that supports your opinion.' Do I not
already know that my ideas are sound?"

Rabbi Yochanan went about in grief. He tore his
clothes, wept, and called out, "Where are you,
Reish Lakish? Where are you, Reish Lakish?"

Strength in Perspectives

The Rebbe, Rabbi Menachem Mendel Schneerson,
Sefer Hasichot 5749:2, pp. 436–437

דֶער אוֹיבֶּערשְׁטֶער הָאט בַּאשַׁאפַן מֶענטשְׁן אִין אַן
אוֹפֶן אַז "אֵין דֵעוֹתֵיהֶן שָׁווֹת", וָואס דָאס גִיט אַן
אֶפְשָׁרִיוּת אַז מִצַד דִי חִילוּקֵי דֵעוֹת צְווִישְׁן מֶענטשְׁן
זָאל ווֶערן אַ מַצָּב פוּן "לֹא נָהֲגוּ כָּבוֹד זֶה לָזֶה".

דִי כַּוָּנָה אִין דֶעם וָואס דֶער אוֹיבֶּערשְׁטֶער הָאט אַזוֹי
בַּאשַׁאפַן מֶענטשְׁן אִיז אָבֶּער נִיט בִּכְדֵי דֶערפוּן זָאל
אַרוֹיס חַס וְשָׁלוֹם מַחְלוֹקֶת, כַּמוּבָן וּפָשׁוּט, נָאר אַדְרַבָּה
- צוּלִיב דֶעם עִילוּי וָואס קוּמְט אַרוֹיס פוּן שָׁלוֹם וְאַחְדוּת
אַנשְׁטָאט וּבִמְקוֹם הַהִתְחַלְּקוּת (דִי מַעֲלָה פוּן שְׁלֹשָׁה):

דוּרךְ דֶעם וָואס עֶס זַיינֶען פַאראן פַארשִׁידֶענֶע דֵעוֹת
קוּמֶען אַרוֹיס אַ רִיבּוּי סְבָרוֹת אוּן חִידוּשִׁים, וָואס יֶעדֶערֶער
טוּט אוֹיף מִצַד זַיין (טֶבַע הַ)שֵׂכֶל, בִּיז אַז דָאס קֶען
בְּרֶענגֶען אוּן בְּרֶענגְט אַ גְלַייכֶערֶע אוּן בֶּעסֶערֶע מַסְקָנָא
וְהַכְרָעָה . . . דוּרךְ דֶעם וָואס פַארשִׁידֶענֶע מֶענטשְׁן
מִיט בַּאזוּנדֶערֶע סְבָרוֹת רֶעדְן זִיךְ צוּנוֹיף (נִיט אַז אֵיינֶער
אִיז מַעֲלִים אָדֶער מְוַותֵּר אוֹיף זַיין סְבָרָא - הֵיפֶּךְ הַטֶּבַע
שֶׁהִטְבִּיעַ בּוֹ הַקָּדוֹשׁ בָּרוּךְ הוּא), זֶעט מֶען דֶעם עִנְיָן פוּן
כַּמָה צְדָדִים, בְּמֵילָא בְּרֶענגְט דָאס צוּ אַ אוֹיסְרִיכְטִיקֶע
מַסְקָנָא (ווי ווֶען נָאר אֵיינֶער וָואלְט גֶעזָאגְט זַיין דֵעָה),

וּבִשְׁעַת מְ'רֶעדְט זִיךְ צוּזַאמֶען בְּאוֹפֶן זֶה אִיז מוּבָן
אַז דָאס אִיז מִתּוֹךְ שָׁלוֹם וְכָבוֹד זֶה לָזֶה.

The Almighty deliberately created humans with diverse perspectives, although that allows the possibility that, due to differing opinions, humans could wind up "not treating each other with respect."

Obviously, G-d's intention in creating people this way was not to enable conflict but its exact opposite: to facilitate a *superior* unity that emerges on the heels of division— the advantage of the number *three*.

The presence of multiple opinions yields multiple fresh points and ideas. Each individual contributes from their unique intellect, eventually leading to a better conclusion and decision. . . . When different individuals with dissimilar perspectives discuss a matter jointly (without any individual suppressing or forfeiting their viewpoint, for that would *contradict* the nature imbued in us by G-d), the matter can be viewed from several angles, leading to a truer conclusion than any single viewpoint.

Needless to say, if parties set this as their goal, they will conduct their discussion peacefully and with mutual respect.

Rabbi Aryeh Weinstein:
Judaism respects
individuality, and so
should you!
myjli.com/relationships

EXERCISE 3.2

In light of Texts 6 and 7, identify attitudes that you consider constructive to navigating disagreements effectively, as well as contrasting attitudes that invite strife.

CONSTRUCTIVE ATTITUDES	NONCONSTRUCTIVE ATTITUDES

IV. PRACTICAL TIPS

With healthy attitudes firmly in place, we can consider practical communication skills that will lend these attitudes concrete expression. These skills will ensure that disagreements are worked through appropriately, without putting others on the defensive.

INTERESTING CONVERSATION
Hans Borchardt (1865–1917), 1912, Munich (Jewish Museum, Berlin, Germany)

Wisdom's Whisper

Ecclesiastes 9:17

דִּבְרֵי חֲכָמִים בְּנַחַת נִשְׁמָעִים, מִזַּעֲקַת מוֹשֵׁל בַּכְּסִילִים.

Softly spoken words of the wise are heard louder than the roars of foolish rulers.

Tentative Talk

Kerry Patterson, *Crucial Conversations: Tools for Talking When Stakes Are High* (New York: McGraw-Hill, 2002), pp. 143–144

Talking tentatively simply means that we tell our story as a story rather than disguising it as a hard fact. "Perhaps you were unaware . . ." suggests that you're not absolutely certain. "In my opinion . . ." says you're sharing an opinion and no more.

When sharing a story, strike a blend between confidence and humility. Share in a way that expresses appropriate confidence in your conclusions while demonstrating that, if called for, you want your conclusions challenged. To do so, change "The fact is" to "In my opinion." Swap "Everyone knows that" for "I've talked to three of our suppliers who think that." Soften "It's clear to me" to "I'm beginning to wonder if."

ECCLESIASTES

Biblical book. Written by King Solomon, Ecclesiastes is part of the Writings (Ketuvim) section of the Tanach. Addressing the existential question of the meaning of life, Ecclesiastes exposes the futility of materialism, concluding that Divine worship and mitzvah observance is the only true meaning of life. This book is traditionally read in many communities during the holiday of Sukkot.

KERRY PATTERSON

Author of many articles and training programs on communication for success, Patterson cofounded Interact Performance Systems, where he served as vice president of research and development for 10 years. Patterson coauthored several best-selling titles, including *Change Anything* (2011).

Why soften the message? Because we're trying to add meaning to the pool, not force it down people's throats. If we're too forceful, the information won't make it into the pool.

One of the ironies of dialogue is that, when talking with those holding opposing opinions, the more convinced and forceful you act, the more resistant others become. Speaking in absolute and overstated terms does not increase your influence, it decreases it. The converse is also true—the more tentatively you speak, the more open people become to your opinions.

DIALOGUE
Mariska Pisam,
oil painting, 2013, Holland

FIGURE 3.5

Forceful Phrases and Words

FORCEFUL PHRASES	FORCEFUL WORDS
"This is what went wrong."	Absolutely
"This is what we have to do."	Must
"That won't work."	Always
"This is the best idea!"	Never
"The fact is . . ."	Can't
"Everyone knows that . . ."	Certainly
"It's clear that . . ."	Worst

TEXT 10

Moderated Assertions

Rabbi Chaim Chizkiyahu Medini, *Sedei Chemed* 9,
Kelalei Haposkim 16:1

מָצִינוּ שֶׁכָּתְבוּ הַפּוֹסְקִים בְּלָשׁוֹן אֶפְשָׁר, וְהַבָּאִים
אַחֲרָיו כָּתְבוּ שֶׁכֵּן דַּעְתּוֹ בְּוַדַּאי, וּפָסְקוּ הַלָכָה כֵּן . . .
דְאֵינוּ לָשׁוֹן סָפֵק, אֶלָּא דֶּרֶךְ עֲנָוָה הוּא לִכְתּוֹב כֵּן.

It is common for halachic authorities to state
their opinions with a term of moderation: *efshar*,
meaning, "perhaps this is so." Nevertheless,
subsequent halachic authorities will proceed
to cite such an opinion as the unequivocal view
of the earlier sage, omitting the modification,
and they will base their rulings on the stated
opinion. . . . This is done because *efshar* does
not [necessarily] imply doubt; rather, it's an
unpretentious way to express oneself.

**RABBI CHAIM
CHIZKIYAHU MEDINI**
1833–1905

Scholar and prolific
author. A Jerusalem
native, Rabbi Medini was
born into a distinguished
Sefardic family. He
served as the rabbi of
Constantinople and later
in the Crimea, during
which time he authored
many volumes of Torah
scholarship. His most
famous work is the
18-volume *Sedei Chemed*,
a comprehensive
encyclopedia of the
Talmud. He eventually
returned to Israel, where
he passed away in 1905.

Is there anyone we *can't*
learn from? **Mrs. Fruma
Gottlieb** shares a unique
perspective.
myjli.com/relationships

Guidelines for Constructive Dialogue in Challenging Conversations

Based on Angela Haupt, "How to Actually Change Someone's Mind," *Time*, October 26, 2022; Rachel Hartman, et al., "Interventions to Reduce Partisan Animosity," *Nature Human Behaviour* 6 (September 2022), pp. 1197–1205

1. **ENTER CALMLY**

   Ensure you are calm, cool, and collected before starting the conversation.

2. **DISCLOSE NERVOUSNESS**

   Be open about any nervousness or vulnerability you may feel; it's disarming.

3. **DON'T ASSUME HOSTILITY**

   Do not assume the person you're talking to dislikes you.

4. **POSITIVE MOMENTS**

   Zoom in on a positive moment you've had with this person, or think about some aspiration of theirs that you support, to foster a better environment for a tough conversation.

5. **CONSIDER OTHER VIEWS**

   Demonstrate that you are willing to consider views that you disagree with.

6. **FIND COMMON GROUND**

   Start by finding something you can both agree on.

7. **AGREE BEFORE CHALLENGING**

   Even in the subject of disagreement, agree with something embedded in their statement before challenging their view.

8. **SHOW RESPECT**

   Be sure you aren't implying that the
   other is stupid or gullible.

9. **AVOID MORALIZING**

   Instead of framing an argument around moral
   imperatives, focus on its practical benefits.

10. **TELL STORIES**

    Instead of facts, share personal experiences
    that led you to your views.

11. **ENCOURAGE INTROSPECTION**

    Ask questions that prompt the person to
    think about their reasons and beliefs.

12. **USE THE REWIND**

    If the person you're talking to says
    something insulting, say: "I want to go
    back to just before you said X."

13. **TAKE BREAKS**

    Use a pause to compose yourself and to decide
    whether to continue the conversation.

14. **STAY DETACHED**

    Don't allow your emotional and mental health to
    depend on the other person changing their mind.

15. **THINK LONG-TERM**

    View the conversation as the first of multiple
    attempts to help the other learn.

V. CONCLUSION: RELATIONSHIP REFLECTIONS

An individual can initiate a constructive attitude and demeanor during a disagreement, with the reasonable hope of triggering collaboration from the other.

TEXT 11

Mirrored Emotions

Proverbs 27:19

כַּמַּיִם הַפָּנִים לַפָּנִים, כֵּן לֵב הָאָדָם לָאָדָם.

As water mirrors a face, so does one human heart reflect another.

PROVERBS

Biblical book. The book of Proverbs appears in the Writings (Ketuvim) section of the Bible and contains the wise teachings, aphorisms, and parables of King Solomon, who lived in the 9th century BCE. The ethical teachings of Proverbs give counsel about overcoming temptation, extol the value of hard work, laud the pursuit of knowledge, and emphasize loyalty to G-d and His commandments as the foundation of true wisdom.

FIDDLER ON THE FALLS
Israel Rubinstein, oil painting, New York

KEY POINTS

1   Perspective diversity is hardwired into human nature. When it surfaces in a relationship, it indicates that the parties are in touch with themselves and comfortable enough to express it. It does not imply that the relationship is in crisis.

2   Love alone is not the solution to navigating relationship disagreements. Love may actually backfire, spurring us to seek to convince others, in vain, to abandon their apparent imprudence, even when they are determined to see things differently.

3   A relationship requires both love and respect. This respect entails honoring the existence of a differing view as a valid product of each person's unique G-d-given personality.

4   Many disagreements are best left untouched. Life unfolds on a vast stage, offering ample opportunities for connection beyond the subject of disagreement.

5   Disagreements can provide opportunities to discover fresh perspectives and gain better understandings, leading to a situation superior to the pre-disagreement state. That is precisely why G-d created humankind with its radically diverse perspectives. Accordingly, disagreements can be exercises in friendship rather than instances of discord.

6   Our views on various matters are not concepts to be worshipped but merely our best current understanding of the truth. This leaves us open to gain fresh understandings and to modify our views. When both parties are committed to this approach, they will emerge with a mutually-agreed-upon enhanced understanding.

7   Disagreements are often seen as a battle between egos, where each party aims to dominate. This adversarial view is nothing but an instinct of the animal soul. The Divine soul serves as the driving force behind the mindset that appreciates disagreement as a pathway to a doubled portion of goodness.

8   We express the attitude of respect by employing proper listening skills and using a gentle tone and non-domineering words. This raises the chances that our words will leave an impression on the listener.

Enlightening Edits

"Softly spoken words of the wise are heard louder than the roars of foolish rulers."

Ecclesiastes 9:17

The Lubavitcher Rebbe placed great importance on effective communication and consistently led by personal example. Many of the Rebbe's transcribed talks were meticulously edited by him before publication. He also revised numerous letters that he had dictated and occasionally reviewed and refined material submitted by others. The Rebbe's inclination to soften language is wonderfully apparent in many of his edits. The following are a few samples of this practice.

Instructions vs. Suggestions

In the summer of 1971, the Rebbe called for intensified focus on Torah study and charitable giving during the annual three-week mourning period that culminates with the Fast of the Ninth of Av—the anniversary of the Destruction of both Jerusalem Temples. A summary of his address on the topic was prepared for publication in *The New York Times*; here is a copy of an introduction to the talk, with the Rebbe's edits: ▶

All vs. Many

The Rebbe's birthday in 1981 arrived while the world was still reeling from the attempt on President Ronald Reagan's life just two weeks prior. In his public talks on that day (11 Nisan, 5741 / April 15, 1981), the Rebbe highlighted a critical underlying crisis: the absence of character education in American public schools—a deficiency that, as he passionately asserted, directly contributed to the rise in crime. Here is an excerpt from an English summary of that address, with the Rebbe's handwritten edits: ▶

FROM THE SECRETARIAT OF THE LUBAVITCHER REBBE

RABBI MENACHEM M. SCHNEERSON

In response to numerous inquiries about the special instructions announced by the Rebbe in his public address on the Sabbath preceding the month of Av, concerning the 'Nine Days' (which commemorate the destruction of the Holy Temple in Jerusalem of old), we publish the following excerpt from his talk:

Original	Edited
"In response to numerous inquiries about the special instructions announced by the Rebbe in his public address . . ."	"In response to numerous inquiries about the special *suggestions contained in* the Rebbe's public address . . ."

in his case, but to all children. The failure to instill in children an awareness of G-d causes the egocentric, self-centered life style of today's youth - the "me" generation. Unfortunately, parents today do not or cannot provide such an education; the responsibility to do so must devolve on the public school system. I have stressed this on many occasions, and indeed, a special Education Day has been enacted to emphasize the importance of education. An education that provides not just knowledge, but that trains our children to be decent and productive citizens.

Original	Edited
". . . this applies not just in his case but to all children."	". . . this applies not just in his case but to *many, many* children."
"The failure to instill in children an awareness of G-d causes the egocentric, self-centered life style of today's youth."	"The failure to instill in children an awareness of G-d causes the egocentric, self-centered life style in a *large portion* of today's youth."
". . . parents today do not or cannot provide such an education. . . ."	". . . *many* parents today do not or cannot provide such an education. . . ."

Inevitable vs. Very Often

In the late 1970s, Professor Susan Handelman authored an essay, titled "The Search for Truth—'Religion' and 'Secularism,'" for the *Der Yiddishe Heim* journal that was published by the Chabad women's organization. Her article explored the interplay between secular knowledge, Torah, and science. Before its publication, the Rebbe personally edited the essay, including the following excerpt:

> The Rebbe Shlite explains in a <u>sicha</u> (<u>Likutei Sichos</u> IV, p. 1101) that all secular sciences are limited and imperfect. They do not possess anything outside of themselves, or/of reason--and, furthermore, reason itself has its own inner limitations. Nevertheless, the Rebbe points out, it is precisely these limitations that satisfy a person, because he can grasp the entire system and contain it. He feels the satisfaction of mastering a body of knowledge, and hence, secular knowledge very often leads to arrogance.
>
> The opposite is the case with the study of Torah, which is absolutely true, and contains all wisdom; it is unlimited, infinite, and contains no defects (ח"ו) whatsoever. Thus one can never contain Torah, master it. A person always feels how far he is from grasping the whole of it and fathoming its infinite depth. Therefore, he does not become arrogant, but on the contrary--humble. And the more he learns, the humbler he becomes, and the greater is his thirst for learning Torah.

Original	Edited
"…*all* secular sciences are limited and imperfect."	"…secular sciences are limited and imperfect."
"…secular knowledge leads to arrogance."	"…secular knowledge *very often* leads to arrogance."

Must vs. Proper

Rabbi Moshe Feller contributed a regular column to the Chabad women's organization's journal, *Der Yiddishe Heim*. The following are some of the Rebbe's edits on excerpts from his articles regarding the Previous Chabad Rebbe, Rabbi Yosef Yitzchak Schneersohn (1880–1950):

> "His father replied, 'In his prayers, a Jew requests of G‑d to fulfill all his needs and he is certain that his request will be granted, for it is directed to G‑d Who is the Father of every Jew - young or old, man or woman. When you ask something of a father *it is proper* you must first *to* cause him satisfaction. The greatest satisfaction to a father is when his children, who are many and diverse, live amongst each other with brotherly love, loving one another as one's self -

> of Torah study, performance and dissemination because "it is easier".
> What a terrible *mistake* crime we Jews are committing by not taking maximum advantage of the great freedom of religion and respect of religion which we experience here in America! We are free to keep publicly all of the 613 Mitzvos and we are respected for doing so! It is heartbreaking to realize how *relatively* pathetically few of our brethren take advantage of this freedom and respect.
> in the midst of establishing our

Original	Edited
"When you ask something of a father you must first cause him satisfaction."	"When you ask something of a father *it is proper* first to cause him satisfaction."
"It is heartbreaking to realize how pathetically few of our brethren take advantage of this freedom and respect."	"It is heartbreaking to realize how *relatively* few of our brethren take advantage of this freedom and respect."

Deficient vs. Sometimes Deficient

In 1972, a record of Chabad Chasidic music was released, featuring a Chasidic tune by Reb Peretz Chein. The following text, edited by the Rebbe, was prepared for the record jacket:

> This nigun was introduced by Reb Peretz B'Reb Meir Simcha Chein when he came to the U.S.A. in 5729 - 1959.
> He learned this nigun in his youth from the Chassidim of Nevel, Russia. It expresses hope that the Almighty will grant all his blessings to his people even though they might *sometimes* be deficient in their total commitment to Him.

Original	Edited
"…the Almighty will grant all his blessings to his people even though they might be deficient in their total commitment to Him."	"…the Almighty will grant all his blessings to his people even though they might be *sometimes* deficient in their total commitment to Him."

A Sampling of Disputations between Rabbi Yochanan and Reish Lakish

Disagreements can foster enhanced understandings, as exemplified by the interactions between Rabbi Yochanan and Reish Lakish. Their debates were not driven by a desire for victory or dominance but by a pursuit of clarity and refined comprehension. The following selection delves into some of their most renowned disagreements as recorded in the Talmud.

| **THE FICKLE SELLER** | Talmud, Bava Metzi'a 47b |

Question

When purchasing an object, when does the transfer of ownership take place: when the money changes hands, or when the purchaser takes physical possession of the object?

Example

Nancy owns a book that Sarah wants to purchase. They agree on a price of $25. Sarah gives Nancy the money, and they agree that Sarah will come pick it up the next day. But the next day Nancy changes her mind: she wants to refund the money and keep the book. Sarah claims that the book is already hers and the sale cannot be revoked.

The Dispute

Rabbi Yochanan	Reish Lakish
The transfer of ownership happens when the money is paid. Sarah is the owner of the book.	The transfer of ownership happens when Sarah picks up the book with her hands (or otherwise takes possession of it). The book is still Nancy's.

Discussion

On the one hand, it seems logical that the buyer, having paid the money, should be able to claim ownership immediately. On the other hand, having the ownership take effect while the object is in a different location invites all sorts of problematic situations. What if the object is damaged or destroyed in the interim by an "act of G-d"? Will the seller be able to claim that the loss occurred when it was already owned by the buyer, and they have no obligation to refund the money?

THE DISSENTING JUDGE

 Talmud, Sanhedrin 30a

Question

**When the court issues a verdict, should it also
specify how the individual judges voted?**

Example

Frank sues Jim, claiming that he owes him $100, while Jim denies
the claim. The two litigants present their arguments and evidence
before a panel of three judges (as Torah law stipulates). Two of the
judges are of the opinion that Jim owes the money, while the opinion
of the third judge is that he does not. When the court announces its
decision, should it also specify what the individual opinions of the
judges were?

The Dispute

Rabbi Yochanan	Reish Lakish
The verdict should only say what the court collectively ruled by majority vote.	The verdict should also include the information of which two judges voted to uphold the claim and which judge voted to deny it.

Discussion

On the one hand, we have the value of transparency, and the ability
to hold individual judges accountable for erroneous or corrupt
rulings. On the other hand, this will expose judges to being slandered
and defamed by those who are dissatisfied with their rulings.

THE NEGLIGENT FIREBUG

Talmud, Bava Kama 22a–23a

Question

What is the extent of a person's responsibility for damages caused by a fire they started?

Example

Harry started a fire in his yard, which then spread beyond his property and injured his neighbor Joe. Joe sues Harry for one million dollars, claiming permanent damage to his person, medical bills, mental anguish, and a host of other damages. Harry argues that Joe's claim is excessive because he was only an indirect cause of Joe's injuries.

The Dispute

Rabbi Yochanan	Reish Lakish
Harry must pay damages for up to five different categories: (1) monetary value of the damage caused to Joe's person, (2) pain and suffering, (3) cost of healing, (4) loss of work and productivity, (5) embarrassment.	Harry is obligated to pay damages of the first category, but is absolved of liability for categories 2, 3, 4, and 5.

Discussion

Torah law differentiates between damages that result from a person's own actions and damages caused by a person's property. While a person is liable in both cases, the type of restitution differs. If Harry throws a stone at Joe and injures him, Harry is obligated to pay the five different types of restitution listed above. On the other hand, if Harry's horse kicks Joe and injures him, Harry's responsibility is more limited. The court estimates the monetary value of the damage caused to Joe's person and obligates Harry to pay Joe that amount in restitution, and that is the extent of his liability.

In the case of the fire, we can argue—as does Rabbi Yochanan—that "your fire is like your arrow." If you shoot an arrow, then any damage it causes as it flies through the air is the direct outcome of your action. But another way of looking at it—and this is Reish Lakish's position—is that "your fire is your property." Your initial act of lighting the fire did not directly injure your neighbor. But it was your responsibility to ensure that it does not cause damage to others, in the same way that you are responsible to prevent your animal or other possessions from damaging others or their property.

THE POWER OF REPENTANCE

 Talmud, Berachot 34b and Yoma 86b; *Tanya, Likutei Amarim,* ch. 7

Question

Who is greater: a perfectly righteous person who never sinned, or someone who sinned and repented?

The Dispute

Rabbi Yochanan	Reish Lakish
The perfectly righteous person is greater.	The penitent is greater.

Discussion

The Torah provides a path for repentance for even the most egregious sinner. When a person sincerely regrets their negative deeds, acknowledges their guilt, makes restitution to those who were hurt by their actions, resolves to change their behavior, and follows through on this resolve, they achieve atonement and forgiveness. Still one can argue that this does not change the fact that bad things were done in the past. Certainly, then, the person who avoids evil altogether is on a higher spiritual level, as Rabbi Yochanan posits.

On the other hand, the very experience of having become distanced and alienated from G-d—and from the core goodness of one's soul—will create a powerful yearning to reconnect. As a result, the true *baal teshuvah* ("returnee") will serve G-d with a passion and desire that far exceed those of a person who never experienced the agony of distance. In such a penitent, says Reish Lakish, "sins are transformed into merits."

Psychology References

Itzchakov G, et al. (2020) Can high-quality listening predict lower speakers' prejudiced attitudes? *Journal of Experimental Social Psychology*, 91, 104022. doi.org/10.1016/j.jesp.2020.104022. Epub 2020 Aug 6. PMID: 32834106; PMCID: PMC7409873.

Itzchakov G, Reis, HT. (2021) Perceived responsiveness increases tolerance of attitude ambivalence and enhances intentions to behave in an open-minded manner. *Personality and Social Psychology Bulletin*, 47(3), 468–485. doi.org/10.1177/0146167220929218.

Mallick L, Guha Thakurta A. (2024) Exploring conflict resolution skills and the imperative for educational programs in fostering peaceful coexistence of mankind. *International Journal of Advanced Academic Studies*, 6(2):20–25. doi.org/10.33545/27068919.2024.v6.i2a.1111.

Overall N, McNulty JK. (2017) What type of communication during conflict is beneficial for intimate relationships? *Current Opinion in Psychology*, 13, 1–5, ISSN 2352-250X. doi.org/10.1016/j.copsyc.2016.03.002.

Overton AR, Lowry AC. (2013) Conflict management: difficult conversations with difficult people. *Clinics in Colon and Rectal Surgery, 26*(4):259–64. doi.org/10.1055/s-0033-1356728. PMID: 24436688; PMCID: PMC3835442.

Vandermeer J, et al. (2019) Escalation of negative social exchange: Reflexive punishment or deliberative deterrence? *Journal of Experimental Social Psychology*, 84, Article 103823, ISSN 0022-1031, doi.org/10.1016/j.jesp.2019.103823.

APPENDIX A—DIVINELY-ENDOWED UNIQUENESS

TEXT 12

Human Singularity

Mishnah, Sanhedrin 4:5

לְפִיכָךְ נִבְרָא אָדָם יְחִידִי, לְלַמֶּדְךָ שֶׁכָּל הַמְאַבֵּד
נֶפֶשׁ אַחַת מִיִּשְׂרָאֵל מַעֲלֶה עָלָיו הַכָּתוּב כְּאִילוּ
אָבֵּד עוֹלָם מָלֵא, וְכָל הַמְקַיֵּם נֶפֶשׁ אַחַת מִיִּשְׂרָאֵל
מַעֲלֶה עָלָיו הַכָּתוּב כְּאִילוּ קִיֵּם עוֹלָם מָלֵא . . .

וּלְהַגִּיד גְּדוּלָתוֹ שֶׁל הַקָּדוֹשׁ בָּרוּךְ הוּא, שֶׁאָדָם טוֹבֵעַ
כַּמָה מַטְבְּעוֹת בְּחוֹתָם אֶחָד וְכֻלָּן דּוֹמִין זֶה לָזֶה, וּמֶלֶךְ
מַלְכֵי הַמְּלָכִים הַקָּדוֹשׁ בָּרוּךְ הוּא טָבַע כָּל אָדָם בְּחוֹתָמוֹ
שֶׁל אָדָם הָרִאשׁוֹן וְאֵין אֶחָד מֵהֶן דּוֹמֶה לַחֲבֵרוֹ.

לְפִיכָךְ, כָּל אֶחָד וְאֶחָד חַיָּב לוֹמַר בִּשְׁבִילִי נִבְרָא הָעוֹלָם.

The reason why initially only a single human was
created is to teach us that someone who destroys a
single life is regarded as having destroyed an entire
world—and conversely, someone who saves a single
life is regarded as having saved an entire world. . . .

It also communicates G-d's greatness: When a human
uses a single mold to mint numerous coins, the coins are
all identical. G-d, however, mints each human using the
mold of the first human, and yet, no two people are alike.

For that reason, each individual must declare,
"The world was created for me."

MISHNAH

The first authoritative
work of Jewish law that
was codified in writing.
The Mishnah contains
the oral traditions that
were passed down from
teacher to student; it
supplements, clarifies,
and systematizes the
commandments of
the Torah. Due to the
continual persecution
of the Jewish people,
it became increasingly
difficult to guarantee
that these traditions
would not be forgotten.
Rabbi Yehudah Hanasi
therefore redacted the
Mishnah at the end
of the 2nd century. It
serves as the foundation
for the Talmud.

Between Light and Dark

Rabbi Yehudah Loew, *Chidushei Agadot*, Shabbat 25b

כִּי אֵין נִקְרָא שָׁלוֹם רַק הָאוֹר בִּלְבַד, מִפְּנֵי שֶׁהוּא נוֹתֵן הֶבְדֵּל
בֵּין הַדְּבָרִים, וְזֶהוּ הַשָּׁלוֹם כַּאֲשֶׁר יֵשׁ הֶבְדֵּל בֵּין הַדְּבָרִים.

כִּי כַּאֲשֶׁר נִקְרָא הַחוֹשֶׁךְ עֶרֶב, מִפְּנֵי שֶׁבְּחוֹשֶׁךְ הַדְּבָרִים הֵם
מְעוּרָבִים, וְאֵין נִכָּר זֶה בִּפְנֵי זֶה, וְהֵם מְעֹרָבִים יַחַד. וְהָאוֹר נִקְרָא
בּוֹקֶר שֶׁעַל יְדֵי הָאוֹר יֵשׁ בִּיקוּר בֵּין הַדְּבָרִים בֵּין זֶה לָזֶה.

וְכַאֲשֶׁר יֵשׁ בִּקוּר בֵּין דָּבָר לְדָבָר הוּא הַשָּׁלוֹם
אֲשֶׁר הוּא בֵּין הַדְּבָרִים, וְאֵין אֶחָד נִכְנָס וּמִתְעָרֵב
בַּחֲבֵירוֹ רַק כָּל אֶחָד בִּפְנֵי עַצְמוֹ.

וּלְפִיכָךְ נִקְרָא נֵר שַׁבָּת שָׁלוֹם.

The root of the Hebrew word for morning, *boker*,
implies examination, because light enables us to examine
and distinguish between one entity and another.

The root of the Hebrew word for evening,
erev, implies *mixture*, because in darkness,
all entities are jumbled together and we are
unable to distinguish one from the other.

When we use light to determine the distinctions between
things, we introduce peace to them, for we prevent one
entity from invading or interfering with the domain
of the other; each remains within its rightful place.

For that reason, the Shabbat candles
are associated with peace.

APPENDIX B—ADVERSARIAL COLLABORATION

The Ideal of Science

TEXT 14

Daniel Kahneman, "Experiences of Collaborative Research," *American Psychologist* 58:9 (September 2003), pp. 729–730

I began to champion a procedure of adversarial collaboration as a substitute for the format of critique-reply-rejoinder in which debates are currently conducted in the social sciences.

Adversarial collaboration involves a good-faith effort to conduct debates by carrying out joint research—in some cases an agreed-upon arbiter may be needed to lead the project and collect the data. Because the contestants are not expected to reach complete agreement at the end of the exercise, adversarial collaborations will usually lead to an unusual type of joint publication, in which disagreements are laid out as part of a jointly authored paper. I have had three adversarial collaborations . . . all three ended with some new facts accepted by all, narrowed differences of opinion, and considerable mutual respect. . . . The result was much more enlightening than what we would have done in the conventional format.

My hope is that these and other variants of adversarial collaboration may eventually become standard. This is not a mere fantasy: It would be

**DANIEL KAHNEMAN, PHD
1934–2024**

Psychologist and economist. Raised in Paris, Dr. Kahneman spent his childhood running from the Nazis until his family immigrated to Israel. He studied psychology and mathematics at Hebrew University and went on to receive his doctorate at UC Berkeley. Kahneman is most noted for his work on the psychology of decision-making and behavioral economics, for which he was awarded the 2002 Nobel Memorial Prize in Economic Sciences.

easy for journal editors to require critics of the published work of others—and the targets of such critiques—to make a good-faith effort to explore differences constructively. I believe that the establishment of such procedures would contribute to an enterprise that more closely approximates the ideal of science as a cumulative social product.

APPENDIX C—THE SAGES' ATTITUDE

TEXT 15

Exemplary Attitude
Mishnah, Eduyot 1:3–4

עַד שֶׁבָּאוּ שְׁנֵי גַרְדְּיִּים מִשַּׁעַר הָאַשְׁפּוֹת שֶׁבִּירוּשָׁלַיִם וְהֵעִידוּ מִשּׁוּם שְׁמַעְיָה וְאַבְטַלְיוֹן . . . וְקִיְּמוּ אֶת דִּבְרֵיהֶם.

וְלָמָה מַזְכִּירִין אֶת דִּבְרֵי שַׁמַּאי וְהִלֵּל לְבַטְּלָן? לְלַמֵּד לְדוֹרוֹת הַבָּאִים שֶׁלֹּא יְהֵא אָדָם עוֹמֵד עַל דְּבָרָיו, שֶׁהֲרֵי אֲבוֹת הָעוֹלָם לֹא עָמְדוּ עַל דִּבְרֵיהֶם.

The matter remained in dispute until two weavers arrived from Jerusalem's Dung Gate and shared personal testimony that Shemayah and Avtalyon had taught [contrary to the views of both Hillel and Shamai]. . . . Thereupon, all of the sages—including Hillel and Shamai—ratified their words.

But why are the opinions of Hillel and Shamai recorded in this instance, if their views are ultimately negated? To teach future generations that we should not stubbornly cling to our opinions, for despite their remarkable stature, Hillel and Shamai were not stubborn in their opinions.

Two Models of Disagreement

TEXT 16

Mishnah, Avot 5:17

כָּל מַחֲלוֹקֶת שֶׁהִיא לְשֵׁם שָׁמַיִם, סוֹפָהּ לְהִתְקַיֵּם.
וְשֶׁאֵינָהּ לְשֵׁם שָׁמַיִם, אֵין סוֹפָהּ לְהִתְקַיֵּם.

אֵיזוֹ הִיא מַחֲלוֹקֶת שֶׁהִיא לְשֵׁם שָׁמַיִם?
זוֹ מַחֲלוֹקֶת הִלֵּל וְשַׁמַּאי.

וְשֶׁאֵינָהּ לְשֵׁם שָׁמַיִם, זוֹ מַחֲלוֹקֶת קֹרַח וְכָל עֲדָתוֹ.

Every argument that is for the sake of Heaven is destined to endure, whereas any argument that is not for the sake of Heaven is destined not to endure.

What is an example of an argument for the sake of Heaven? The debates of Hillel and Shamai.

What is an example of an argument that is not for the sake of Heaven? The dispute of Korah and his following.

Reaching the Goal

Rabbi Ovadiah of Bartenura, ad loc.

הַמַּחֲלוֹקֶת שֶׁהִיא לְשֵׁם שָׁמַיִם, הַתַּכְלִית וְהַסוֹף הַמְבוּקָשׁ מֵאוֹתָהּ מַחֲלוֹקֶת לְהַשִּׂיג הָאֱמֶת. וְזֶה מִתְקַיֵּים, כְּמוֹ שֶׁאָמְרוּ, מִתּוֹךְ הַוִּיכּוּחַ יִתְבָּרֵר הָאֱמֶת. וּכְמוֹ שֶׁנִּתְבָּאֵר בְּמַחֲלוֹקֶת הִלֵּל וְשַׁמַּאי שֶׁהֲלָכָה כְּבֵית הִלֵּל.

וּמַחֲלוֹקֶת שֶׁאֵינָהּ לְשֵׁם שָׁמַיִם, תַּכְלִית הַנִּרְצֶה בָּהּ הִיא בַּקָּשַׁת הַשְּׂרָרָה וְאַהֲבַת הַנִּיצוּחַ. וְזֶה הַסּוֹף אֵינוֹ מִתְקַיֵּים, כְּמוֹ שֶׁמָּצִינוּ בְּמַחֲלוֹקֶת קוֹרַח וַעֲדָתוֹ שֶׁתַּכְלִית וְסוֹף כַּוָּנָתָם הָיְתָה בַּקָּשַׁת הַכָּבוֹד וְהַשְּׂרָרָה, וְהָיוּ לְהֵיפֶךְ.

In a dispute conducted for the sake of Heaven, where the desired goal is discovering the truth, that end goal will be achieved. As the sages taught, truth is crystallized through debate. This was precisely the result of the debates between Hillel and Shamai: in the end, the truth was achieved and the law was [typically] ratified per Hillel.

By contrast, in a dispute that is not for the sake of Heaven, the desired end goal is the attainment of dominance and a sense of personal victory. This goal will not be achieved, as demonstrated in the dispute of Korah and his following: they desired prestige and dominance but ended up with the exact opposite.

RABBI OVADIAH OF BARTENURA C. 1445–1524

Scholar and author. Born in Italy, Rabbi Ovadiah is commonly known as "the Bartenura," after the city in which he held the rabbinate. Arriving in Jerusalem in 1488, he quickly became an effective leader of the oppressed Jewish community, especially focusing his energies on the influx of Sefardic Jews to Jerusalem following the Spanish expulsion. His highly acclaimed commentary on the Mishnah appears in almost every printed edition.

APPENDIX D—THIRD PARTY

Rabbi Meir's Advice

TEXT 18

Midrash, *Kohelet Rabah* 4:14

רַבִּי מֵאִיר כַּד הֲוָה חָמֵי חַד נָפֵיק לְאִיסְטְרַטָא,
הֲוָה צָוַח לֵיהּ: "זִיל שְׁלָם עֲלָךְ מָרֵי מִיתָה".

תְּרֵין, הֲוָה צָוַח לוֹן: "שְׁלָם לְכוֹן מָרֵי קְטָטָה".

תְּלַת, צָוַח לוֹן: "שְׁלָם לְכוֹן מָרֵי שְׁלָמָא".

If Rabbi Meir saw a person setting out
on the road alone, he would call out,
"Go, peace on you, mister death!"

If he saw two people setting out together, he
would call out, "Peace to you, disputants!"

If he saw three people setting out together, he
would call out, "Peace to you, peaceful folk!"

KOHELET RABAH

A Midrashic text
on the book of
Ecclesiastes. Midrash
is the designation of
a particular genre of
rabbinic literature.
The term "Midrash" is
derived from the root
d-r-sh, which means "to
search," "to examine,"
and "to investigate."
This particular Midrash
provides textual
exegeses and develops
and illustrates moral
principles. It was first
published in Pesaro,
Italy, in 1519, together
with 4 other Midrashic
works on the other 4
biblical *Megillot.*

APPENDIX E—JOSEPH AND JUDAH

TEXT 19A

Judah Approached Joseph

Genesis 44:18

וַיִּגַּשׁ אֵלָיו יְהוּדָה, וַיֹּאמֶר, בִּי אֲדֹנִי, יְדַבֶּר נָא עַבְדְּךָ דָבָר בְּאָזְנֵי אֲדֹנִי, וְאַל יִחַר אַפְּךָ בְּעַבְדֶּךָ, כִּי כָמוֹךָ כְּפַרְעֹה.

Judah approached Joseph and said, "Please, my lord, allow your servant to speak a word in my lord's ears, and do not become angry at your servant, for you are [as esteemed] as Pharaoh [in my eyes]."

An Emotional Approach

TEXT 19B

Rabbi Chaim ibn Atar, ad loc.

יִתְבָּאֵר אָמְרוֹ "וַיִּגַּשׁ אֵלָיו" עַל דֶּרֶךְ אָמְרוֹ
"כַּמַּיִם הַפָּנִים לְפָנִים, כֵּן לֵב הָאָדָם לָאָדָם".

וְלָזֶה נִתְחַכֵּם יְהוּדָה לְהַטּוֹת לֵב יוֹסֵף עָלָיו לְרַחֲמִים,
וְהִקְרִיב דַּעְתּוֹ וּרְצוֹנוֹ אֵלָיו לְאַהֲבוֹ וּלְחַבְּבוֹ כְּדֵי
שֶׁתִּתְקָרֵב דַּעְתּוֹ שֶׁל יוֹסֵף אֵלָיו לְקַבֵּל דְּבָרָיו וּפִיּוּסוֹ.

We can explain the phrase "Judah approached" according to the proverb, "As water mirrors a face, so does one human heart reflect another."

Judah devised a strategy to cause Joseph to experience a change of heart and have mercy on him. Judah mentally and emotionally "approached" Joseph, inducing a sense of affinity for Joseph within himself, so that Joseph would be inclined to listen to his message and accept his conciliatory efforts.

RABBI CHAIM IBN ATAR (OR HACHAYIM) 1696–1743

Biblical exegete, kabbalist, and Talmudist. Rabbi Atar, born in Meknes, Morocco, was a prominent member of the Moroccan rabbinate and later immigrated to the Land of Israel. He is most famous for his *Or Hachayim,* a popular commentary on the Torah. The famed Jewish historian and bibliophile Rabbi Chaim Yosef David Azulai was among his most notable disciples.

4

THE ART OF POSITIVITY

Our biases influence how we perceive and process problematic behavior in others, often undermining our relationships. How can we train ourselves to overcome these biases to see more virtue in the people we know?

CLIFFHANGER
Chris Veeneman,
oil on wood, 2017, Paris

I. INTRODUCTION

Today's study focuses on the way we regard others and their behaviors. As we will see, "negativity bias" and the "fundamental attribution error" can cause or exacerbate relationship problems.

RELATION 92
Santhosh C H, watercolor
on paper, 2019, India

TEXT 1

Negativity Bias

Roy F. Baumeister, et al., "Bad Is Stronger than Good,"
Review of General Psychology 5:4 (2001), pp. 346–347

The greater power of bad in the sphere of moral behavior was the focus of Riskey and Birnbaum (1974) in an article with the revealing subtitle, "Two Rights Don't Make Up for a Wrong." They found that morally bad actions create a powerful effect on [one's] overall judgment [of others], and this effect is only slightly mitigated by adding morally good actions. Riskey and Birnbaum's conclusion was "the overall goodness of a person is determined mostly by his worst bad deed, with good deeds having lesser influence.... Given a person has done evil, an infinite number of good deeds may not produce a favorable overall impression." ...

Hiring and personnel decisions constitute an especially important sphere of impression formation.... Bolster and Springbett (1961) studied how interviewers' opinions changed as a function of new, good, or bad information about a candidate. Across a variety of measures and procedures, they found consistently that bad information exerted a more powerful effect than good information. For example, if the initial judgment favored hiring (i.e., acceptance), only 3.8 unfavorable bits of information were required to shift the decision to rejection; whereas 8.8 favorable pieces of information were necessary to shift an initially negative decision toward acceptance.

ROY FREDERICK BAUMEISTER
1953–

Social psychologist and author. Roy Baumeister received his PhD in psychology from Princeton University and has taught at universities in the U.S. and Australia. He is known for his research on the nature of the self and its impact on human behavior.

Fundamental Attribution Error

Daniel R. Stalder, *The Power of Context: How to Manage Our Bias and Improve Our Understanding of Others* (Amherst, New York: Prometheus Books, 2018), pp. 33–37

Traffic jams are no fun. . . . So when you see an impatient jerk pull onto the shoulder and start passing everyone because he obviously doesn't think traffic laws pertain to him, you might get really mad. Who does he think he is? Right? What arrogance. . . .

You might be committing the fundamental attribution error or FAE. . . . The FAE has two co-occurring parts. First, we quickly overestimate the causal role of dispositional factors, such as the individual's traits, attitudes, feelings, preferences, motives, abilities, or inadequacies. Arrogant jerk. These explanations are called internal or dispositional attributions. Second, we overlook or underestimate the possible contribution of situational factors or specific circumstances. Running out of gas. Explanations involving such circumstances are called external or situational attributions. . . .

Of course, sometimes the person or persons who behave negatively do indeed have negative personal characteristics or intentions—end of story. But what is clear from decades of research is that it's not nearly as often as most people think.

DANIEL R. STALDER

Social psychologist. Dr. Daniel Stalder is a professor of psychology at the University of Wisconsin-Whitewater. His publications focus on biases, individual differences, and cognitive dissonance theory. He is the author of *The Power of Context: How to Manage Our Bias and Improve Our Understanding of Others.*

QUESTIONS

1. How might negativity bias and the fundamental attribution error affect our relationships?

2. What options might we have to reduce the impact of these biases?

II. THE POSITIVITY BIAS

Jewish ethical works encourage a behavioral approach to shaping character. In this model, we combat negativity bias by making a conscious effort to tilt toward the opposite extreme—to identify the positive in all things. The Talmud similarly highlights the need to be a "good guest," referring to the desired trait of augmenting the positive in others rather than seeking to diminish it.

THERE IS HOPE!
George Psaroudakis, acrylic
on canvas, 2016, Greece

Behavior Influences Character

TEXT 3A

Maimonides, *Mishneh Torah*, Laws of Character Development 1:7

וְכֵיצַד יַרְגִּיל אָדָם עַצְמוֹ בְּדֵעוֹת אֵלּוּ עַד שֶׁיִּקָּבְעוּ בּוֹ? יַעֲשֶׂה, וְיִשְׁנֶה, וִישַׁלֵּשׁ, בַּמַּעֲשִׂים שֶׁעוֹשֶׂה עַל פִּי הַדֵּעוֹת הָאֶמְצָעִיּוֹת, וְיַחֲזֹר בָּהֶם תָּמִיד, עַד שֶׁיִּהְיוּ מַעֲשֵׂיהֶם קַלִּים עָלָיו, וְלֹא יִהְיֶה בָּהֶם טֹרַח עָלָיו, וְיִקָּבְעוּ הַדֵּעוֹת בְּנַפְשׁוֹ.

How can we cultivate proper attitudes and traits so that they become ingrained features of our personality? We engage once, then a second time, and yet a third time in behaviors that embody the balanced ideal. We repeat the desired behavior consistently. Eventually, the proper actions become natural rather than difficult, seamlessly integrated into our character.

RABBI MOSHE BEN MAIMON (MAIMONIDES, RAMBAM) 1135–1204

Halachist, philosopher, author, and physician. Maimonides was born in Córdoba, Spain. After the conquest of Córdoba by the Almohads, he fled Spain and eventually settled in Cairo, Egypt. There, he became the leader of the Jewish community and served as court physician to the vizier of Egypt. He is most noted for authoring the *Mishneh Torah*, an encyclopedic arrangement of Jewish law; and for his philosophical work, *Guide for the Perplexed*. His rulings on Jewish law are integral to the formation of Halachic consensus.

Extreme Situations

TEXT 3B

Maimonides, ibid., 2:2

אִם הָיָה רָחוֹק לַקָּצֶה הָאֶחָד, יַרְחִיק עַצְמוֹ לַקָּצֶה הַשֵּׁנִי, וְיִנְהֹג בּוֹ זְמַן רַב.

If you are already swayed to one extreme, distance yourself from it by moving to the opposite extreme, and accustom yourself to it for a long time.

Is what we say really that powerful? **Rabbi Mendel Kalmenson** explains. myjli.com/relationships

TEXT 4

Canine Encounter

Rabbi Bachya ibn Pakudah, *Chovot Halevavot*,
The Gate of Submission 6

וְנֶאֱמַר עַל אֶחָד מִן הַחֲסִידִים שֶׁעָבַר עַל נִבְלַת כֶּלֶב מַסְרַחַת
מְאֹד. וְאָמְרוּ לוֹ תַּלְמִידָיו: כַּמָּה מַסְרַחַת נְבֵלָה זֹאת!

אָמַר לָהֶם: כַּמָּה לְבָנִים שִׁנֶּיהָ!

וְנִתְחָרְטוּ עַל מָה שֶׁסִּפְּרוּ בִּגְנוּתָהּ.

וְכֵיוָן שֶׁהוּא גְּנַאי לְסַפֵּר בִּגְנוּת כֶּלֶב מֵת, כָּל שֶׁכֵּן בְּאָדָם
חַי. וְכֵיוָן שֶׁהוּא טוֹב לְשַׁבֵּחַ נִבְלַת כֶּלֶב בְּלוֹבֶן שִׁנֶּיהָ, כָּל
שֶׁכֵּן שֶׁהוּא חוֹבָה לְפִי זֶה לְשַׁבֵּחַ אָדָם מַשְׂכִּיל וּמֵבִין.

וְהָיְתָה כַּוָּנָתוֹ לְהוֹכִיחָם שֶׁלֹּא יְלַמְּדוּ לְשׁוֹנָם
לְדַבֵּר רַע וְיָשׁוּב לָהֶם טֶבַע. וְכֵן כְּשֶׁיְּלַמְּדוּ
לְשׁוֹנָם לְדַבֵּר טוֹב, יָשׁוּב לָהֶם טֶבַע קָבוּעַ.

It is related that when a pious teacher passed
the foul smelling carcass of a dog, his disciples
exclaimed, "How terribly this carcass smells!"

Whereupon the teacher replied,
"How white are its teeth!"

The students understood and regretted
having disparaged the carcass.

Consider: If it is improper to speak disparagingly of
an animal carcass, all the more so of a living human.
The reverse is also true: If it is proper to praise an

**RABBI BACHYA
IBN PAKUDAH
11TH CENTURY**

Moral philosopher and
author. Ibn Pakudah lived
in Muslim Spain, but
little else is known about
his life. *Chovot Halevavot*
(*Duties of the Heart*),
his major work, was
intended to be a guide
for attaining spiritual
perfection. Originally
written in Judeo-Arabic
and published in 1080, it
was later translated into
Hebrew and published
in 1161 by Judah ibn
Tibbon, a scion of
the famous family of
translators. Ibn Pakudah
had a strong influence on
Jewish pietistic literature.

animal carcass for the whiteness of its teeth, how much more so is it our duty to praise a human—a being endowed with intelligence and understanding.

With his retort, the teacher intended to teach his disciples to avoid discussing the negative, lest the habit become part of their nature. Instead, through habitually mentioning the positive, it would become part of their nature to speak positively.

EXERCISE 4.1

1. Choose an individual from one of your circles of support with whom you would like to enjoy an enhanced relationship:

2. Identify three of this individual's positive qualities:

   a.

   b.

   c.

3. Think of three true incidents involving this individual that illustrate the above three qualities:

   a.

   b.

   c.

TEXT 5

The Two Guests

Talmud, Berachot 58a

הוּא הָיָה אוֹמֵר:

אוֹרֵחַ טוֹב מַהוּ אוֹמֵר?

כַּמָּה טְרָחוֹת טָרַח בַּעַל הַבַּיִת בִּשְׁבִילִי! כַּמָּה בָּשָׂר
הֵבִיא לְפָנַי! כַּמָּה יַיִן הֵבִיא לְפָנַי! כַּמָּה גְּלוּסְקָאוֹת
הֵבִיא לְפָנַי! וְכָל מַה שֶּׁטָּרַח לֹא טָרַח אֶלָּא בִּשְׁבִילִי!

אֲבָל אוֹרֵחַ רַע מַהוּ אוֹמֵר?

מַה טוֹרַח טָרַח בַּעַל הַבַּיִת זֶה? פַּת אַחַת אָכַלְתִּי, חֲתִיכָה
אַחַת אָכַלְתִּי, כּוֹס אֶחָד שָׁתִיתִי, כָּל טוֹרַח שֶׁטָּרַח
בַּעַל הַבַּיִת זֶה לֹא טָרַח אֶלָּא בִּשְׁבִיל אִשְׁתּוֹ וּבָנָיו.

עַל אוֹרֵחַ טוֹב מַהוּ אוֹמֵר? "זְכֹר כִּי תַשְׂגִּיא
פָּעֳלוֹ אֲשֶׁר שֹׁרְרוּ אֲנָשִׁים" (איוב לו, כד).

עַל אוֹרֵחַ רַע כְּתִיב: "לָכֵן יְרֵאוּהוּ אֲנָשִׁים" וגו' (איוב לז, כד).

Ben Zoma used to say:

What does a good guest say?

"My host extended himself remarkably for me!
Look how much meat he brought before me! How
much wine he set before me! How many fine rolls he
laid out before me! My host did this all just for me!"

BABYLONIAN TALMUD

A literary work of
monumental proportions
that draws upon the legal,
spiritual, intellectual,
ethical, and historical
traditions of Judaism.
The 37 tractates of the
Babylonian Talmud
contain the teachings of
the Jewish sages from
the period after the
destruction of the 2nd
Temple through the 5th
century CE. It has served
as the primary vehicle
for the transmission
of the Oral Law and
the education of Jews
over the centuries; it
is the entry point for
all subsequent legal,
ethical, and theological
Jewish scholarship.

What does a bad guest say?

"Can I consider this host as having extended himself for me? All I ate was one piece of bread. I ate just one slice. I drank just one cup. If this host exerted himself, it was only for his own wife and children."

With regard to the good guest, the verse proclaims, "He remembers to augment what was done, singing people's praises" (JOB 36:24).

With regard to a bad guest, it is stated, "People therefore fear him" (JOB 37:24).

ABRAHAM'S TENT
Michoel Muchnik, mixed media, 2003, New York

1. Reflect on a recent benevolent act or gesture that someone extended to you.

2. Conceive a plausible scenario detailing how this person needed to make a substantial effort, whether practical or emotional, to perform the aforementioned act.

3. Consider the possibility that this act was a manifestation of genuine love, care, and respect for you.

4. How will you express gratitude to this person?

III. NAVIGATING FLAWS

The fundamental attribution error magnifies misbehavior, making others less than worthy in our eyes. The Torah combats this relationship blocker by encouraging us and guiding us toward judging favorably, an important trait with multiple layers of expression.

WIND AND RAIN IN JERUSALEM
Chana Helen, oil on canvas

An Employee in Anguish

Talmud, Shabbat 127b

וּמַעֲשֶׂה בְּאָדָם אֶחָד שֶׁיָּרַד מִגָּלִיל הָעֶלְיוֹן, וְנִשְׂכַּר
אֵצֶל בַּעַל הַבַּיִת אֶחָד בַּדָּרוֹם שָׁלֹשׁ שָׁנִים.

עֶרֶב יוֹם הַכִּפּוּרִים אָמַר לוֹ: תֶּן לִי שְׂכָרִי, וְאֵלֵךְ
וְאָזוּן אֶת אִשְׁתִּי וּבָנַי. אָמַר לוֹ: אֵין לִי מָעוֹת.

אָמַר לוֹ: תֶּן לִי פֵּירוֹת.

אָמַר לוֹ: אֵין לִי.

תֶּן לִי קַרְקַע - אֵין לִי.

תֶּן לִי בְּהֵמָה - אֵין לִי.

תֶּן לִי כָּרִים וּכְסָתוֹת - אֵין לִי.

הִפְשִׁיל כֵּלָיו לַאֲחוֹרָיו, וְהָלַךְ לְבֵיתוֹ בְּפַחֲי נֶפֶשׁ . . .

A fellow once traveled south from the Upper Galilee
and was hired by a landowner for a three-year term.

On the eve of Yom Kippur, the Galilean
asked his employer, "Give me my wages so
I can go and feed my wife and children."

The employer replied, "I have no money."

The employee rejoined, "In that case, give me
my wages in the form of produce," to which
the employer insisted that he had none.

"Give me my wages in the form of land," he pressed,
but the employer replied that he owned no land.

"Give me animals."

"I have none."

"Give me cushions and blankets."

"I have none."

The worker slung his tools over his shoulder
and left for home in anguish. . . .

FIGURES IN SAFED
Moshé Elazar Castel, oil on canvas, c. 1930

Circumstantial Attribution

TEXT 6B Talmud, ibid.

לְאַחַר הָרֶגֶל נָטַל בַּעַל הַבַּיִת שְׂכָרוֹ בְּיָדוֹ, וְעִמּוֹ מַשּׂוֹי שְׁלֹשָׁה
חֲמוֹרִים, אֶחָד שֶׁל מַאֲכָל, וְאֶחָד שֶׁל מִשְׁתֶּה, וְאֶחָד שֶׁל מִינֵי
מִגְדִּים, וְהָלַךְ לוֹ לְבֵיתוֹ. אַחַר שֶׁאָכְלוּ וְשָׁתוּ נָתַן לוֹ שְׂכָרוֹ.

אָמַר לוֹ: בְּשָׁעָה שֶׁאָמַרְתָּ לִי "תֶּן לִי שְׂכָרִי"
וְאָמַרְתִּי "אֵין לִי מָעוֹת", בַּמֶּה חֲשַׁדְתַּנִי?

אָמַרְתִּי: שֶׁמָּא פְּרַקְמַטְיָא בְּזוֹל נִזְדַּמְּנָה לְךָ, וְלָקַחְתָּ בָּהֶן.

וּבְשָׁעָה שֶׁאָמַרְתָּ לִי "תֶּן לִי בְּהֵמָה", וְאָמַרְתִּי
"אֵין לִי בְּהֵמָה", בַּמֶּה חֲשַׁדְתַּנִי?

אָמַרְתִּי: שֶׁמָּא מוּשְׂכֶּרֶת בְּיַד אֲחֵרִים.

בְּשָׁעָה שֶׁאָמַרְתָּ לִי "תֶּן לִי קַרְקַע", וְאָמַרְתִּי
לְךָ "אֵין לִי קַרְקַע", בַּמֶּה חֲשַׁדְתַּנִי?

אָמַרְתִּי: שֶׁמָּא מוּחְכֶּרֶת בְּיַד אֲחֵרִים הִיא.

וּבְשָׁעָה שֶׁאָמַרְתִּי לְךָ "אֵין לִי פֵּירוֹת" בַּמֶּה חֲשַׁדְתַּנִי?

אָמַרְתִּי: שֶׁמָּא אֵינָן מְעוּשָּׂרוֹת.

וּבְשָׁעָה שֶׁאָמַרְתִּי לְךָ "אֵין לִי כָּרִים וּכְסָתוֹת" בַּמֶּה חֲשַׁדְתַּנִי?

אָמַרְתִּי: שֶׁמָּא הִקְדִּישׁ כָּל נְכָסָיו לַשָּׁמַיִם . . .

After the festival, the employer took the worker's
wages in his hand and set off for the worker's
home. He took three donkeys, the first laden

with food, the second with beverages, and the third with assorted delicacies. After they ate and drank together, the employer handed him his wages.

The employer then asked the Galilean, "Tell me, when you requested your wages and I replied I had no money—what did you suspect?"

Responded the employee, "I told myself that perhaps the opportunity to purchase merchandise inexpensively had just presented itself, and you purchased it with the money you had, and so you had no money available."

"And when you requested animals and I said I had none—what did you suspect?"

Replied the employee, "I told myself that perhaps the animals are rented to others."

"When you asked for land and I claimed to own no land—what did you suspect?"

"Perhaps the land is leased to others."

"And when you asked for produce and I said I had none—what did you suspect?"

"Perhaps they are not tithed."

"And when I insisted that I owned no cushions or blankets—what did you suspect?"

"Perhaps he consecrated all his property to Heaven." . . .

The End of the Story

Talmud, ibid.

אָמַר לוֹ: הָעֲבוֹדָה! כָּךְ הָיָה. הִדַּרְתִּי כָּל נְכָסַי
בִּשְׁבִיל הוּרְקָנוֹס בְּנִי שֶׁלֹּא עָסַק בַּתּוֹרָה.

וּכְשֶׁבָּאתִי אֵצֶל חֲבֵירַי בַּדָּרוֹם הִתִּירוּ לִי כָּל נְדָרַי.

וְאַתָּה, כְּשֵׁם שֶׁדַּנְתַּנִי לִזְכוּת, הַמָּקוֹם יָדִין אוֹתְךָ לִזְכוּת.

The employer exclaimed, "I swear that it was so!
I had made a vow concerning all of my property
[consecrating it to the Temple]. I did this because
I was upset at my son Hyrcanus for not engaging
in Torah study [and I sought to disinherit him].

"When I later came to the sages of the
south, they released all my vows.

"As for you, just as you judged me favorably,
so may G-d judge you favorably!"

EXERCISE 4.3

1. Circle one relationship category.

2. Describe a behavior that might arise in that type of relationship that is likely to come across as frustrating, annoying, or confusing.

3. Identify a character flaw that might be regarded as the cause for that undesired behavior.

4. Identify a *circumstantial* attribution that would reasonably explain the behavior.

CIRCLE OF SUPPORT	SCENARIO	PERSONALITY ATTRIBUTION	CIRCUMSTANTIAL ATTRIBUTION
INTIMACY			
FRIENDSHIP			
PARTICIPATION			
EXCHANGE			

TEXT 7A

Drop the Gavel

Mishnah, Avot 2:4

וְאַל תָּדִין אֶת חֲבֵרְךָ עַד שֶׁתַּגִּיעַ לִמְקוֹמוֹ.

Do not judge others until you
have reached their place.

TEXT 7B

External and Internal Challenge

Rabbi Shneur Zalman of Liadi, *Tanya*, *Likutei Amarim*, ch. 30

"אַל תָּדִין אֶת חֲבֵרְךָ עַד שֶׁתַּגִּיעַ לִמְקוֹמוֹ": כִּי
מְקוֹמוֹ גּוֹרֵם לוֹ לַחֲטֹא, לִהְיוֹת פַּרְנָסָתוֹ לֵילֵךְ
בַּשּׁוּק כָּל הַיּוֹם, וְלִהְיוֹת מִיּוֹשְׁבֵי קְרָנוֹת, וְעֵינָיו
רוֹאוֹת כָּל הַתַּאֲווֹת, וְהָעַיִן רוֹאָה וְהַלֵּב חוֹמֵד.

וְיִצְרוֹ בּוֹעֵר כְּתַנּוּר בֹּעֲרָה מֵאֹפֶה . . .
כִּי אֵין הַיֵּצֶר שָׁוֶה בְּכָל נֶפֶשׁ.

"Do not judge others until you have reached
their place." This is because their place, that
is, their environment, causes them to engage
in the undesirable behavior. Their livelihood
requires of them to navigate the marketplace
all day and to linger at the street corners.
Thus, their eyes witness all temptations.
And what the eye sees, the heart desires.

**AVOT
(ETHICS OF THE
FATHERS; PIRKEI AVOT)**

A 6-chapter work on
Jewish ethics that is
studied widely by Jewish
communities, especially
during the summer. The
first 5 chapters are from
the Mishnah, tractate Avot.
Avot differs from the rest of
the Mishnah in that it does
not focus on legal subjects;
it is a collection of the sages'
wisdom on topics related
to character development,
ethics, healthy living, piety,
and the study of Torah.

**RABBI SHNEUR
ZALMAN OF LIADI
(ALTER REBBE)
1745–1812**

Chasidic rebbe, Halachic
authority, and founder of
the Chabad movement.
The Alter Rebbe was
born in Liozna, Belarus,
and was among the
principal students of the
Magid of Mezeritch. His
numerous works include
the *Tanya*, an early
classic containing the
fundamentals of Chabad
Chasidism; and *Shulchan
Aruch HaRav*, an
expanded and reworked
code of Jewish law.

Additionally, the nature of their instinctive impulse leads them to undesirable action, for it burns in them like a baker's fiery oven. . . . The instinctive impulse is not the same in everyone.

KING DAVID STREET, JERUSALEM
Gustav Bauernfeind, oil on canvas, 1887

Is it possible to not be judgmental? **Mrs. Leah Rosenfeld** shares the crucial mindset shift.
myjli.com/relationships

IV. THE PHILOSOPHICAL TRUTH

Working to reduce the impact of negativity bias and the fundamental attribution error is beneficial for our relationships. Yet Jewish mysticism takes it one step further: combating these tendencies taps the deepest mystical truth regarding the soul.

LOVE YOUR FELLOW JEW
Yoram Raanan, Israel

Zebra Question

Shel Silverstein, "Zebra Question," *A Light in the Attic*
(New York: Harper & Row, 1981), p. 125

I asked the zebra,

Are you black with white stripes?

Or white with black stripes?

And the zebra asked me,

Are you good with bad habits?

Or are you bad with good habits?

Are you noisy with quiet times?

Or are you quiet with noisy times?

Are you happy with some sad days?

Or are you sad with some happy days?

Are you neat with some sloppy ways?

Or are you sloppy with some neat ways?

And on and on and on and on

And on and on he went.

I'll never ask a zebra

About stripes

Again.

**SHEL SILVERSTEIN
1930-1999**

American poet, singer-songwriter, musician, composer, cartoonist, and screenwriter. Sheldon Allan Silverstein, better known as Shel Silverstein, was a famous composer and lyricist. He was also a cartoonist, well known for his provocative illustrations. Silverstein was famous among kids as Uncle Shelby and was admired for his children's books.

What is the message of this poem?
Do you agree with it?

TEXT 9

Divine Image

Genesis 1:26

וַיֹּאמֶר אֱלֹקִים, נַעֲשֶׂה אָדָם בְּצַלְמֵנוּ כִּדְמוּתֵנוּ . . .

Then G-d said, "Let us make humankind
in our image, in our likeness. . . ."

TEXT 10

Not Your Fault!

The Rebbe, Rabbi Menachem Mendel Schneerson,
Torat Menachem 5742:1, pp. 53–54

וּכְיָדוּעַ פִּתְגָּם רַבּוֹתֵינוּ נְשִׂיאֵינוּ
(לִיקוּטֵי דִיבּוּרִים ח"ד, תקפא, א):

"כְּשֵׁם שֶׁצְּרִיכִים לֵידַע אֶת הַחֶסְרוֹנוֹת,
כְּמוֹ כֵן צְרִיכִים לֵידַע מַעֲלוֹת עַצְמוֹ".

**RABBI MENACHEM
MENDEL SCHNEERSON
1902–1994**

The towering Jewish
leader of the 20th
century, known as "the
Lubavitcher Rebbe," or
simply as "the Rebbe."
Born in southern
Ukraine, the Rebbe
escaped Nazi-occupied
Europe, arriving in
the U.S. in June 1941.
The Rebbe inspired
and guided the revival
of traditional Judaism
after the European
devastation, impacting
virtually every Jewish
community the world
over. The Rebbe often
emphasized that the
performance of just
one additional good
deed could usher in
the era of Mashiach.
The Rebbe's scholarly
talks and writings have
been printed in more
than 200 volumes.

וּבָזֶה יֵשְׁנוֹ דִיוּק נִפְלָא: כַּאֲשֶׁר מְדוּבָּר אוֹדוֹת הַמַעֲלוֹת,
הַלָשׁוֹן הוּא מַעֲלוֹת עַצְמוֹ, וְאִילוּ כַּאֲשֶׁר מְדוּבָּר אוֹדוֹת
הַחֶסְרוֹנוֹת, הַלָשׁוֹן הוּא חֶסְרוֹנוֹת סְתָם, וְלֹא חֶסְרוֹנוֹת עַצְמוֹ.

וְהַבִּיאוּר בָּזֶה עַל פִּי מַה שֶׁכָּתוּב בְּזֹהַר (ח"ג יג, ב):
"וְנֶפֶשׁ כִּי תֶחֱטָא (וַיִקְרָא ד, ב)–תְּוָוהָא".

יְהוּדִי מִצַד עַצְמוֹ אֵינוֹ שַׁיָּיךְ לְעִנְיָן שֶׁל חֵטְא כְּלָל.
וְגַם כַּאֲשֶׁר נִכְשַׁל בְּעִנְיָן שֶׁל חֵטְא חַס וְשָׁלוֹם, אֵין זֶה
חִסָרוֹן עַצְמוֹ אֶלָא זֶהוּ דָבָר שֶׁמְחוּץ הֵימֶנוּ שֶׁנִדְבַּק אֵלָיו.

The rebbes of Chabad crafted an adage
(*LIKUTEI DIBURIM* 4, P. 581A):

"Just as we need to know the shortcomings,
so we need to know our advantages."

The anomaly in this phrase is that it refers
to "*our* advantages," whereas with regard
to shortcomings it merely refers to "*the*
shortcomings"—not "*our* shortcomings."

The explanation: The Torah [introduces its
discussion of the atonement process with the words]
"If a soul sinned . . ." (LEVITICUS 4:2). The *Zohar*
(3:13B), however, reads this as a rhetorical
exclamation: "A soul sinned? Is that possible?"

The concept of sin is completely alien to our being.
Even when we stumble, G-d forbid, our lapse does
not undermine our identity; rather, it is something
external to our nature that has latched on to us.

Mrs. Sara Blau shares
how to offer guidance.
myjli.com/relationships

The Mashiach

Isaiah 11:3

TEXT 11A

וְלֹא לְמַרְאֵה עֵינָיו יִשְׁפּוֹט וְלֹא לְמִשְׁמַע אָזְנָיו יוֹכִיחַ.

Neither with the sight of his eyes shall he judge,
nor with the hearing of his ears shall he reprove.

ISAIAH

Biblical book. The book of
Isaiah contains the prophecies
of Isaiah, who lived in the
7th–6th centuries BCE.
Isaiah's prophecies contain
stern rebukes for the personal
failings of the contemporary
people of Judea and the
corruption of its government.
The bulk of the prophecies,
however, are stirring
consolations and poetic visions
of the future Redemption.

The Full Picture

Rabbi Yosef Yitzchak Schneersohn, *Likutei Diburim* 2, pp. 317–322

TEXT 11B

דֶער דִין וּמִשְׁפָּט פוּן בְּנֵי אָדָם אִיז נָאר וָואס בְּעֵינָיו
יִרְאֶה אוּן בְּאָזְנָיו יִשְׁמַע . . . עֶר גֶעהט נִיט אַרַיין אִין
דֶעם לֶעבְּן פוּן דֶעם וֶועלְכָן עֶר מִשְׁפָּט. עֶר רֶעכְנְט זִיךְ
נִיט מִיט זַיין אוּמְשְׁטַאנְד אוּן מִיט דֶעם וָואס רִינְגְלְט
אִים אַרוּם, דָאס הֵייסְט, עֶר גֶעהט נִיט אַרַיין אִין זַיין
אִינֶערְלִיכְן לֶעבְּן אוּן פַאֹרְטִיפְט זִיךְ נִיט אִין דִי סִבּוֹת
וָואס הָאבֶּן אִיהם גֶעבְּרַאכְט צוּ אַזַא לֶעבְּן . . . אַזַא
מִשְׁפָּט אִיז נִיט קֵיין אֶמֶת'עֶר מִשְׁפָּט . . . מִשְׁפְּטִ'ן
קָאן מֶען נָאר דַאמָאלְט וֶוען מִ'שְׁטֶעלְט זִיךְ אַנִידֶער
אוֹיף יֶענֶעמְ'ס אָרְט, אוּן מִ'לֶעבְּט עֶס דוּרְךְ . . .

דֶער מִשְׁפָּט פוּן מָשִׁיחַ'ן אִיז, אַז "לֹא לְמַרְאֵה עֵינָיו
יִשְׁפּוֹט וְלֹא לְמִשְׁמַע אָזְנָיו יוֹכִיחַ", מָשִׁיחַ'ס מִשְׁפָּט וֶועט
נִיט זַיין וָוי אַ מֶענְשְׁלִיכֶער מִשְׁפָּט, אַז מֶעהר נִיט וָואס
עֶר זֶעהט אוּן הֶערְט. מָשִׁיחַ'ס מִשְׁפָּט וֶועט זַיין אַז עֶר

**RABBI YOSEF YITZCHAK
SCHNEERSOHN
(RAYATZ, FRIERDIKER REBBE,
PREVIOUS REBBE)
1880–1950**

Chasidic rebbe, prolific writer,
and Jewish activist. Rabbi
Yosef Yitzchak, the 6th leader
of the Chabad movement,
actively promoted Jewish
religious practice in Soviet
Russia and was arrested for
these activities. After his
release from prison and exile,
he settled in Warsaw, Poland,
from where he fled Nazi
occupation and arrived in
New York in 1940. Settling in
Brooklyn, Rabbi Schneersohn
worked to revitalize American
Jewish life. His son-in-law
Rabbi Menachem Mendel
Schneerson succeeded
him as the leader of the
Chabad movement.

וֶועט קוּקֶען זֶעהֶען אוּן פיהלֶען אוֹיךְ דִי סְבּוֹת וָואס הָאבּן
מִיטְגֶעבּרַאכְט דֶעם זִינְדִיגֶער אוֹיף זִינְדִיגֶען, עֶר וֶועט אוֹיךְ
פיהלֶען וִוי דֶער זִינְדִיגֶער הָאט דָאס נִיט גֶעוָואלְט טָאהן,
אָבֶּער עֶר הָאט זִיךְ נִיט גֶעקָאנְט גוֹבֵר זַיין אוֹיף זַיין תַּאֲוָה.

Human judgment is confined to what the eyes
see and what the ears hear. . . . We do not enter
into the lives of the people being judged, nor do
we consider their circumstances or environment.
We do not delve into their internal experience or
explore the factors that led them to their current
situation. . . . This type of judgment is not true
judgment. . . . True judgment can only be given
when we place ourselves in another's situation
and experience that which they experience.

Regarding Mashiach it is stated, "Neither with the
sight of his eyes shall he judge, nor with the hearing
of his ears shall he reprove." Mashiach's judgment
will not be like typical human judgment, based
solely on what one sees and hears. Mashiach will
understand and feel the circumstances that led
wrongdoers to err. Mashiach will recognize that
the wrongdoers did not want to stray but simply
could not overcome their passionate desires.

KEY POINTS

1   We possess the freedom to act in defiance
of our biases and tendencies. By doing so
repeatedly and consistently, we gradually
steer ourselves toward healthier attitudes.

2   We alter our negativity bias by becoming radically
profuse in describing the virtues of the people
connected to us. We battle this bias even more
fundamentally by training ourselves to search
for the beauty and positivity in all things.

3   When someone benefits us, in addition to
focusing on this virtue, it is also advisable
to *augment* the virtue by assuming that it
required much effort and that it is a result
of the benefactor's genuine kindness.

4   The Torah regards our essence to be the G-dly
soul, even if our animal soul speaks louder and has
more influence on our daily choices. We are "good
with bad habits," not "bad with good habits."
When we tap this truth, it makes sense to dwell
on another person's virtues instead of their vices
and to augment their good rather than reduce it.

5   We overcome the tendency to commit attribution errors by relating stories of those who excelled in judging favorably, which makes us conscious of the problem and motivates us to overcome it. Practically: When a cynical attribution surfaces, ask yourself whether there is a reasonable circumstantial explanation that is worth accommodating.

6   Even when unique circumstances are not the cause for misbehavior, we can judge favorably by taking into account the wrongdoer's disposition and surroundings, acknowledging that under similar pressures, we might have acted similarly. This empathetic perspective does not justify wrongdoing but it eliminates our own undeserved sense of superiority that generates discord.

7   The Torah regards our essence to be the G-dly soul. It is therefore logical to attribute failings to an extra-challenging animal soul or another circumstantial cause.

8   To truly appreciate the soul in others and regard it as their primary identity, we must prioritize *our own* soul's importance in *our own* lives. You cannot reach deeper within another than you reach within your own self.

Power of Phraseology

"The teacher intended to teach his disciples to avoid discussing the negative, lest the habit become part of their nature. Instead, through habitually mentioning the positive, it would become part of their nature to speak positively" (Rabbi Bachya ibn Pakudah, *Chovot Halevavot*, The Gate of Submission 6).

This teaching from the medieval Jewish classic resonates profoundly in the talks and writings of the Lubavitcher Rebbe. Even a cursory examination of his works reveals a deliberate and remarkable avoidance of negative words and phrases.

Positive Suggestions

Here are four instances where the Rebbe recommended replacing a commonly used term with a more positive alternative because the original term had a negative connotation.

LOVE, NOT DISTANT

" The rebbes of Chabad did not use the term *kiruv rechokim*—'drawing closer those who are far.' Rather, they emphasized the importance of loving another Jew, including a Jew one has never met, even one who lives on the other side of the world. This is the terminology they used to advocate for lending support to enhance Jewish practice. But they did not use the term *kiruv rechokim*. The reason: It is contrary to Jewish law to inform another Jew that they are distant and that you seek to draw them close. Moreover, in truth, there is no such a thing as a Jew who is distant from Judaism."

—Address on Shabbat *Behar-Bechukotai* 5740 (May 10, 1980), *Sichot Kodesh* 5740:3, pp. 102–103

HEALING, NOT ILLNESS

" I hope you recall my suggestion to use the term *bet refuah*, 'institution of healing,' instead of *bet cholim*, 'institution for the ill.' Although it may sound like semantics, the change can bring encouragement to those undergoing treatment. Moreover, 'institution of healing' matches the true nature of the institution!"

—Letter dated 3 Adar, 5737 (February 21, 1977) to Professor Mordechai Shani, director of Tel Hashomer Hospital, Tel Aviv, *Igrot Kodesh* 32, p. 130

SIMPLE, NOT IGNORANT

" Rather than using the term *am haaretz* (ignoramus) to describe a Jewish person with limited knowledge, my father-in-law would refer to them as *anashim peshutim* (simple people), which also reflects their unique bond with *peshitut haAtzmut*, the abstract simplicity of G-d's Essence that's beyond definable characteristics."

—In conversation with Mr. Zalman Shazar, 5 Shevat, 5733 (January 8, 1973), *Torat Menachem* 5733:2 (71), p. 49

EXCEPTIONAL, NOT HANDICAPPED

" When, for some reason, a person is lacking in the physical sense . . . it means that the Creator endowed them with special spiritual power, which enables them to overcome that which ordinary eyes perceive as a physical lack. Such individuals can show that they are on par with others, and furthermore, possess an exceptional spirit that allows them to surpass their limitations, in order to thrive and progress in significant fields, achieving more than what is expected of the average individual.

"For this reason, I am uncomfortable when the term 'handicapped' is applied to someone, because it suggests some kind of inferiority. To the contrary, we must emphasize that the Creator has made them special and exceptional. . . .

"In keeping with the Jewish 'custom' of offering advice even regarding areas that are not quite one's own business, I would like to suggest that the designation be changed from 'handicapped' to 'exceptional' (*metzuyanim*). . . . This name change is not merely semantics but rather depicts the situation most truly."

—Address to exceptional Israeli soldiers, 23 Av, 5736 (August 19, 1976), *Sichot Kodesh* 5736:2, pp. 634–635

Positive Rephrasing

The Rebbe's communications are replete with citations from across the spectrum of Torah literature. Notably, when a source text included less-than-positive phraseology, the Rebbe often refrained from direct quotations and settled instead for a paraphrase, taking pains to balance the need to convey the original intent while exemplifying his dedication to positive expression. Here are some examples.

LIFE'S CHOICE

" Behold, I have set before you today life and good, and death and evil."

Deuteronomy 30:15

" G-d desired that it should be in such a way that 'I have set before you today life and good' and the opposite."

—The Rebbe, 10 Shevat, 5740 (January 28, 1980)

HAMAN'S HATRED

" Haman sought to destroy all the Jews who were throughout Ahasuerus's entire kingdom."

Esther 3:6

" Haman desired the opposite of Jewish continuity."

—The Rebbe, Purim 5732 (March 26, 1972)

THE INNER CHALLENGE

" Those who destroy you and those who lay you waste will go forth from you."

Isaiah 49:17

" When a Jew states that unholiness has power and that we need to yield to it, we face the problem that Isaiah referred to as 'will go forth from you'—with the few words that precede it. This behavior leads to matters that are the opposite of building and the opposite of all that is good."

—The Rebbe, 18 Iyar, 5730 (May 24, 1970)

THE FOUR CHILDREN

" The Torah discusses four children: one is wise, one is wicked, one is simple, and one does not know how to ask. . . . The wicked child, what does he say? 'What is this service to you?'"

Passover *Haggadah*

" The child who is the opposite of the wise one states, 'What is this service to you?'"

—The Rebbe, 11 Nisan, 5733 (April 13, 1973)

CYCLE OF DEEDS

" One mitzvah leads to another mitzvah, and a transgression leads to another transgression."

Mishnah, Avot 4:2

" Just as one mitzvah leads to another mitzvah in the sphere of good, the same is true in the opposite sphere."

—The Rebbe, 18 Iyar, 5730 (May 24, 1970)

THE JERUSALEM TEMPLE

" A generation that does not merit to build the Holy Temple is akin to the generation in which it was destroyed!"

Jerusalem Talmud, Yoma 1:1

" A generation that does not merit to build the Temple is akin to, etc.!"

—The Rebbe, 15 Av, 5739 (August 8, 1979)

ABUNDANT VIRTUE

" The sinners of the Jewish people are filled with good deeds like a pomegranate."

Talmud, Eiruvin 19a

" Even those who are the opposite of righteous are filled with good deeds like a pomegranate."

—The Rebbe, 24 Tevet, 5738 (January 2, 1978)

JETHRO'S JOURNEY

" There was no form of idolatry in the world that Jethro didn't pursue and worship [before he ultimately recognized G-d]."

Mechilta, Exodus 18:11

" The Midrash teaches that Jethro knew all of the theories, philosophies, and opinions that were contrary to the Torah and contrary to worshipping G-d."

—The Rebbe, 10 Shevat, 5740 (January 28, 1980)

FAITH IN THE HOLY LAND

" Anyone who resides outside of the Land of Israel is considered as one who does not have a G-d."

Talmud, Ketubot 110b

" Anyone who resides outside of the Land of Israel is considered as one who, etc."

—The Rebbe, 20 Av, 5715 (August 8, 1955)

INCLUSIVE CONGREGATION

" "The Hebrew word for a congregation, *tzibur*, is an acronym for *tzadikim*, *beinonim*, and *resha'im*."

Rabbi Chaim Yosef David Azulai, *Kikar Laaden*, Avot 2:4

" The Hebrew word for a congregation, *tzibur*, is an acronym for *tzadikim*, *beinonim*—and the third category, which is alluded to with the letter *reish*."

—The Rebbe, 10 Tevet 5750 (January 7, 1990)

Positive Diction

The following is a selection of twenty examples of common negative words that the Rebbe took pains to avoid. He averted some of these frequently while sidestepping others only on occasion. Regardless, the Rebbe was consistent in this overall effort: nearly every address and communication included at least a couple of such instances, highlighting the significance of choosing positive language.

Hebrew Term	Translation	The Rebbe's Alternative	Translation
Ra	Bad/evil	*Hepech hatov*	Opposite of good
Kelipah	The negative forces	*Hepech hakedushah*	Forces that are the opposite of holiness
Tumah	Impurity	*Hepech hataharah*	Opposite of purity
Aveirah	Sin	*Hepech haTorah*	That which is contrary to the Torah
Shechitut	Corruption/immorality	*Hepech hatzedek*	Opposite of justice/morality
Yetzer Hara	Evil inclination	*Der yetzer hepech fun der yetzer tov*	The inclination that is the opposite of the good inclination
Rasha	Wicked person	*Hepech fun a tzadik*	Opposite of a righteous person
Sinah	Hate	*Hepech hakiruv vehaachdut*	Opposite of closeness and unity

Hebrew Term	Translation	The Rebbe's Alternative	Translation
Sheker	Lie	*Hepech ha'emet*	Opposite of truth
Shetut	Foolishness	*Hepech hasechel*	Opposite of intelligence
Sone Yisrael	Antisemite	*Hepech fun an ohev Yisrael*	Opposite of a lover of Jews
Atzvut	Sadness	*Hepech hasimchah*	Opposite of joy
Tzaar	Pain	*Hepech hanachat ruach*	Opposite of pleasure
Daagah	Anxiety	*He'eder menuchat hanefesh*	Absence of tranquility
Mavet	Death	*Hepech hachayim*	Opposite of life
Kelalah	Curse	*Hepech haberachah*	Opposite of blessing
Onesh	Punishment	*Hepech hasechar*	Opposite of reward
Gehinom	Purgatory	*Hepech fun Gan Eden*	Opposite of Paradise
Churban Beit Hamikdash	The Temple's destruction	*Hepech fun kiyum Beit Hamikdash*	The opposite of the Temple's endurance
Baya	Problem	*Inyan hadoresh tikun*	A matter that requires repair

Negativity Bias: The Human Tendency to Dwell on the Negative Over the Positive

This curated collection summarizes the findings from numerous studies exploring the concept of negativity bias, a psychological phenomenon in which negative events and emotions significantly impact our thoughts, behaviors, and overall well-being to a greater extent than positive emotions and events. These findings offer profound insight into how deeply rooted and influential this bias is in our daily lives. Understanding this tendency permits us to harness it constructively and identify ways to prevent it from negatively affecting ourselves and those around us.

SOURCES: Paul Rozin and Edward B. Royzman, "Negativity Bias, Negativity Dominance, and Contagion," *Personality and Social Psychology Review* 5:4 (2001), pp. 296–320; Roy F. Baumeister, et al., "Bad Is Stronger than Good," *Review of General Psychology* 5:4 (2001), pp. 323–370

ENDOWMENT EFFECT

People demand more to give up something they own than they are willing to pay to acquire it.

QUANTITY OF INFORMATION

If an initial judgment favored hiring, only 3.8 unfavorable bits of information were required to shift the decision to rejection; whereas 8.8 favorable pieces of information were necessary to shift an initially negative decision toward acceptance.

PHOTOGRAPHS

People spent more time viewing photographs of negative behaviors than positive ones.

POST-BET REFLECTION

A study found that participants who lost bets on sporting events spent more time discussing and reflecting on their losses than those who won spent on discussing their gains.

BAD MOODS

People have more strategies to escape bad moods than to induce good ones. Efforts to terminate unpleasant states were reported more frequently than efforts to prolong pleasant states.

RECALLING AND SHARING

When people were asked to recall a recent, important emotional event, they were more likely—by a four-to-one margin—to recall and share negative emotional events than positive ones.

DEPRESSION

The presence of upsetting individuals in one's social network was a stronger predictor of depression than the presence of helpful individuals.

SAVING LIVES TO OFFSET MURDER

Psychology undergraduates were asked how many lives one would need to save to be forgiven for one murder. The median response was twenty-five.

DETECTING FACES

The task was to scan a "crowd" of black-and-white schematically drawn faces and identify the one face that was inconsistent with the others, whether it was happy or angry. Reaction times were much faster for identifying a frowning and angry face than for identifying a smiling and happy face.

SEEKING EXPLANATIONS

People seek more explanations for negative events than for positive ones.

LOSS AVERSION

In the context of wager options, some consistently made choices with the best-expected value. Others went to an extreme: making choices that reflected an overconcern with losing money or assuming extra risk for added gain. Of those who went to an extreme, 83 percent showed a preference for avoiding losses.

WELL-BEING MEASURES

Social conflict has a stronger relationship with well-being measures than social support.

AFTER FAILURE

Participants who completed a task were divided into groups: some were told they had succeeded, some were told they had failed, and some (the control group) weren't given any feedback. All were then asked to estimate how other people would likely do on the same task. Those who had failed rated failure as more common and likely. Success, in contrast, yielded no departure from the control group.

REVERTING TO BASELINE

An interview of lottery winners, accident victims, and a control group showed that while lottery winners' happiness quickly returned to baseline, accident victims remained less happy even a year later.

REWARD AND PUNISHMENT

A study examined what would motivate children to walk as slowly as possible and to wait as long as possible before speaking up. The children performed better in the punishment conditions (losing marbles) than in the reward conditions (gaining the same number of marbles).

LACK OF POSITIVE OPPOSITES

Many common negative terms in the English language, such as "risk," "accident," "catastrophe," and "murderer," lack simple, common positive opposites.

PREFERENCE OF NEWS

When asked whether they preferred to hear good or bad news first, most participants preferred to hear the bad news first.

WORDS FOR NEGATIVE EMOTION

In a compilation of 558 terms of emotion, there were significantly more words for negative emotions than positive ones (62 percent vs. 38 percent).

"CONTAGION"

Contact with lower castes in the Hindu system has a more potent and lasting effect than contact with higher castes.

SELF-ESTEEM

Participants were told that they had either been selected by other members to be included in a group, excluded from it, or had been *randomly* included or excluded. The intentional rejection led to a change in self-esteem, but the intentional acceptance did not have an effect.

SOCIAL REJECTION

Social rejection among children was more consistently recognized than social popularity: children, teachers, and parents showed higher agreement on who was rejected than on who was popular.

LOSS AND GAIN

People reported greater distress over losing money than happiness over gaining the same amount of money.

ASSOCIATIONS IN TASTE

Pairing neutral flavors with unpleasant tastes led participants to develop a strong dislike for those neutral flavors, whereas pairing those neutral flavors with pleasant tastes did not enhance a liking for those neutral flavors.

INFANT FACES

Adults were able to identify infants' negative emotions more accurately than positive ones.

MARITAL SATISFACTION

Stress has a greater impact on marital satisfaction than positive factors like social support and resources: stress added more than 20 percent to the amount of variance in marital satisfaction, whereas positive support and resources added only 5 percent.

NEGATIVE EVALUATIONS

Participants in a study received either a positive or a negative evaluation from another person. The participants then watched the evaluations on video. The negative evaluation videos were watched for longer than the positive ones, especially when expecting future interactions with the evaluator.

BAD TRAITS

In a study using the Stroop paradigm, participants took longer to name the ink color of words describing bad traits than good traits, suggesting that the meanings of bad traits had greater power for attracting attention.

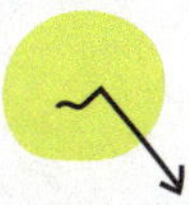

ECONOMIC DOWNTURNS AND VOTING

Economic downturns reduce votes for incumbent parties in U.S. presidential elections, while upturns have little effect.

The Fundamental Attribution Error

The Fundamental Attribution Error is also known as the *correspondence bias* (Gilbert & Malone, 1995). It refers to the tendency to attribute the behavior of others to internal characteristics such as personality traits, beliefs, or attitudes, while overlooking the impact of external factors such as environmental circumstances or social pressure.

The Fundamental Attribution Error can lead to misunderstandings, stereotypes, and prejudice, as we may inaccurately judge others based on limited information and biased attributions (Dovidio, et al., 2018).

Three Causes of the Fundamental Attribution Error

Several factors contribute to the occurrence of the Fundamental Attribution Error. Following are three of the most relevant causes.

1. Perceptual salience

When observing behavior, we tend to focus on what is easiest to perceive, the clearly visible actions of the person instead of more subtle aspects of the surrounding context. This amplifies the tendency to attribute behavior to internal characteristics (Gilbert & Malone, 1995).

2. Cognitive simplification

The human mind often seeks to simplify complex phenomena by categorizing them into easily understandable theories and attributions. As a result, we may default to the person's character and disposition to make sense of their behavior, neglecting the nuances and complexities of a variety of situational influences (Heider, 1958).

3. Cultural norms

In cultures that emphasize personal agency and achievement (like the USA), the Fundamental Attribution Error may be more pronounced than in collectivist cultures, which prioritize social harmony and interdependence. (Miller, 1984; Markus & Kitayama, 1991; Nisbett, 2003; Lee & Fiore, 2020).

Four Steps to Recognize Fundamental Attribution Error

To overcome negativity bias, we can be mindful and alert about an underlying cause, the Fundamental Attribution Error.

Let us look at these steps in order.

1. Pause and reflect.

Before jumping to conclusions about someone's behavior, take a moment to consider alternative explanations and situational factors that may have influenced their actions.

2. Consider context.

Pay attention to the situational context in which behavior occurs, as it can provide valuable insights into the motives and constraints shaping individuals' actions.

3. Practice empathy.

Put yourself in the other person's shoes and try to understand their perspective and experiences. Empathizing with others can help mitigate the tendency to make overly simplistic attributions.

4. Seek information.

Gather additional information or perspectives before forming judgments about someone's behavior. Avoid relying solely on first impressions or limited observations.

Psychology References

Baumeister RF, et al. (2001) Bad is stronger than good. *Review of General Psychology*, *5*(4), 346–347. doi.org/10.1037/1089-2680.5.4.323.

Bolster B, Springbett BM. (1961) The reaction of interviewers to favorable and unfavorable information. *Journal of Applied Psychology 45*(2), pp. 97–103. doi.org/10.1037/h0048316.

Chen-Xia XJ, et al. (2023) Cultural variations in perceptions and reactions to social norm transgressions: a comparative study. *Frontiers in Psychology*, 14, 1243955. doi.org/10.3389/fpsyg.2023.1243955.

Dong P. (2022) Explaining the unexplained: Situational differences in fundamental attribution error. *International Journal of Social Science Research*, *10*(2). 210. doi.org/10.5296/ijssr.v10i2.19927.

Dovidio JF, et al. (2018) Physical health disparities and stigma: Race, sexual orientation, and body weight. In B. Major, J. F. Dovidio, & B. G. Link (Eds.), *The Oxford Handbook of Stigma, Discrimination, and Health* (pp. 29–51). Oxford University Press.

Gilbert, DT, Malone PS. (1995) The correspondence bias. *Psychological Bulletin, 117*(1), 21–38. doi.org/10.1037/0033-2909.117.1.21.

Heider, F. (1958) *The Psychology of Interpersonal Relations.* John Wiley & Sons Inc. doi.org/10.1037/10628-000.

Hirozawa PY, et al. (2019) Intention matters to make you (im)moral: Positive-negative asymmetry in moral character evaluations. *The Journal of Social Psychology*, *160*(4). 401-415. doi.org/10.1080/00224545.2019.1653254.

Norris CJ. (2021) The negativity bias, revisited: Evidence from neuroscience measures and an individual differences approach. *Social Neuroscience, 16*(1), 68–82. doi.org/10.1080/17470919.2 019.1696225.

Riskey DR, Birnbaum MH. (1974) Compensatory effects in moral judgment: Two rights don't make up for a wrong. *Journal of Experimental Psychology, 103*:1, 171–173. doi.org/10.1037/h0036892.

Ross L. (1977) The intuitive psychologist and his shortcomings: Distortions in the attribution process. In L. Berkowitz (Ed.), *Advances in Experimental Social Psychology, 10*. New York: Academic Press, 173–220. ISSN 0065-2601. ISBN 9780120152100. doi.org/10.1016/S0065-2601(08)60357-3.

Soroka S, et al. (2019) Cross-national evidence of a negativity bias in psychophysiological reactions to news. *Proceedings of the National Academy of Sciences of the United States of America,* 116(38), 18888–18892 doi.org/10.1073/pnas.1908369116.

Stalder D. (2018) *The Power of Context: How to Manage Our Bias and Improve Our Understanding of Others* (Amherst, New York: Prometheus Books), pp. 33–37

APPENDIX A—THE POWER OF SPEECH

Love Your Fellow

Maimonides, *Mishneh Torah*, Laws of Character Development 6:3

TEXT 12A

מִצְוָה עַל כָּל אָדָם לֶאֱהוֹב אֶת כָּל אֶחָד וְאֶחָד מִיִּשְׂרָאֵל
כְּגוּפוֹ, שֶׁנֶּאֱמַר: "וְאָהַבְתָּ לְרֵעֲךָ כָּמוֹךָ" (וַיִקְרָא יט, יח).

לְפִיכָךְ צָרִיךְ לְסַפֵּר בְּשִׁבְחוֹ וְלָחוּס עַל מָמוֹנוֹ,
כַּאֲשֶׁר הוּא חָס עַל מָמוֹן עַצְמוֹ וְרוֹצֶה בִּכְבוֹד עַצְמוֹ.

We are obligated to love each of our fellow Jews as
we love our own selves, as it is stated, "Love your
fellow as yourself" (LEVITICUS 19:18).

Therefore, we must speak the praises of others and
be concerned for their assets, to the same extent that
we care about our own assets and desire respect.

The Value of Praise

The Rebbe, Rabbi Menachem Mendel Schneerson,
Likutei Sichot 27, pp. 163–164

TEXT 12B

די אייגנשאפט פון דיבור איז ארויסצוברענגען אן עניָן פון הָעוֹלָם
(מַחֲשָׁבָה) צו גילוי. און דעריבער, ווען מען רעדט ווענן יענעמס רע און
מ'ברענגט עס אל הגילוי בדיבור, איז דאס עלול צו שאטן יענעם. ווען
מ'וואלט ווענן דעם ניט גערעדט - וואלט יענעמס רע אפשר געבליבן
בְּהֶעלֶם און עס וואלט ניט ארויסגערופן די תוצאות הבלתי רצויות.

סְ'אִיז דָאךְ אַ כְּלָל אַז "מִדָּה טוֹבָה מְרוּבָּה מִמְדַת פּוּרְעָנִיּוֹת"
(סוֹטָה יא, א), אִיז מָה-דָאךְ אַז דָאס רֵיידְן װעגְן צְװײיטְנְס
גְנוּת הָאט שֶׁעדְלֶעכֶע װירְקוּנְג אוֹיף יֶענֶעם, אִיז מִכָּל שֶׁכֵּן
אַז עֶס אִיז אַזוֹי (אוּן נָאךְ מֶער) אִין דֶער מִדָּה טוֹבָה, אַז
בְּעֵת מֶען רֶעדְט װעגְן יֶענֶעמְס טוֹב אוּן מַעֲלוֹת הָאט עֶס
אַװַדַאי אַ גוּטֶע װירְקוּנְג אוֹיף דֶעם װעלְכְן מ'לוֹיבְּט, אוּן
עֶס גִיט אִים אַ חִיזּוּק וְסִיוּּעַ אִין זַיין עֲבוֹדָה - מֶען בְּרֶענְגְט
אַרוֹיס בְּגִילּוּי אוּן בְּפוֹעַל זַיין טוֹב אוּן זַיינֶע מַעֲלוֹת.

The function of speech is to deliver something hidden—one's thoughts—into revealed form. Consequently, if we speak about someone else's negativity, it can potentially harm the individual under discussion. If we had not discussed it, that person's negativity might have remained concealed, without causing undesirable consequences.

There is a principle that "a positive force is greater than its negative counterpart" (TALMUD, SOTAH 11A). Therefore, if discussing someone's faults harms that individual, then this is certainly the case (and to a far greater extent) regarding the positive: If we speak about someone's positive qualities and virtues, our words undoubtedly have a beneficial influence on the person we are praising. Our words deliver that individual's goodness and virtues into clear and tangible manifestation, thereby strengthening and assisting that individual in achieving their purpose in life.

APPENDIX B—JUDGING FAVORABLY

TEXT 13

Enabler of Peace

Sefer Hachinuch, Mitzvah 235

"בְּצֶדֶק תִּשְׁפֹּט עֲמִיתֶךָ" (וַיִּקְרָא יט, טו). וּבָא הַפֵּירוּשׁ
שֶׁנִּצְטַווּ הַדַּיָּנִין לְהַשְׁווֹת בַּעֲלֵי הָרִיב, כְּלוֹמַר, שֶׁלֹּא
יְכַבֵּד הַדַּיָּן אֶחָד מִבַּעֲלֵי הַדִּין יוֹתֵר מִן הָאַחֵר . . .

וְעוֹד יֵשׁ בִּכְלַל מִצְוָה זוֹ: שֶׁרָאוּי לְכָל אָדָם לָדוּן אֶת חֲבֵרוֹ
לְכַף זְכוּת, וְלֹא יְפָרֵשׁ מַעֲשָׂיו וּדְבָרָיו אֶלָּא לְטוֹב . . .
יִהְיֶה סִיבָּה לִהְיוֹת בֵּין אֲנָשִׁים שָׁלוֹם וְרֵעוּת.

The Torah commands us, "Judge your neighbor with righteousness" (LEVITICUS 19:15). According to the standard interpretation, this is a command for judges to treat litigants equally, so that a judge does not honor one party over the other. . . .

Another obligation embedded within this same commandment is that it is appropriate for each individual to judge others favorably, interpreting their actions and words only in a positive light. . . . This fosters peace and harmony among people.

SEFER HACHINUCH

A work on the biblical commandments. Four aspects of every mitzvah are discussed in this work: the definition of the mitzvah; ethical lessons that can be deduced from the mitzvah; basic laws pertaining to the observance of the mitzvah; and who is obligated to perform the mitzvah, and when. The work was composed in the 13th century by an anonymous author who refers to himself as "the Levite of Barcelona."

A Father's Wisdom

TEXT 14

Rabbi Yehudah Hachasid, *Sefer Chasidim* 655

מַעֲשֶׂה בְּבֵן שֶׁכִּבֵּד אֶת אָבִיו בְּיוֹתֵר. אָמַר לוֹ אָבִיו: אַתָּה מְכַבְּדֵינִי בְּחַיַּי, תְּכַבְּדֵנִי בְּמוֹתִי. אֲנִי מְצַוְּךָ שֶׁתָּלִין כַּעַסְךָ לַיְלָה אֶחָד, וַעֲצוֹר רוּחֲךָ שֶׁלֹא תְדַבֵּר.

לְאַחַר פְּטִירַת אָבִיו הָלַךְ לִמְדִינַת הַיָּם, וְהִנִּיחַ אִשְׁתּוֹ מְעוּבֶּרֶת וְהוּא לֹא יָדַע, וְעִכֵּב בַּדֶּרֶךְ יָמִים וְשָׁנִים.

וּכְשֶׁחָזַר בָּעִיר, בָּא בַּלַּיְלָה, וְעָלָה לַחֶדֶר שֶׁאִשְׁתּוֹ הָיְתָה שָׁם שׁוֹכֶבֶת, וְשָׁמַע קוֹלוֹ שֶׁל בָּחוּר שֶׁהָיָה מְנַשֵּׁק אוֹתָהּ. שָׁלַף חַרְבּוֹ וְרָצָה לַהֲרוֹג שְׁנֵיהֶם, וְזָכַר מִצְוַת אָבִיו וְהֵשִׁיבוֹ לְתַעֲרָהּ.

שָׁמַע שֶׁאָמְרָה לְאוֹתוֹ בָּחוּר, בְּנָהּ שֶׁאֲצָלָהּ: כְּבָר יֵשׁ שָׁנִים רַבּוֹת שֶׁהָלַךְ אָבִיךְ מֵאֶצְלִי. אִילוּ הָיָה יוֹדֵעַ שֶׁנּוֹלַד לוֹ בֵּן, כְּבָר הִגִּיעַ לְהַשִׂיא לְךָ אִשָׁה.

כְּשֶׁשָּׁמַע זֶה הַדָּבָר אָמַר: פִּתְחִי לִי אֲחוֹתִי רַעְיָיתִי! בָּרוּךְ ה' שֶׁעָצַר כַּעֲסִי, וּבָרוּךְ אָבִי שֶׁצִּיוַּנִי לַעֲצוֹר כַּעֲסִי לַיְלָה אֶחָד, שֶׁלֹא הָרַגְתִּי אוֹתָךְ וְאֶת בְּנִי.

There was once an individual who showed his father tremendous respect. Toward the end of his life, the father told him, "Just as you honored me during my lifetime, please honor me after my passing [by observing this final directive]: always allow one night to pass before you act on or verbally express your anger."

RABBI YEHUDAH HACHASID
1140–1217

Mystic and ethicist. Born in Speyer, Germany, he was a rabbi, a mystic, and one of the initiators of Chasidei Ashkenaz, a Jewish German moralist movement that stressed piety and asceticism. Rabbi Yehudah settled in Regensburg in 1195. He is best known for his work *Sefer Chasidim*, on the ethics of day-to-day concerns.

After his father's passing, the son traveled overseas, leaving behind a wife who, unknown to him, was pregnant. Circumstances forced him to be delayed overseas for many long years.

When he finally returned, he entered his hometown at night. As he approached his wife's room, he heard the sound of a young man giving her a kiss. Instinctively, he drew his sword—intending to kill them both. Just then, he recalled his father's parting directive and he returned his sword to its sheath.

He then overheard his wife telling the young man, "Your father has been gone for so many years! If he only knew that I had given birth to his son, he would certainly return to help you get married."

When the husband heard that, he called out, "Open up for me, my dear! Blessed be G-d for tempering my anger, and blessed is my father who instructed me to never act upon my anger until a night has passed—so that I did not end up killing you and my son!"

TEXT 15

A Matter of Perspective

Valerie Cox, "A Matter of Perspective," in Jack Canfield and Mark Victor Hansen, *A 3rd Serving of Chicken Soup for the Soul: 101 More Stories to Open the Heart and Rekindle the Spirit* (Deerfield Beach, Fla.: Health Communications, Inc., 1996), pp. 199–200

A woman was waiting at an airport one night,
with several long hours before her flight. She
hunted for a book in the airport shops, bought
a bag of cookies, and found a place to drop.

She was engrossed in her book but happened to
see, that the man sitting beside her, as bold as could
be . . . grabbed a cookie or two from the bag in
between, which she tried to ignore to avoid a scene.

So she munched the cookies and watched the
clock, as the gutsy cookie thief diminished
her stock. She was getting more irritated
as the minutes ticked by, thinking, "If I
wasn't so nice, I would blacken his eye."

With each cookie she took, he took one too; when
only one was left, she wondered what he would
do. With a smile on his face and a nervous laugh,
he took the last cookie and broke it in half.

He offered her half, as he ate the other, she
snatched it from him and thought, "Oh, brother.
This guy has some nerve and he's also rude.
Why he didn't even show any gratitude!"

VALERIE COX
1946–2017

Poet. Valerie Cox was the author of *Inspirational and Humorous Poems, Prose and Prayers* and contributed poems and short stories to various books and publications.

She had never known when she had been so galled
and sighed with relief when her flight was called.
She gathered her belongings and headed to the
gate, refusing to look back at the thieving ingrate.

She boarded the plane and sank in her seat, then she
sought her book, which was almost complete. As she
reached in her baggage, she gasped with surprise—
there was her bag of cookies, in front of her eyes.

If mine are here, she moaned in despair, the
others were his, and he tried to share. Too late
to apologize, she realized with grief, that she
was the rude one, the ingrate, the thief.

APPENDIX C—A CONCEALING LOVE

Inconsequential Faults

TEXT 16A

Rabbi Menachem Mendel of Lubavitch,
Derech Mitzvotecha 29a

"אֵין אָדָם רוֹאֶה חוֹב לְעַצְמוֹ" (כְּתוּבוֹת קה, ב), אֵין
הַפֵּירוּשׁ שֶׁאֵינוֹ יוֹדֵעַ כְּלָל כְּלָל חוֹבוֹתָיו. אַדְרַבָּה, יוּכַל לִרְאוֹת
וּלְהָבִין הֵיטֵב עֲמָקוֹת פְּחִיתוּתוֹ יוֹתֵר מֵרְאִיַּת זוּלָתוֹ עָלָיו,
שֶׁהֲרֵי זוּלָתוֹ אֵינוֹ רוֹאֶה אֶלָּא לָעֵינַיִם וְהוּא יִרְאֶה לַלֵּבָב.

אֶלָּא הַכַּוָּנָה שֶׁאֵין הַחוֹב תּוֹפֵס מָקוֹם אֶצְלוֹ כְּלָל לְהִתְפָּעֵל
מִזֶּה, וּכְאִילוּ אֵינוֹ רוֹאֶה אוֹתוֹ כְּלָל, כִּי מִפְּנֵי הָאַהֲבָה

הַגְּדוֹלָה אֲשֶׁר הוּא אוֹהֵב מְאֹד אֶת עַצְמוֹ, עַל כָּל פְּשָׁעָיו שֶׁיּוֹדֵעַ בְּדַעְתּוֹ, תְּכַסֶּה הָאַהֲבָה בִּבְחִינַת מַקִּיף שֶׁלֹּא יִמְשָׁךְ מִן הַיְדִיעָה לִידֵי הִתְפַּעֲלוּת בַּמִּדּוֹת, וְלָכֵן אֵין תּוֹפְסִים מָקוֹם כְּלָל לְהִתְפָּעֵל מִזֶּה . . .

וְכַאֲשֶׁר יִרְאֶה זוּלָתוֹ עַל הַחוֹב שֶׁלּוֹ וְיָבִין אוֹתוֹ, יִרְגַּז מְאֹד, אַף עַל פִּי שֶׁיּוֹדֵעַ בְּעַצְמוֹ שֶׁאֱמֶת הוּא . . . שֶׁיְּדִיעַת חֲבֵירוֹ אֶת פְּחִיתוּתוֹ הוּא בִּבְחִינַת יֵשׁ וְהִתְפַּעֲלוּת. מַה שֶּׁאֵין כֵּן כְּשֶׁהוּא יוֹדֵעַ, הָאַהֲבָה מְכַסָּה.

Our sages taught that "people fail to see their own faults" (TALMUD, KETUBOT 105B). It is not that we are *unaware* of our faults; to the contrary, we perceive and appreciate the depth of our deficiencies to a far greater degree than others do: whereas others only see what is visible, we know what transpires within our hearts.

Rather, our sages' statement refers to the phenomenon whereby we do not consider our faults to be significant enough to upset our equanimity. We treat our faults as if they are invisible to us, for we smother them with an extremely thick layer of self-love. True, we are intellectually aware of our deficiencies, but we do not allow that awareness to evoke any emotional response. We do not permit them to matter to us in the slightest. . . .

When *someone else* notices or knows about our flaw, we grow extremely upset, although we know that we truly bear the flaw. . . . We become upset because the other person perceives our shortcomings as something substantial, as something that genuinely matters. This is not the case when we know our own shortcomings, because we blanket them with love.

Love Despite Faults

Rabbi Menachem Mendel of Lubavitch, ibid.

וְזֶהוּ "מַה דְּסָנֵי לָךְ": גְּלוּי זֶה, "לְחַבְרָךְ לֹא תַעֲבִיד"
(שַׁבָּת לא, ב), שֶׁלֹּא תִרְאֶה חוֹבוֹתָיו וּפְשָׁעָיו, הֵן
בְּמִילֵי דְעָלְמָא בִּדְבָרִים שֶׁבֵּין אָדָם לַחֲבֵירוֹ וְהֵן בְּמִילֵי
דִשְׁמַיָּא, לְיֵשׁ וּדְבַר מָה, אֶלָּא יִהְיֶה הָאַהֲבָה שֶׁלְּךָ לוֹ
גְּדוֹלָה כָּל כָּךְ עַד שֶׁתִּתְכַּסֶּה עַל הַפְּשָׁעִים, וְלֹא תַנִּיחַ
אוֹתָם מִן הַיְּדִיעָה לָבֹא לְהִתְפַּעֲלוּת בַּמִּדּוֹת.

On this basis, we can appreciate Hillel's statement,
"Whatever you find hateful when done to you,
do not do to your fellow" (TALMUD, SHABBAT
31A). The intention is: Do not permit your
fellow's faults and imperfections—regardless
of whether they are social flaws or spiritual
misbehavior—to achieve significance in your
perception. Do not regard the flaws as noticeable
and consequential. Instead, allow your love for your
fellow to grow so great that it covers their flaws
and refuses to permit your intellectual awareness
of them to evoke any emotional response.

**JEWISH WOMEN ON
THE BALCONY, ALGIERS**
Théodore Chassériau,
oil on wood panel, 1849
(The Louvre, Paris)

THE ART OF INFLUENCE

*In healthy relationships, offering guidance or critique
is sometimes essential. How can we guide and inspire
effectively without generating resentment and
emotional distress?*

I. INTRODUCTION

In healthy relationships, it is at times necessary to provide guidance or to give critique. Thankfully, the Torah provides illuminating direction in this area. One of its 613 commandments is to guide, influence, and reprove, and the sages' commentaries on this obligation hold valuable insights on the methods of doing so effectively.

FIGURES ON THE STREET (DETAIL)
Zvi Raphaeli (1924–2005),
oil on canvas, Israel

Challenges of Critique

Talmud, Arachin 16b

אָמַר רַבִּי טַרְפוֹן: תָּמֵהַ אֲנִי אִם יֵשׁ בַּדּוֹר הַזֶּה שֶׁמְּקַבֵּל תּוֹכָחָה. אִם אָמַר לוֹ: טוֹל קֵיסָם מִבֵּין שִׁנֶּיךָ, אָמַר לוֹ: טוֹל קוֹרָה מִבֵּין עֵינֶיךָ.

אָמַר רַבִּי אֶלְעָזָר בֶּן עֲזַרְיָה: תְּמִיהַנִי אִם יֵשׁ בַּדּוֹר הַזֶּה שֶׁיּוֹדֵעַ לְהוֹכִיחַ.

Rabbi Tarfon exclaimed, "I wonder if there is anyone in this generation who knows how to accept critique! If one person tells another, 'Remove the sliver from between your teeth,' the second retorts, 'Remove the beam from between your eyes!'"

Rabbi Elazar ben Azariah commented, "I wonder if there is anyone in this generation who knows how to properly *provide* critique."

BABYLONIAN TALMUD

A literary work of monumental proportions that draws upon the legal, spiritual, intellectual, ethical, and historical traditions of Judaism. The 37 tractates of the Babylonian Talmud contain the teachings of the Jewish sages from the period after the destruction of the 2nd Temple through the 5th century CE. It has served as the primary vehicle for the transmission of the Oral Law and the education of Jews over the centuries; it is the entry point for all subsequent legal, ethical, and theological Jewish scholarship.

EXERCISE 5.1

Think of an individual who once provided criticism that you did *not* take well. What was it about this person's style of communication that closed your heart and mind?

1.

2.

Think of an individual who provided criticism that you *did* take well. What was it about this person's style of communication that made you receptive?

1.

2.

TEXT 2

An Interpersonal Mitzvah

Leviticus 19:17

לֹא תִשְׂנָא אֶת אָחִיךָ בִּלְבָבֶךָ, הוֹכֵחַ תּוֹכִיחַ אֶת עֲמִיתֶךָ.

Do not hate your brother in your heart;
you shall surely reprove your fellow.

II. GUIDANCE WITH LOVE

Abraham and Moses demonstrated by personal example that words of guidance, critique, and inspiration are most effective when expressed with genuine, loving intentions that are palpable to the intended recipient. When love is our primary motivating factor, we also take care to ensure that the recipient is ready to listen and thus able to grow from our words.

MOTHER WITH KIDS
Elena Flerova, oil on canvas

TEXT 3

Reversed Roles

Midrash, *Devarim Rabah* 1:4

רְאוּיוֹת הָיוּ הַתּוֹכָחוֹת לוֹמַר מִפִּי בִלְעָם, וְהַבְּרָכוֹת מִפִּי מֹשֶׁה.

אֶלָּא, אִילוּ הוֹכִיחָם בִּלְעָם, הָיוּ יִשְׂרָאֵל אוֹמְרִים: שׂוֹנֵא מוֹכִיחֵנוּ.

וְאִילוּ בֵּרְכָם מֹשֶׁה, הָיוּ אוּמוֹת הָעוֹלָם אוֹמְרִים: אוֹהֲבָן בֵּרְכָן.

אָמַר הַקָּדוֹשׁ בָּרוּךְ הוּא: יוֹכִיחָן מֹשֶׁה שֶׁאוֹהֲבָן, וִיבָרְכֵן בִּלְעָם שֶׁשׂוֹנְאָן.

Would it not have been more appropriate for critique to emerge from the mouth of Balaam and blessing from the mouth of Moses?

However, if Balaam had provided critique, the Jewish people would have dismissed it, claiming, "The person who hates us is critiquing us!"

And if Moses had offered blessing, other nations would have downplayed it, arguing, "The person who loves them is blessing them!"

G-d therefore declared, "Let Moses, who loves them, offer them criticism; and let Balaam, who hates them, provide them with blessing."

DEVARIM RABAH

A homiletic commentary on the book of Deuteronomy. It was first printed in Constantinople in 1512, with 4 other Midrashic works on the other 4 books of the Pentateuch. The homilies are structured similarly: each episode begins with a question of religious law and is followed by an answer, which opens with the words, "Our sages taught." Most commentaries end with reassurances and promises of the Redemption.

TEXT 4

Absence of Enmity

Rabbi Yosef Yitzchak Schneersohn, *Igrot Kodesh* 2, pp. 475–476

אָנוּ מוֹצְאִים אֲשֶׁר קוֹדֶם צִוּוּי "הוֹכֵחַ תּוֹכִיחַ אֶת עֲמִיתֶךָ" נֶאֱמַר בַּתּוֹרָה "וְלֹא תִשְׂנָא אֶת אָחִיךָ בִּלְבָבֶךָ" . . . הַכַּוָּונָה אֲשֶׁר טֶרֶם שֶׁמּוֹכִיחִים אֶת מִי שֶׁהוּא, צָרִיךְ הַמּוֹכִיחַ לְהַרְחִיק מֵעַצְמוֹ כָּל עִנְיָן וְדָבָר שֶׁיָּכוֹל לָשֵׂאת עָלָיו חוֹתָם שֶׁל הִתְרַגְּשׁוּת . . . שֶׁלֹּא יִהְיֶה לְהַמּוֹכִיחַ שׁוּם רֶגֶשׁ שֶׁאֵינוֹ אַהֲבָה, וְרַק אָז יָכוֹל לִהְיוֹת "הוֹכֵחַ תּוֹכִיחַ".

The Torah prefaces the directive, "You shall surely reprove your fellow," with the instruction, "Do not hate your brother in your heart." . . . This informs us that before we criticize someone, we must first eliminate from ourselves anything that bears the mark of agitation . . . so that while we provide critique we are free of any feelings other than love. Only on the heels of this effort can our critique be effective.

Is all feedback good feedback? **Rabbi Aryeh Weinstein** examines this topic.
myjli.com/relationships

Noah's Shortcoming

The Rebbe, Rabbi Menachem Mendel Schneerson,
Likutei Sichot 15, p. 91

וֶוען אֵיינֶער אִיז מוֹכִיחַ אַ צְווֵייטְן בְּלוֹיז צוּ מְקַיֵּים זַיין דֶעם
צִיווּי "הוֹכֵחַ תּוֹכִיחַ אֶת עֲמִיתֶךְ" (וַיִקְרָא יט, יז), אִיז אֲפִילוּ
וֶוען עֶר טוּט עֶס "מֵאָה פְּעָמִים" וֶוירְקְט עֶס נִיט אוֹיף יֶענֶעם
אַזוֹי שְׁטַארְק ווִי אַ תּוֹכָחָה וָואס אִיז אוֹיסְן יֶענֶעם'ס טוֹבָה.

וְיֵשׁ לוֹמַר, שֶׁזֶּהוּ גַם הַטַּעַם מַה שֶׁתּוֹכַחְתּוֹ שֶׁל
נֹחַ לֹא פָּעֲלָה עֲלֵיהֶם שֶׁיִּתְעוֹרְרוּ בִּתְשׁוּבָה.

Critique extended simply for the sake of
observing the Torah's instruction, "You shall
surely reprove your fellow," even if repeated one
hundred times, will not have nearly the same
effect as critique motivated by a sincere desire
to bring benefit to the intended recipient.

This can explain why Noah's admonitions failed
to inspire the people to mend their ways.

The Litmus Test

The Rebbe, Rabbi Menachem Mendel Schneerson,
Sefer Hasichot 5751:1, p. 252

כְּתִיב "שְׁמַע בְּנִי מוּסַר אָבִיךָ" (מִשְׁלֵי א, ח),
וְאוֹהֲבוֹ (בְּנוֹ) שִׁחֲרוֹ מוּסָר" (שָׁם יג, כד) - דִּבְרֵי
מוּסָר צְרִיכִים לִהְיוֹת כְּמוֹ שֶׁל אָב לִבְנוֹ,

שֶׁהָאָב אוֹהֵב בְּעֶצֶם וְתָמִיד תָּמִיד אֶת בְּנוֹ, וְגַם
כְּשֶׁמוֹכִיחוֹ בִּדְבָרִים (וְלִפְעָמִים גַּם מַעֲנִישָׁן), נִכֶּרֶת
בִּשְׁעַת מַעֲשֶׂה עַצְמוֹ אַהֲבָתוֹ הָאֲמִיתִּית לִבְנוֹ . . .

וְעַל דֶּרֶךְ זֶה בְּנוֹגֵעַ לְהַצִּיוּוּי "הוֹכֵחַ תּוֹכִיחַ אֶת עֲמִיתֶךָ" -
שֶׁדִּבְרֵי הַתּוֹכֵחָה צְרִיכִים לִהְיוֹת חֲדוּרִים בְּאַהֲבַת יִשְׂרָאֵל . . .

וְהַבְּחִינָה לָזֶה - כְּשֶׁהַשׁוֹמֵעַ אֶת דִּבְרֵי הַהוֹכָחָה
מַרְגִּישׁ שֶׁהַדְּבָרִים נֶאֱמָרִים אַךְ וְרַק מִתּוֹךְ אַהֲבָה.

Proverbs teaches us, "Listen, my child, to the
critique of your father" (1:8), and similarly,
"Those who love [their children] are diligent
to critique them" (13:24). These verses link
critique to a child-parent relationship, thereby
informing us that all critique must resemble the
redirection parents provide to their children.

Parents bear an intrinsic and constant love for their
children. Even when they offer verbal criticism
(and discipline when warranted), their true love for
their children is apparent at that same moment. . . .

The same is true of the Torah's directive, "You shall surely reprove your neighbor." Our words of critique must be suffused with love. . . .

The litmus test is if the *listener* can *feel* that the message is delivered purely out of love.

TEXT 7

Timely Wisdom

Mishnah, Avot 4:18

רַבִּי שִׁמְעוֹן בֶּן אֶלְעָזָר אוֹמֵר:

אַל תְּרַצֶּה אֶת חֲבֵרְךָ בְּשַׁעַת כַּעֲסוֹ,

וְאַל תְּנַחֲמֵהוּ בְּשָׁעָה שֶׁמֵּתוֹ מֻטָל לְפָנָיו.

Rabbi Shimon ben Elazar says:

"Do not attempt to soothe someone's anger during the time of their wrath.

"Do not attempt to console them at the time when their deceased lies before them."

AVOT
(ETHICS OF THE FATHERS; PIRKEI AVOT)

A 6-chapter work on Jewish ethics that is studied widely by Jewish communities, especially during the summer. The first 5 chapters are from the Mishnah, tractate Avot. Avot differs from the rest of the Mishnah in that it does not focus on legal subjects; it is a collection of the sages' wisdom on topics related to character development, ethics, healthy living, piety, and the study of Torah.

TEXT 8

The Goal in Mind

Talmud, Yevamot 65b

כְּשֵׁם שֶׁמִּצְוָה עַל אָדָם לוֹמַר דָּבָר הַנִּשְׁמָע,
כָּךְ מִצְוָה עַל אָדָם שֶׁלֹּא לוֹמַר דָּבָר שֶׁאֵינוֹ נִשְׁמָע.

Just as it's a mitzvah to share words that *will* be accepted, so it's a mitzvah *not* to deliver words that *won't* be accepted.

HELPING HANDS
Suzy Norris, mixed media
painting, 2014, California

III. GUIDING WITH GENTLENESS

Effective critique requires respecting the other's personal space, avoiding even the semblance of an attack or a desire to dominate. One way to achieve this is through using a gentle tone and tentative language. An amusing but brilliant habit of two famous Chasidic masters exemplifies this approach.

TWO RABBIS IN JERUSALEM
Isaac Snowman (1874–1947),
oil on canvas

Siblings of Influence

TEXT 9

Rabbi Chaim Mordechai Perlow, *Likutei Sipurim*, p. 279

RABBI CHAIM MORDECHAI PERLOW 1889–1977

Rabbi and author. Born in Kherson, Ukraine, Rabbi Mordechai Perlow studied at the renowned Yeshivat Tomchei Temimim in the town of Lubavitch, Russia. Under Communist rule, he served as a rabbi in various cities in the U.S.S.R., and spent years in a Siberian gulag for his work to maintain Jewish life. After World War II, he served as a rabbi in Milan, Italy, and Melbourne, Australia. Rabbi Perlow wrote *Get Lemaaseh*, a Halachic work on the laws of divorce, and *Likutei Sipurim*, a record of the Chasidic stories he heard and witnessed while studying in Lubavitch.

יָדוּעַ שֶׁהָרַב הַקָּדוֹשׁ ר' אֱלִימֶלֶךְ זֵכֶר צַדִּיק לִבְרָכָה מִלִּיזֶענְסְק וְאָחִיו הָרַב הַקָּדוֹשׁ ר' זוּסְיָא מֵהַאנִיפָּאלִי זֵכֶר צַדִּיק לִבְרָכָה הָיוּ הוֹלְכִים לִישׁוּבִים שׁוֹנִים. הָיוּ אָז יְהוּדִים בּוֹדְדִים, שְׁנַיִם אוֹ שָׁלֹשׁ מִשְׁפָּחוֹת . . .

וְשָׁם הָיוּ מוֹכְרִים לַהַנָּכְרִים יֵין שָׂרָף וּמִינֵי מַאֲכָלִים, וּמִזֶּה הָיוּ מִתְפַּרְנְסִים . . . עַל פִּי רוֹב הָיוּ אֵלֶּה אֲנָשִׁים פְּשׁוּטִים. הָיוּ בֵּינֵיהֶם גַּם הַרְבֵּה מְאֹד תְּמִימִים וְיִרְאֵי אֱלֹקִים, אֲבָל מִפְּנֵי שֶׁהִתְגּוֹרְרוּ יַחַד עִם לֹא יְהוּדִים, וְכָל עִסְקָם הָיוּ אִתָּם, הָיוּ בֵּינֵיהֶם גַּם כָּאֵלֶּה שֶׁנִּכְשְׁלוּ בִּדְבָרִים גַּסִּים רַחֲמָנָא לִיצְלַן.

הָרַב הַקָּדוֹשׁ הַמַּגִּיד מִמֶּעזְרִיטְשׁ הָיָה שׁוֹלֵחַ אֶת תַּלְמִידָיו הַנִּזְכָּרִים לְעֵיל לַבֹּקֶר אֵצֶל יְהוּדִים אֵלֶּה לְעוֹדְדָם וּלְחַזְּקָם בַּתּוֹרָה וְיִרְאַת שָׁמַיִם. דַּרְכָּם שֶׁל אַחִים קְדוֹשִׁים אֵלֶּה הָיְתָה כָּךְ:

הָרַב הַקָּדוֹשׁ ר' זוּסְיָא הָיָה מַתְחִיל לְפָרֵט עַל עַצְמוֹ אֶת כָּל הַחֲטָאִים שֶׁרָאָה עַל הַיִּשׁוּבְנִיק, כְּאִילוּ הוּא עַצְמוֹ עָשָׂה אוֹתָם חַס וְשָׁלוֹם, עַד שֶׁהַיִּשׁוּבְנִיק הָיָה מַתְחִיל לְהִתְחָרֵט וּלְהַרְהֵר בְּלִבּוֹ: "הֲלֹא כָּל הַדְּבָרִים הָאֵלֶּה אֲנִי עָשִׂיתִי".

וְאָז הָיָה אָחִיו הָרַב הַקָּדוֹשׁ ר' אֱלִימֶלֶךְ זֵכֶר צַדִּיק לִבְרָכָה אוֹמֵר לוֹ אֶת הַתִּקּוּנִים לַעֲבֵירוֹת אֵלּוּ, עַד שֶׁהַיִּשׁוּבְנִיק הָיָה שׁוֹמֵעַ וּמַרְגִּישׁ, וְנַעֲשָׂה בַּעַל תְּשׁוּבָה גָּמוּר.

The saintly brothers, Rabbi Elimelech of Lizhensk and Rabbi Zusha of Anipoli, were known to frequent the numerous outlying villages in which very few Jews lived—typically, two or three lonely Jewish families per village. . . .

Back in those days, these Jewish households usually earned their living through peddling food and alcohol to local peasant populations. . . . The overwhelming majority of these Jews were simple and uneducated. Many were pure-hearted and G-d-fearing individuals, but due to the abysmal moral standards of their local environments, some of these Jews adopted ways that were less than desirable.

The Magid of Mezeritch would dispatch the saintly brothers to these villages so that they could encourage and strengthen their fellow Jews in their Torah observance and awe of Heaven. The brothers chose a unique method of operation:

Rabbi Zusha would deliberately address his brother loud enough for the nearby Jewish villager—the true target of their efforts—to overhear their conversation. He would lament to his brother that he had failed in several ways, describing precisely the matters in which he noticed this Jewish villager was failing. Overhearing this conversation, the villager would be struck with powerful pangs of regret, telling himself, "Didn't *I* do all the same things myself?"

The villager would continue listening eagerly, as Rabbi Elimelech proceeded to inform Rabbi Zusha of the methods through which the latter was able to rectify these particular transgressions. The eavesdropping villager would take Rabbi Elimelech's words to heart, and return to the proper path.

QUESTION

What motivated these rabbis to employ such an unusual method? What might be its benefits?

Human Nature

Orchot Tzadikim, The Gate of Anger

בַּתְּחִלָּה תּוֹכִיחַ אוֹתוֹ בְּנַחַת וּבַסֵּתֶר, וְתֹאמַר לוֹ
בְּלָשׁוֹן רַכָּה וְתַחֲנוּנִים כִּי לְטוֹבָתוֹ אַתָּה אוֹמֵר לוֹ,
וְאָז לֹא תְקַבֵּל עָלָיו חֵטְא. אֲבָל אִם תּוֹכִיחַ אֶת חֲבֵרְךָ
מִתְּחִלָּה בְּקוֹל רַעַשׁ וּבְזַעַם וּתְבַיֵּשׁ אוֹתוֹ, אָז תְּקַבֵּל
עָלָיו חֵטְא. וְאוֹתוֹ חָבֵר לֹא יְקַבֵּל תּוֹכָחָה מִמְּךָ.

כִּי כֵן דֶּרֶךְ בְּנֵי אָדָם: כְּשֶׁאָדָם בָּא עַל חֲבֵרוֹ בְּחָזְקָה,
אָז חֲבֵרוֹ מִתְקַשֶּׁה כְּנֶגְדּוֹ וְלֹא יִכָּנַע תַּחְתָּיו.

וְעַל זֶה אָמַר הֶחָכָם (קֹהֶלֶת ט, יז):
"דִּבְרֵי חֲכָמִים בְּנַחַת נִשְׁמָעִים".

ORCHOT TZADIKIM
C. 14TH CENTURY

A classic work on Jewish ethics. The identity of the author of *Orchot Tzadikim* (*The Ways of the Righteous*) is unknown, but it is believed to have been written by a French scholar, probably in the 14th century. Drawing much material from earlier ethicists Rabbi Shlomo ibn Gabirol, Maimonides, and Rabbi Bachya ibn Pakudah, *Orchot Tzadikim* focuses on character refinement and on explaining the core values of Jewish religious life.

Criticism should be conveyed gently and in private. Use soft speech and plead with your intended audience to realize that you have their good in mind. If you do this, you will be free of blame. By contrast, if you rebuke them in an angry voice and with rage, and you thereby shame them, then you are blameworthy, and your audience will not accept your words.

Such is human nature: if someone is approached forcefully, they will counter with a forcefulness of their own and refuse to concede.

King Solomon the Wise therefore declared, "*Softly spoken* words of the wise are heard" (ECCLESIASTES 9:17).

TEXT 11

Tentative Talk

Rabbi Chaim Yosef David Azulai, *Nachal Kedumim* 5

שֶׁלֹּא יַגְבִּיהַ לוֹ הַחֵטְא וְיֹאמַר לוֹ "כַּמָּה גָדוֹל חַטָאתְךָ, כַּמָּה כָּבֵד עֲוֹנְךָ", כִּי יִכְבְּדוּ עָלָיו דְּבָרָיו, וְיִטְעוֹן נֶגְדְּךָ.

אֲבָל יֹאמַר לוֹ דֶּרֶךְ אַהֲבָה: "אָחִי, כִּמְדוּמַנִי שֶׁשָּׁגִיתָ בָּזֶה", וְכַיּוֹצֵא דְּבָרִים רַכִּים וְלָשׁוֹן קַלָּה כְּדֵי שֶׁיִּתְקַבֵּל.

Do not magnify the wrong by informing the individual you seek to redirect, "You committed a really big sin! Your guilt is truly heavy!" Such words will weigh heavily upon the recipient, prompting them to lash out against you in response.

Instead, address them with love. Tell them, "My friend, it seems to me that you made a mistake." Use this kind of gentle phraseology and soft language so that your message will be accepted.

RABBI CHAIM YOSEF DAVID AZULAI (CHIDA) 1724–1806

Talmudist and noted bibliophile. Born in Jerusalem, scion to a prominent rabbinic family, he studied under Rabbi Chaim ibn Atar. A prolific writer on various Jewish topics, his *Shem Hagedolim* is particularly famous, chronicling short biographies of Jewish authors with overviews of their works. He traveled extensively in Europe to raise funds on behalf of the Jewish community in the Land of Israel, and he died in Italy.

Rabbi Shais Taub:
Humility is not humiliation.
myjli.com/relationships

IV. GUIDANCE WITH HUMILITY

Critique is most effective when the person delivering it also identifies related areas for self-improvement, thereby turning the critique inward as well. Chasidism reveals that this is not simply a strategy for heightened effectiveness but is the Divine purpose behind the phenomenon of observing a flaw in a fellow.

IDENTITY
Osnat Tzadok, acrylic
on canvas, Toronto

Contrasting Spirits

TEXT 12

Midrash, *Kohelet Rabah* 10:4

"וְרוּחַ אֱלֹקִים לָבְשָׁה אֶת זְכַרְיָה וְגוֹ' וַיַּעֲמֹד מֵעַל לָעָם"
(דִּבְרֵי הַיָּמִים ב, כד, כ): וְכִי מֵעַל רָאשֵׁי הָעָם הָיָה הוֹלֵךְ?

אֶלָּא שֶׁרָאָה עַצְמוֹ גָּדוֹל מִכָּל הָעָם - חֲתַן הַמֶּלֶךְ, וְכֹהֵן,
וְנָבִיא, וְדַיָּן. הִתְחִיל מְדַבֵּר גְּדוֹלוֹת וְאוֹמֵר לָהֶם "לָמָּה
אַתֶּם עוֹבְרִים אֶת מִצְוֹת ה' וְלֹא תַצְלִיחוּ וְגוֹ'" (שָׁם).

מִיָּד "וַיִּקְשְׁרוּ עָלָיו וַיִּרְגְּמוּ אוֹתוֹ אֶבֶן
בְּמִצְוַת הַמֶּלֶךְ" (שָׁם כד, כא) . . .

אֲבָל יַחֲזִיאֵל לֹא עָשָׂה כֵן, אֶלָּא "וְיַחֲזִיאֵל בֶּן זְכַרְיָה . . .
הָיְתָה עָלָיו רוּחַ ה' בְּתוֹךְ הַקָּהָל" (שָׁם כ, יד):
מַהוּ בְּתוֹךְ הַקָּהָל? שֶׁהִשְׁוָה עַצְמוֹ לַקָּהָל.

"The spirit of G-d enveloped Zechariah son of Jehoiada the priest, and he stood above the people" (II CHRONICLES 24:20).

Did he literally walk above the heads of the people? Rather, the phrase indicates that he considered himself greater than all the people. After all, he was the king's son-in-law, a priest, a prophet, and a judge! He therefore began to speak arrogantly and told them, "Why do you transgress G-d's commandments? It will not succeed!" (IBID.).

KOHELET RABAH

A Midrashic text on the book of Ecclesiastes. Midrash is the designation of a particular genre of rabbinic literature. The term "Midrash" is derived from the root *d-r-sh,* which means "to search," "to examine," and "to investigate." This particular Midrash provides textual exegeses and develops and illustrates moral principles. It was first published in Pesaro, Italy, in 1519, together with 4 other Midrashic works on the other 4 biblical *Megillot.*

What's the difference between humility and low self-esteem? **Rabbi David Aaron** responds. myjli.com/relationships

Immediately, "They conspired against him and stoned him to death by the king's command" (IBID., 24:21). . . .

Yachaziel, by contrast, did not behave this way. Rather, it is reported that "the spirit of G-d was upon Yachaziel . . . in the midst of the assembly" (IBID., 20:14). What does "in the midst of the assembly" imply? That he considered himself an equal of the assembled.

RAINBOW PROPHET
Yoram Raanan, Israel

A Literal Translation

Leviticus 19:17

TEXT 13A

לֹא תִשְׂנָא אֶת אָחִיךָ בִּלְבָבֶךָ, הוֹכֵחַ תּוֹכִיחַ
אֶת עֲמִיתֶךָ, וְלֹא תִשָּׂא עָלָיו חֵטְא.

Do not hate your brother in your heart;
reprove you shall reprove your fellow—
and do not bear a sin upon him.

Self-Inclusion

Rabbi Yaakov Yosef of Polonye, *Toledot Yaakov Yosef*,
Kedoshim, ad loc.

TEXT 13B

וּבֶאֱמֶת שֶׁצָּרִיךְ לְכָלוֹל עַצְמוֹ עִמָּהֶן. וּכְמוֹ שֶׁכָּתַבְתִּי "הוֹכֵחַ"
- לְעַצְמְךָ כְּשֶׁ"תּוֹכִיחַ אֶת עֲמִיתֶךָ, וְלֹא תִשָּׂא עָלָיו חֵטְא".

We must truly include ourselves in the words
of critique we supply to others. The Torah
therefore directs us—if we translate the verse
literally—"Reprove you shall reprove your fellow."
This means, "Reprove *yourself when* you shall
reprove your neighbor." Indeed, the Torah further
clarifies, "Do not bear a sin upon him"—do not
consider that the sin he committed is *only* upon
his shoulders and not upon yours as well.

RABBI YAAKOV YOSEF OF POLONYE C. 1710–1784

Chasidic pioneer and author. Rabbi Yaakov Yosef was a dedicated disciple of the Baal Shem Tov, the founder of the Chasidic movement, and is credited with taking a leading role in the dissemination of the philosophy of Chasidism in its nascent years. He authored *Toledot Yaakov Yosef*, the first printed work of Chasidic philosophy. This work is cherished in Chasidic circles.

TEXT 14

Mirroring Faults

Rabbi Yisrael Baal Shem Tov, cited in Rabbi Menachem Nachum Twerski, *Me'or Einayim, Chukat*

מִי שֶׁרוֹאֶה שׁוּם רַע בַּחֲבֵירוֹ, הָעִנְיָן הוּא כְּמוֹ שֶׁמִּסְתַּכֵּל בַּמַרְאָה:

אִם פָּנָיו מְטוּנָפִין, רוֹאֶה גַם כֵּן בַּמַרְאָה כָּךְ.

וְאִם פָּנָיו נְקִיִּים, אֵינוֹ רוֹאֶה בַּמַרְאָה שׁוּם דּוֹפִי.

כְּמוֹ שֶׁהוּא כָּךְ רוֹאֶה.

Seeing a fault in another is like gazing into a mirror:

If our face is dirty, we observe a dirty face.

If our face is clean, we observe a clean face.

As we are, so we see.

RABBI YISRAEL BAAL SHEM TOV (BESHT)
1698–1760

Founder of the Chasidic movement. Born in Slutsk, Belarus, the Baal Shem Tov was orphaned as a child. He served as a teacher's assistant and clay digger before founding the Chasidic movement and revolutionizing the Jewish world with his emphasis on prayer, joy, and love for every Jew, regardless of his or her level of Torah knowledge.

V. GUIDANCE WITH POSITIVITY

When we observe a flaw in others, it is highly effective to emphasize that the individual is greater than their shortcomings. By extension, it is preferable to refrain from labeling the negative behavior itself as unqualified evil.

TEXT 15A

Whom to Reprove

Proverbs 9:8

אַל תּוֹכַח לֵץ פֶּן יִשְׂנָאֶךָּ,

הוֹכַח לְחָכָם וְיֶאֱהָבֶךָּ.

Do not reprove scoffers, for they will hate you.

Reprove the wise and they will love you.

PROVERBS

Biblical book. The book of Proverbs appears in the Writings (Ketuvim) section of the Bible and contains the wise teachings, aphorisms, and parables of King Solomon, who lived in the 9th century BCE. The ethical teachings of Proverbs give counsel about overcoming temptation, extol the value of hard work, laud the pursuit of knowledge, and emphasize loyalty to G-d and His commandments as the foundation of true wisdom.

Speak Up

Rabbi Yeshayahu Halevi Horowitz, *Shenei Luchot Haberit, Devarim*

כְּשֶׁאַתָּה רוֹצֶה לְהוֹכִיחַ אֶת אֶחָד, אַל תֹּאמַר לוֹ: "כָּךְ וְכָךְ אַתָּה גָּרוּעַ", כִּי אָז יִשְׂנָאֶךְ וְלֹא יִשְׁמַע לִדְבָרֶיךָ. וְזֶהוּ שֶׁאָמַר, "אַל תּוֹכַח לֵץ", שֶׁלֹּא תוֹכִיחַ אוֹתוֹ בְּדֶרֶךְ זִלְזוּל לוֹמַר לוֹ: "לֵץ אַתָּה".

רַק, אַדְּרַבָּה, תֹּאמַר לוֹ: "חָכָם אַתָּה, וְאִם כֵּן חֶרְפָּה הִיא לְאִישׁ כָּמוֹךָ לַעֲשׂוֹת כֹּה וָכֹה". זֶהוּ "הוֹכַח לְחָכָם", כְּלוֹמַר, תַּעֲשֵׂהוּ לְךָ לְחָכָם, אָז יֶאֱהָבְךָ וְיִשְׁמַע לְקוֹל דְּבָרֶיךָ וִיקַבֵּל מוּסָר.

If you wish to offer criticism, do not tell the person how awful they are. If you do, they will despise you and not heed your words. This is the meaning of the verse: "Do not reprove *scoffers*," meaning, do not reprove them by diminishing them, labeling them as scoffers.

To the contrary, explain to them how unbefitting it is for a wise person like them to behave in such a manner. This is the implication of the phrase, "Reprove the *wise*," meaning, consider them as wise, and they will then heed your words and accept the critique.

RABBI YESHAYAHU HALEVI HOROWITZ (SHALAH) 1565–1630

Kabbalist and author. Rabbi Horowitz was born in Prague and served as rabbi in several prominent Jewish communities, including Frankfurt am Main and his native Prague. After the passing of his wife in 1620, he moved to Israel. In Tiberias, he completed his *Shenei Luchot Haberit*, an encyclopedic compilation of kabbalistic ideas. He is buried in Tiberias, next to Maimonides.

Introduce Ambiguity

TEXT 16

Rabbi Chaim Yosef David Azulai, *Devarim Achadim, Derush 12*

אַל תּוֹכַח . . . בְּדֶרֶךְ תּוֹכָחָה לוֹמַר לוֹ שֶׁמַּעֲשָׂיו רָעִים
וְאַתָּה מוֹכִיחוֹ. שֶׁאִם אַתָּה עוֹשֶׂה כֵן - יִשְׂנָאֶךָ.

רַק יִהְיוּ דְבָרֶיךָ בְּדֶרֶךְ הוֹכָחָה, כְּלוֹמַר: מַעֲשֶׂה זֶה שֶׁעָשִׂיתָ יֵשׁ
צְדָדִין לְכָאן וּלְכָאן, כִּי יֵשׁ כַּף זְכוּת לִטְעוֹן כָּךְ, אֲבָל חֲדַל לְךָ
מִזֶּה, כִּי אֵין הַכֹּל יוֹדְעִים טוֹבָתְךָ, וַאֲנִי מַכְרִיעַ לְהִתְרַחֵק מִזֶּה.

וּבְדֶרֶךְ זֶה . . . וְיֶאֱהָבְךָ וַדַּאי, שֶׁהוּא מַרְגִּישׁ בַּכָּבוֹד
שֶׁעָשִׂיתָ לוֹ לוֹמַר לוֹ בְּדֶרֶךְ הוֹכָחָה וְלֹא תוֹכָחָה.

Do not offer critique . . . with an unequivocal
reprimand, informing others that their actions
are bad and that you are compelled to criticize
them. If you do so, they will despise you.

Rather, deliver your message couched as your personal
opinion. Tell them, "What you have done can be
seen two ways; there are grounds to justify it but also
reasons to criticize it. In my opinion, it would be better
for you to refrain from this kind of thing because
not everyone knows your good nature like I do."

If you formulate your message like this . . .
your audience will certainly like you. They will
appreciate the dignity you provided them by
couching a critique as your personal opinion rather
than delivering an unequivocal reprimand.

VI. CONCLUSION

To process all of the above, it would be useful to consider a hypothetical scenario that plays out all the time.

EXERCISE 5.2

Together with a partner, consider the following case of a husband critiquing his wife. Mark down what he did right and what he did wrong, in line with the values and techniques that we discussed in this lesson.

Sarah and Benjamin are at a restaurant along with their friends, the Steins. Conversation flows freely, but one participant—Sarah—has gotten lost on social media and is oblivious to the conversation. Someone asks her a question and receives no response. "I'm mortified," Benjamin thinks to himself. "I can't stand when this happens."

"Sarah," says her husband good-naturedly, "We've been trying to get your attention, trying to rescue you from your phone!"

When they are alone on their way home, Benjamin decides to address the topic.

"You know, Sarah," says Benjamin calmly. "I've been meaning to tell you this for a while: You've become addicted to your phone. When I come home at the end of the day, you aren't there for me. The twins sometimes get into fights over some silly doll, and they screech loud enough for the windows to shatter, but you don't hear a thing. You need to make a no-phone time zone that expires only once the kids are safely in bed."

"Oh come on!" she replies angrily, with a denial. "It happened once, and you're making it sound like it happens every day! I'm usually too busy with the kids to even touch my phone!"

Benjamin is taken aback. "Why are you getting all defensive on me? I'm just telling the truth and trying to help you!"

What was done well:

What was not done well:

KEY POINTS

1   The Torah entrusts each of us with a duty
to care for the welfare of others. Within
this culture of care, Judaism emphasizes
the importance of positively influencing
others to help them reach their full potential
and become greater forces for good.

2   Criticism that stems from a desire to control—or
a need to showcase expertise or superiority—is
unlikely to succeed. Likewise, criticism that
flows from anger is unlikely to be effective.

3   While our initial motivation to critique may
be to protect our interests, our words will
be more effective if we ground them in care
and love. When people feel that the speaker
genuinely cares about their well-being,
they become receptive to the message.

4   Even when our words are infused with love, if the
listener isn't in the right frame of mind to hear
them, it's better to postpone the conversation.

5   If our words are perceived as an attack
or an attempt to control, people will
find ways to dismiss them. Therefore,
it's essential to guide gently, using a
delicate tone and tentative language.

6   Instead of positioning ourselves as superior figures fixing others, it's more effective to identify a related flaw in ourselves and direct our words inward as well. A collaborative spirit is more likely to inspire change.

7   The doctrine of Divine Providence teaches us that noticing faults in others is not accidental but personally relevant. G-d reveals to us specific flaws in others to indicate that we harbor a version—even if a much more subtle one—of that vice ourselves.

8   An effective way to offer critique is to emphasize the person's virtues and highlight how their actions are unbefitting of someone of their stature.

A Chasidic Approach to Critique

Self-improvement is a cornerstone of Chasidic teachings. Beyond personal growth, Chasidic teachings emphasize the importance of supporting one another in this journey. Intimate gatherings, known as *farbrengens*, create a nurturing environment for offering guidance and encouragement. In the following passages, Rabbi Yosef Yitzchak Schneersohn (1880–1950), the revered sixth leader of the Chabad-Lubavitch movement, eloquently outlines the principles guiding the use of critique in these settings.

A Lesson from an Injection

Medics came today to treat me and administered an injection.

I noticed their overly cautious preparations: they checked that their equipment was sterile; the doctor and his assistant donned white aprons; they rinsed their hands two or three times; they examined their fingernails lest a speck of dirt remained; and finally, they poured a strong disinfectant over their fingertips, and especially their nails, to remove any possibility of contamination. After all that, they scrubbed my leg with a strong disinfectant to remove even microscopic dirt—three times!

Seeing their caution, I asked them why it was necessary to wash my leg, given that I had just bathed and my skin was clean. They replied that this is the strict protocol: Before penetrating living flesh to inject medication, they must clean the site with disinfectant to remove harmful bacteria and other microorganisms. If they fail to do so, a contaminant may enter the body together with the medication, not only canceling the medicinal effect but even triggering severe ailments.

A *farbrengen* of Chasidim is akin to a medicinal injection that heals the body through a needle prick. In the vast majority of these gatherings, speakers passionately urge those present to improve their conduct and ways, to establish dedicated times for studying Chasidic teachings, and to apply these teachings to influence their behavior positively. The exhortations at the *farbrengen*, though motivated by profound internal love and abundant affection, often come in the form of a jab. . . . It is imperative that this needle be absolutely sterile and for the intended target to be first disinfected from contaminants.

Letter dated 21 Adar II, 5695 (March 26, 1935),
Igrot Kodesh 3, pp. 291–292

Misquoted in a Yiddish Newspaper

I was distressed when I read the newspaper article you sent me, which included my letter to the editor of *Das Yiddishe Vort*. Words were added that were not in my letter, namely, "to the editor of a Yiddish newspaper in the cold country of Canada." I am surprised that you . . . allowed this to happen.

Delivering criticism is a complex matter and it must be done per the guidance of the Torah. The Torah prefaces the directive, "You shall surely reprove your fellow," with the instruction, "Do not hate your brother in your heart" (Leviticus 19:17). The passage then continues, "And do not bear a sin upon him." This informs us that before we criticize someone, we must first eliminate from ourselves anything that bears the mark of agitation. "Do not hate your brother in your heart" tells us that the person providing critique should be free of any feelings other than love. Only on the heels of this effort can a critique be effective. If we observe that the attempt at redirection did not bear fruit, then "Do not bear a sin upon him," meaning, the listener is not to blame for its ineffectiveness; the blame is on the speaker because surely the speaker's words did not emanate from the heart. Otherwise, they would have certainly entered the heart, for it is a well-known principle that words emanating from the heart penetrate the heart. Alternatively, perhaps the condition of bearing no antagonism wasn't met.

Therefore, in every critique delivered by an intelligent person, the speaker must remove any stinging words or even hints of a sting that could cause pain to the listener. Before an operation on a bodily limb, the doctors numb the place of surgery to reduce the patient's pain. The same is true of critique that is intended to heal a soul: it is necessary to limit to the greatest possible extent the infliction of pain, and to actively seek only the beneficial elements of the process. . . .

If this is true when communicating with an individual, it is certainly true with a group: extra care is required to avoid stinging remarks. . . . It runs against my deepest beliefs to rebuke an entire country, or any group of people, with the deficiency of coldness.

In fact, after many years of observing various groups of Jews in different countries (and becoming acquainted with various parties, groups, and social strata), I have realized that the Jewish heart is an immeasurable wellspring. Thus, the words "in the cold country of Canada" caused me distress.

Letter dated 1 Kislev, 5693 (November 30, 1932), *Igrot Kodesh* 2, pp. 275–276

Out of Deep Personal Care

Each of us has the obligation and mitzvah to strengthen, aid, and support others to walk on the well-trodden path, the ways revealed to us by our holy ancestors and sages.

We must cleanse our hearts of the slightest trace of a negative character trait and look at others with a kindly and compassionate eye, judging them favorably at all times.

If despite this we notice something that appears negative in a fellow, we should not ignore it but discuss it, so that it can be fixed.

However, it must be done the way parents critique their children and the way loving siblings critique each other. They only critique because they care about their beloved relatives and desire their good. With this mindset, the words spring from the heart and, consequently, find acceptance in the heart of the listener. Even the speaker will be inspired by their own message to further improve themselves.

A basic guideline among us is that when we issue critique, we are critiquing *ourselves*, and our intended audience naturally hears and takes from our words that which is relevant to them. . . .

It must be clear to each of us that all people know who they are and aren't making erroneous self-judgments. . . . If people would only know that someone is genuinely concerned for their welfare and is a faithful friend, they would certainly reveal to them the innermost recesses of their hearts to enlist their aid in bettering their character.

Letter dated 2 Iyar, 5681 (May 10, 1921), *Igrot Kodesh* 1, pp. 148–149

Context Matters: Lesson from a Sauna

Rabbi Sholom Ber Gordon related:

In the summer of 1948, I was about to accept my first pulpit. I asked Rabbi Yosef Yitzchak Schneerson: "I find myself in a certain dilemma. On the one hand, the rabbi has to guide, correct, and chastise. On the other hand, I'm told that you alienate people that way and you'll be left without a congregation. What is the answer?"

Rabbi Yosef Yitzchak replied, "Were you ever in a sauna, a Russian bathhouse?"

I said, "Yes, I went many times with my father."

He said, "Did you notice what they do?"

I answered, "Yes, they ascend the steps, and the steam gets hotter and hotter; then they are massaged—they hit each other with a *besem*, a combination of leaves and branches."

Then the Rebbe said, "Can you picture yourself going down the street, and someone running over to you or anyone else with this *besem*, and beginning to hit them? What would be the reaction? Don't you think they'd hit the person back?"

I said, "Yes!"

He continued, "However, if you are together with them in a warm environment, and you elevate them, and then you hit them—they enjoy it and ask for more!"

Living Torah, Disk 122, Program 487

Finding a Personal Parallel

During one of the travels of Rabbi Dovber of Lubavitch (the "Miteler Rebbe," 1773–1827), he suddenly interrupted his schedule of individual audiences—although hundreds had gathered for their turn to meet him in private—secluded himself for three days, and continuously recited Psalms while shedding bitter tears.

He later explained that during a private audience, it is typically necessary to offer redirection or guidance for something negative within an individual's behavior or character. At that point, he must first examine and discover a parallel—even if only extremely subtle and to the remotest degree—within himself; after correcting that element within himself, he can then provide critique or redirection.

This time, Rabbi Dovber explained, he faced an individual guilty of things so terrible that he could not possibly find a parallel within himself even to the most abstract degree. Nevertheless, he concluded, if G-d had sent him this individual, a parallel must indeed exist; he must harbor a subtle hidden evil of which he is unaware. With that thought, he engaged in three days of intense repentance.

Letter dated Sivan 5695 (June 1935), *Sefer Hamaamarim Kuntreisim* 2, pp. 712–713

Fiery Words, Fleeting Effects

Many educators and counselors err, thinking that their emotional outbursts that are accompanied by much commotion and shouting help them achieve their educational goals. Some assault their students with harsh and angry words and berate and insult them.

In truth, however, even if the pupil is temporarily affected by the fiery words of the educator, even if the pupil's heart contracts from pain, even if the pupil cries bitter tears, this type of education yields no lasting benefit. Any [temporary positive] effect will vanish like a fleeting dream.

Principles of Education and Guidance, ch. 5

Lessons from the Soil

In agriculture, successful germination depends on how well the seed takes root, which is determined by the skill of the sower. If the sower—whose main task is to prepare the soil to host the seed—is an expert, then the seed will sprout successfully. . . .

In the realm of spiritual planting, or mentorship, what truly matters is the attitude of the sower, the mentor. The mentor must invest considerable effort, both spiritually and physically, to make the soil receptive to new growth. This involves digging, weeding, and irrigating, all in due order. Additionally, the sower—the mentor—must be utterly dedicated to his saplings, caring for each one individually. If there is any consideration that may not directly affect germination but could ultimately improve the fruit, the mentor will spare no effort in utilizing it, because the quality of the fruit is of utmost importance to him. . . .

It won't suffice to merely speak as a mentor and simply tell someone how they should act. One needs to toil at refining oneself and thereby influence another.

My mentor, Rabbi Shmuel Betzalel Sheftel, used to say, "If one seeks to show another what a *mentsh* is, one has to be higher than what a *mentsh* is. A *mentsh* remains within the realm of habit; to be higher than a *mentsh* is to reign over habit."

Address delivered on Passover 1943, *Likutei Diburim* 3, pp. 851–852, 856

How to Give Constructive Criticism

From a Place of Love

Criticism is less likely to produce good results when prompted by antagonism, to express superiority, or to exert control. Chances of success are considerably better if the receiver perceives that the critique comes from genuine care and respect, empathy for their circumstances, and the intent to make things better or help them improve.

Be Humble

Reflect on your corresponding struggles, to find an empathetic approach. As a leader, work to create an atmosphere where you are an available and approachable mentor.

Timing Is Everything

We don't repair a leaky roof during a rainstorm. In the heat of the moment, place a bucket. Revisit the underlying issue when you can be calm and nonjudgmental, and the other is in a positive frame of mind and open to listening. Don't wait too long, however: it is good to provide feedback while the events are still fresh in mind.

Be Gentle

Contempt has no place in a critique. Avoid shouting, sarcasm, or putting the person down. Focus on the behavior, not the person. Point out the positives, as well as the problems in the event. If you have a difficult piece of feedback, sandwich the criticism between compliments.

Be Positive

Avoid destructive criticism using labels that focus on the person's bad traits and reinforce a negative self-image. Avoid assumptions about the person as the cause of the failure. Use the "I"-language technique so the criticism is about the situation, not them. Convey faith in their abilities and character.

Be Specific

Communicate clearly and specifically. Examples illustrate what you mean and raise the person's awareness of behavior they may not realize. Provide specific, actionable solutions with practical steps and strategies that help the recipient address the concerns effectively.

Psychology References

Ellison LJ, et al. (2022) Setting the stage: Feedback environment improves outcomes for a 360-degree-feedback leader-development program. *Consulting Psychology Journal, 74*(4), 363–382. doi.org/10.1037/cpb0000236.

Fong CJ, et al. (2018) When feedback signals failure but offers hope for improvement: A process model of constructive criticism. *Thinking Skills and Creativity, 30*, 42–53, ISSN 1871-1871. doi.org/10.1016/j.tsc.2018.02.014.

Mwania JM, Muola JM. (2013) Teachers' labeling of students and its effect on students' self-concept: A case of Mwala District. *International Journal of Education and Research, 1*(10). ISSN: 2201-6333 (Print). ISSN: 2201-6740 (Online).

Nash RA, et al. (2018) A memory advantage for past-oriented over future-oriented performance feedback. *Journal of Experimental Psychology. Learning, Memory, and Cognition, 44*(12), 1864–1879. doi.org/10.1037/xlm0000549. Epub 2018 Mar 5. PMID: 29504785.

Simon LS, et al. (2022) Pain or gain? Understanding how trait empathy impacts leader effectiveness following the provision of negative feedback. *The Journal of Applied Psychology, 107*(2), 279–297. doi.org/10.1037/apl0000882.

Young SF, et al. (2017) How empathic concern helps leaders in providing negative feedback: A two-study examination. *Journal of Occupational and Organizational Psychology, 90*(4), 535–558. doi.org/10.1111/joop.12184.

APPENDIX A—IT'S NOT ABOUT YOU

TEXT 17

"I" Messages Matter

Eboni J. Baugh and Deborah Humphries, *Can We Talk? Improving Couples' Communication* (Gainesville, FL: University of Florida, 2001), p. 2

An effective way to talk to your partner is through "I" messages—statements that describe your feelings and tell how you are affected by your partner's behavior. "I" messages can express emotions in a way that is not threatening as they focus on the speaker's feelings and not blaming the partner.

"I" messages are very different from a "you" message. "You" messages place blame and judge the other person based on their behavior. "You" messages often trigger defensiveness or hostility from your partner and tend to increase conflict. Think about how you feel when you hear *"You always . . ."* or *"You never. . . ."*

EBONI J. BAUGH, PHD

Author and professor. Baugh serves as associate professor of human development and family science at East Carolina University.

DEBORAH HUMPHRIES, MS

Humphries serves as an extension agent for the Taylor County (FL) Cooperative Extension Service.

FIGURE 5.1

Examples of "You" vs. "I" Messages

"YOU" MESSAGES	"I" MESSAGES
"You don't care about me. You never make time for me."	"When you don't pay attention to me or text me, I feel disconnected and lonely."
"You don't help out in the house."	"I'm feeling overwhelmed and underappreciated."
"You spend too much."	"When you spend a lot, it makes me anxious and worried about our financial future."
"You didn't finish the financial report on time."	"I am getting backed up on my work because I don't have the financial report yet."

EXERCISE 5.3

Convert the following "you" messages into productive "I" messages.

YOU MESSAGE	I MESSAGE
"You care more about work than family."	
"You just don't understand me!"	
"Why are you always late?"	
"You spend too much time on your smartphone and social media. It's hurting our relationship."	
"You must study, or you won't score well on your test."	
"You are so insensitive; you just don't care; you don't love me."	
"You have to/ought to/are supposed to . . ."	

LESSON

6

THE ART OF FORGIVENESS

No matter how wonderful the company we keep, there will inevitably be times when we feel insulted, hurt, or even betrayed by someone. What steps can we take to mend bonds and achieve reconciliation?

SIMCHAPHONIC TREE OF SHALOM (DETAIL)
Mordechai Edel, oil painting,
Vancouver, Canada

I. INTRODUCTION

In a world where humans are only human, missteps are inevitable and feelings are often hurt. Today's lesson addresses Judaism's unique view on the art of forgiveness and reconciliation to mend bonds and restore personal connection.

EXERCISE 6.1

WHICH IS HARDER: ASKING FOR FORGIVENESS OR GRANTING IT? WHY?

WHAT DOES "FORGIVENESS" MEAN? HOW WOULD YOU DEFINE IT?

II. TWO MODELS OF FORGIVENESS

Some focus on the fact that forgiveness is a pathway to personal liberation, clearing the clutter of grievances that stifle emotional well-being. In this view, forgiveness can coexist with moving away from and forgetting an offender. The Torah presents a deeper dimension, emphasizing an intrinsic connection between individuals, which naturally drives both parties toward reconciliation. The biblical Aaron (Moses's brother) emphasized this perspective.

SISTERHOOD
Karin Foreman, mixed media,
2017, California

Forgiveness Is for You

Fred Luskin, *Forgive for Good: A Proven Prescription for Health and Happiness* (New York: HarperOne, 2002), pp. vii–viii

Picture the crowded screen in front of a harried air traffic controller. Picture the chaos in the room and the jumble of planes on the screen. Now imagine that your unresolved grievances are the planes on that screen and have been circling for days and weeks on end. Most of the other planes have landed, but your unresolved grievances continue to take up precious air space, draining resources that may be needed in an emergency. Having them on the screen forces you to work harder and increases the chance for accidents. The grievance planes become a source of stress, and burnout is often the result. . . .

- Forgiveness is the peace you learn to feel when you allow these circling planes to land.

- Forgiveness is for you and not for the offender.

- Forgiveness is taking back your power.

- Forgiveness is taking responsibility for how you feel.

- Forgiveness is about your healing and not about the people who hurt you.

- Forgiveness is a trainable skill just like learning to throw a baseball.

FRED LUSKIN

Researcher, lecturer, and author. Dr. Luskin earned his doctorate in counseling and health psychology from Stanford University and serves as the director of the Stanford Forgiveness Project. He serves as a senior consultant in health promotion at Stanford University and is a professor of clinical psychology at the Institute of Transpersonal Psychology. He authored *Forgive for Good* and *Forgive for Love*.

A story of the **Lubavitcher Rebbe** on how forgiveness can liberate us.
myjli.com/relationships

- Forgiveness helps you get control over your feelings.

- Forgiveness can improve your mental and physical health.

TEXT 2

Self-Retaliation

Jerusalem Talmud, Nedarim 9:4

כְּתִיב: "לֹא תִקֹּם וְלֹא תִטֹּר אֶת בְּנֵי עַמֶּךָ" (וַיִּקְרָא יט, יח).

הֵיךְ עָבִיד?

הֲוָה מְקַטַּע קוֹפָּד וּמְחַת סַכִּינָא לְיָדוֹי. תַּחֲזוֹר וְתִמְחֵי לְיָדֵיהּ?

The Torah states, "You shall neither take revenge from nor bear a grudge against the members of your people" (LEVITICUS 19:18).

But how can we be expected to forgive in this way?

Consider this example: If while cutting meat you cut your hand, would you retaliate in kind against the offending hand?

JERUSALEM TALMUD

A commentary to the Mishnah, compiled during the 4th and 5th centuries. The Jerusalem Talmud predates its Babylonian counterpart by 100 years and is written in both Hebrew and Aramaic. While the Babylonian Talmud is the most authoritative source for Jewish law, the Jerusalem Talmud remains an invaluable source for the spiritual, intellectual, ethical, historical, and legal traditions of Judaism.

Inherent Unity

Rabbi Moshe Cordovero, *Tomer Devorah* 1

TEXT 3

שֶׁהַנְּשָׁמוֹת כְּלוּלוֹת יַחַד . . . וּלְכָךְ רָאוּי לָאָדָם לִהְיוֹתוֹ חָפֵץ בְּטוֹבָתוֹ שֶׁל חֲבֵירוֹ, וְעֵינוֹ טוֹבָה עַל טוֹבַת חֲבֵירוֹ, וּכְבוֹדוֹ יִהְיֶה חָבִיב עָלָיו כְּשֶׁלּוֹ, שֶׁהֲרֵי הוּא הוּא מַמָּשׁ. וּמִטַּעַם זֶה נִצְטַוֵּינוּ "וְאָהַבְתָּ לְרֵעֲךָ כָּמוֹךָ" (וַיִּקְרָא יט, יח).

All souls are united as one. . . . It is therefore appropriate to desire good for others, to be happy for their gain, and to consider their dignity as important as your own, for you and they are truly synonymous. For that reason, we are commanded, "Love your fellow as yourself" (LEVITICUS 19:18).

RABBI MOSHE CORDOVERO (RAMAK) 1522–1570

Prominent kabbalist. Ramak belonged to the circle of Jewish mystical thinkers who flourished in 16th-century Safed. The name Cordovero indicates that his family originated in Córdoba, Spain. His most famous kabbalistic work is *Pardes Rimonim*.

Pursuer of Peace

Avot DeRabbi Natan 12:3

TEXT 4

שְׁנֵי בְּנֵי אָדָם שֶׁעָשׂוּ מְרִיבָה זֶה עִם זֶה. הָלַךְ אַהֲרֹן וְיָשַׁב לוֹ אֵצֶל אֶחָד מֵהֶם וְאָמַר לוֹ: בְּנִי, רְאֵה חֲבֵרְךָ מַהוּ אוֹמֵר? מְטָרֵף אֶת לִבּוֹ, וְקוֹרֵעַ אֶת בְּגָדָיו, אוֹמֵר, אוֹי לִי, הֵיאַךְ אֶשָּׂא אֶת עֵינַי וְאֶרְאֶה אֶת חֲבֵרִי? בּוֹשְׁתִּי הֵימֶנּוּ שֶׁאֲנִי הוּא שֶׁסָּרַחְתִּי עָלָיו. הוּא יוֹשֵׁב אֶצְלוֹ עַד שֶׁמֵּסִיר קִנְאָה מִלִּבּוֹ.

וְהוֹלֵךְ אַהֲרֹן וְיוֹשֵׁב לוֹ אֵצֶל הָאַחֵר וְאָמַר לוֹ: בְּנִי, רְאֵה חֲבֵרְךָ מַהוּ אוֹמֵר? מְטָרֵף אֶת לִבּוֹ, וְקוֹרֵעַ אֶת

AVOT DERABBI NATAN

A commentary on, and an elaboration of, the Mishnaic tractate Avot, bearing the name of Rabbi Natan, one of the sages of the Mishnah. The work exists in two very different versions, one of which appears in many editions of the Talmud.

בְּגָדָיו, וְאוֹמֵר, אוֹי לִי, הֵיאַךְ אֶשָּׂא אֶת עֵינַי וְאֶרְאֶה אֶת חֲבֵרִי? בּוֹשְׁתִּי הֵימֶנּוּ שֶׁאֲנִי הוּא שֶׁסָּרַחְתִּי עָלָיו. הוּא יוֹשֵׁב אֶצְלוֹ עַד שֶׁמֵּסִיר קִנְאָה מִלִּבּוֹ.

וּכְשֶׁנִּפְגְּשׁוּ זֶה בָּזֶה, גָּפְפוּ וְנָשְׁקוּ זֶה לָזֶה.

When Aaron became aware that two individuals quarreled and had fallen out with each other, he would go and sit with one of them and say, "My dear, do you know what your friend is saying? He is utterly devastated and is tearing his clothes! He is saying: 'Woe is to me! How can I ever raise my eyes and look at my friend after what I've done to him? I am so ashamed for having wronged him!'" Aaron would continue working with this person until he had removed the grudge from his heart.

Aaron would then go and sit with the other party and say, "My dear, do you know what your friend is saying? He is utterly devastated and is tearing his clothes! He is saying: 'Woe is to me! How can I ever raise my eyes and look at my friend after what I've done to him? I am so ashamed for having wronged him!'" Aaron would stay with this second party until he had similarly removed the grudge from his heart.

When the two individuals would later meet, they would hug and kiss each other in reconciliation.

III. THE PROCESS OF FORGIVENESS

Jewish law presents a model by which two individuals who are suffering from a strained relationship can air out their grievances and rediscover harmony. Each side has responsibilities in this process, and success depends on each person playing their part. The following section delineates this process.

ONE HEART
Yaeli Vogel, New York

TEXT 5

Remaining Silent

Talmud, Chulin 89a

אֵין הָעוֹלָם מִתְקַיֵּם אֶלָּא בִּשְׁבִיל מִי שֶׁבּוֹלֵם אֶת עַצְמוֹ בִּשְׁעַת מְרִיבָה.

The world endures only because of those who choose to remain silent during a quarrel.

FIGURE 6.1

Process of Forgiveness

1. **One party chooses to terminate the active quarrel.**

2.

3.

4.

5.

6.

BABYLONIAN TALMUD

A literary work of monumental proportions that draws upon the legal, spiritual, intellectual, ethical, and historical traditions of Judaism. The 37 tractates of the Babylonian Talmud contain the teachings of the Jewish sages from the period after the destruction of the 2nd Temple through the 5th century CE. It has served as the primary vehicle for the transmission of the Oral Law and the education of Jews over the centuries; it is the entry point for all subsequent legal, ethical, and theological Jewish scholarship.

Reprove, Don't Resent

Maimonides, *Mishneh Torah,* Laws of Character Development 6:6

TEXT 6

כְּשֶׁיֶּחֱטָא אִישׁ לְאִישׁ לֹא יִשְׂטְמֶנּוּ וְיִשְׁתּוֹק . . .
אֶלָּא מִצְוָה עָלָיו לְהוֹדִיעוֹ וְלוֹמַר לוֹ:
לָמָה עָשִׂיתָ לִי כָּךְ וְכָךְ, וְלָמָה חָטָאתָ לִי בְּדָבָר פְּלוֹנִי?
שֶׁנֶּאֱמַר (וַיִּקְרָא יט, יז), "הוֹכֵחַ תּוֹכִיחַ אֶת עֲמִיתֶךָ".

When someone wrongs us, we should not harbor silent resentment. . . . Rather, it is a mitzvah to inform them and to inquire, "Why did you do such and such to me? Why did you wrong me in this way?" This obligation is stated in the passage, "You shall surely reprove your fellow" (LEVITICUS 19:17).

RABBI MOSHE BEN MAIMON (MAIMONIDES, RAMBAM) 1135–1204

Halachist, philosopher, author, and physician. Maimonides was born in Córdoba, Spain. After the conquest of Córdoba by the Almohads, he fled Spain and eventually settled in Cairo, Egypt. There, he became the leader of the Jewish community and served as court physician to the vizier of Egypt. He is most noted for authoring the *Mishneh Torah,* an encyclopedic arrangement of Jewish law; and for his philosophical work, *Guide for the Perplexed.* His rulings on Jewish law are integral to the formation of Halachic consensus.

INSURMOUNTABLE ABYSS
Arthur Segal, from the "Dramas" cycle, oil on canvas, 1918 (Jewish Museum, Berlin, Germany)

Unilateral Forgiveness

Rabbi Shneur Zalman of Liadi, *Shulchan Aruch HaRav,*
Orach Chayim 156:6

וְאִם רוֹצֶה לִמְחוֹל לוֹ וְלֹא לְהוֹכִיחוֹ, הֲרֵי זֶה מִדַּת
חֲסִידוּת, וְלֹא הִקְפִּידָה הַתּוֹרָה אֶלָּא עַל הַמַּשְׂטֵמָה.

We may, if we wish, unilaterally forgive an
offending party without confronting them.
Indeed, this is an act of piety. The Torah's
directive to raise the matter is merely an insistence
against harboring emotional hostility.

**RABBI SHNEUR
ZALMAN OF LIADI
(ALTER REBBE)
1745–1812**

Chasidic rebbe, Halachic
authority, and founder of
the Chabad movement.
The Alter Rebbe was
born in Liozna, Belarus,
and was among the
principal students of the
Magid of Mezeritch. His
numerous works include
the *Tanya,* an early
classic containing the
fundamentals of Chabad
Chasidism; and *Shulchan
Aruch HaRav,* an
expanded and reworked
code of Jewish law.

The Process of Forgiveness

1. One party chooses to terminate the active quarrel.

2. If the offender fails to initiate reconciliation, the
    victim conveys their feelings to the offender.

3.

4.

5.

6.

Is sharing your feelings
the only way to resolve
anger? **Rabbi Manis
Friedman** and **Rabbi David
Aaron** respond.
myjli.com/relationships

Self-Justification

Rabbi Yosef Yitzchak Schneersohn,
Sefer Hamaamarim 5709, pp. 36–37

דְּהִנֵּה אָנוּ רוֹאִים בְּמוּחָשׁ, שֶׁיֵּשׁ טֶבַע בִּבְנֵי אָדָם לְהַצְדִּיק
אֶת עַצְמָם גַּם בְּמָקוֹם שֶׁיּוֹדֵעַ שֶׁאֵין הָאֱמֶת כֵּן ... לֵאמֹר
כִּי צֶדֶק מַעֲשֵׂהוּ, וְטוֹב עָשָׂה, אוֹ עַל כָּל פָּנִים מוֹצֵא
זְכוּת לְעַצְמוֹ בְּטַעַם וְסִבָּה עַל אֲשֶׁר עָשָׂה דָבָר זֶה ...

וָואס בֶּאֱמֶת, אִיז דָאס וָואס אַ מֶענְטשׁ אִיז אַ מַצְדִּיק
אֶת עַצְמוֹ ... מֵבִיא לוֹ הֶיזֵק גָּדוֹל בְּנַפְשׁוֹ ... דְּהִנֵּה
כַּאֲשֶׁר הָאָדָם עוֹשֶׂה דְּבָרִים לֹא טוֹבִים, בֵּין אִם יִהְיוּ
דְּבָרִים שֶׁבֵּין אָדָם לַמָּקוֹם, בֵּין אִם יִהְיוּ דְּבָרִים שֶׁבֵּין
אָדָם לַחֲבֵירוֹ, הִנֵּה כַּאֲשֶׁר יוֹדֵעַ אֲשֶׁר חָטָא וְאָשֵׁם, אָז
הִנֵּה בְּעֵת מִן הָעִתִּים, כַּאֲשֶׁר מִתְעוֹרֵר לְבָבוֹ, הֲרֵי הוּא
עוֹשֶׂה תְּשׁוּבָה, וּמִתְחָרֵט עַל הֶעָבָר, וְעוֹקֵר רְצוֹנוֹ הַקָּדוּם,
וּמְקַבֵּל עָלָיו בְּקַבָּלָה אֲמִיתִּית לְבִלְתִּי יָשׁוּב לְכִסְלָה עוֹד.

שֶׁכָּל זֶה הוּא כַּאֲשֶׁר מוֹדֶה עַל פְּשָׁעָיו וּמַכִּיר
בְּחֶטְאוֹ. אֲבָל כַּאֲשֶׁר מַצְדִּיק אֶת עַצְמוֹ, הֲרֵי אֵינוֹ
מַרְגִּישׁ כְּלָל כְּלָל שֶׁחָטָא ... שֶׁאָז הֲרֵי לֹא יַעֲשֶׂה
תְּשׁוּבָה וְיִשָּׁאֵר מְגוֹאָל וּמְלוּכְלָךְ בַּחֲטָאָיו.

שֶׁכָּל זֶה בָּא מִסִּבַּת נֶפֶשׁ הַטִּבְעִי שֶׁהוּא הַבַּהֲמִי.

**RABBI YOSEF YITZCHAK
SCHNEERSOHN
(RAYATZ,
FRIERDIKER REBBE,
PREVIOUS REBBE)
1880–1950**

Chasidic rebbe, prolific
writer, and Jewish
activist. Rabbi Yosef
Yitzchak, the 6th
leader of the Chabad
movement, actively
promoted Jewish
religious practice in
Soviet Russia and was
arrested for these
activities. After his
release from prison
and exile, he settled in
Warsaw, Poland, from
where he fled Nazi
occupation and arrived
in New York in 1940.
Settling in Brooklyn,
Rabbi Schneersohn
worked to revitalize
American Jewish life.
His son-in-law Rabbi
Menachem Mendel
Schneerson succeeded
him as the leader of the
Chabad movement.

It is a human tendency to justify our wrongful
acts even when we are aware that our justification
is not truthful. . . . We tell ourselves that our
actions were just and good, or we at least find
an excuse for our wrongful behavior. . . .

Such self-justification . . . is self-destructive. . . . If
we commit a wrong, whether it undermines our
relationship with G-d or disrupts our relationship
with a fellow mortal, then as long as we are aware
that we behaved wrongly, we will—eventually,
when our hearts are inspired—repent. We will
regret the past, uproot the former desire, and truly
accept upon ourselves not to repeat such folly.

All of this can occur only if we acknowledge our
error. Conversely, if we justify ourselves, we feel as
though we did no wrong. . . . In that case, we will fail
to repent and remain tainted and sullied with sin.

Flawed self-justification stems from the
natural soul, which is naturally animalistic.

EXERCISE 6.2   **Provide three self-justifications that one might
generate after hurting someone else:**

1.

2.

3.

The Process of Forgiveness

1. One party chooses to terminate the active quarrel.

2. If the offender fails to initiate reconciliation, the victim conveys his or her feelings to the offender.

3. **The offender takes responsibility.**

4.

5.

6.

TEXT 9A

Requesting Forgiveness

Mishnah, Bava Kama 8:1–7

הַחוֹבֵל בַּחֲבֵרוֹ חַיָּיב עָלָיו מִשׁוּם חֲמִשָּׁה דְבָרִים . . . אַף עַל פִּי שֶׁהוּא נוֹתֵן לוֹ, אֵין נִמְחָל לוֹ עַד שֶׁיְּבַקֵּשׁ מִמֶּנּוּ.

One who injures another is obliged to provide five kinds of compensation. . . . Even after providing these payments, G-d will not forgive until the offender requests forgiveness from the victim.

MISHNAH

The first authoritative work of Jewish law that was codified in writing. The Mishnah contains the oral traditions that were passed down from teacher to student; it supplements, clarifies, and systematizes the commandments of the Torah. Due to the continual persecution of the Jewish people, it became increasingly difficult to guarantee that these traditions would not be forgotten. Rabbi Yehudah Hanasi therefore redacted the Mishnah at the end of the 2nd century. It serves as the foundation for the Talmud.

Soothing the Pain

TEXT 9B

Talmud, Yoma 87a

כָּל הַמַּקְנִיט אֶת חֲבֵירוֹ אֲפִילוּ בִּדְבָרִים, צָרִיךְ לְפַיְּיסוֹ.

One who vexes another, even if only
verbally, needs to placate the victim.

More than Once

TEXT 10

Rabbi Shneur Zalman of Liadi, *Shulchan Aruch HaRav,*
Orach Chayim 606:2–3

וְאִם אֵינוֹ מִתְפַּיֵּיס בְּפַעַם רִאשׁוֹן, יַחֲזוֹר וְיֵלֵךְ
לְפַיְּיסוֹ פַּעַם שְׁנִית בְּמִין רִיצּוּי אַחֵר.

וְאִם לֹא נִתְפַּיֵּיס, יַחֲזוֹר וְיֵלֵךְ פַּעַם שְׁלִישִׁית
לְפַיְּיסוֹ בְּמִין רִיצּוּי אַחֵר . . .

וְאִם לֹא נִתְפַּיֵּיס בַּפַּעַם הַשְּׁלִישִׁית שׁוּב אֵין
זָקוּק לוֹ . . . אִם רוֹצֶה לְהַחֲמִיר עַל עַצְמוֹ
וְלֵילֵךְ אֵלָיו כַּמָּה פְּעָמִים, הָרְשׁוּת בְּיָדוֹ.

If the victim is not mollified on the first try,
the offender should return and attempt a
second time, using a different approach.

If the victim is still not placated, the
offender should return and attempt a
third time, using a third approach. . . .

After the third attempt, the offender need
not pursue the matter any longer. . . . If
an offender desires to be extra stringent,
additional attempts are permitted.

The Process of Forgiveness

1. One party chooses to terminate the active quarrel.

2. If the offender fails to initiate reconciliation, the victim conveys his or her feelings to the offender.

3. The offender takes responsibility.

4. The offender engages in an effort to placate the victim, which may include multiple attempts.

5.

6.

When to Forgive

TEXT 11

Maimonides, *Mishneh Torah*, Laws of Injury and Damage 5:10

כֵּיוָן שֶׁבִּקֵשׁ מִמֶּנּוּ הַחוֹבֵל וְנִתְחַנֵּן לוֹ . . .
וְיָדַע שֶׁהוּא שָׁב מֵחֶטְאוֹ וְנִיחַם עַל רָעָתוֹ, יִמְחוֹל לוֹ.

Once the offender has requested and pleaded for
the victim's forgiveness . . . and the victim knows
that the offender has indeed repented of the sin and
regrets the wrongful act, the victim should forgive.

EXERCISE 6.3

Provide three examples of a non-apology apology:

1.

2.

3.

Sometimes forgiveness is
not advisable. **Rabbi YY
Jacobson** shares when
this applies.
myjli.com/relationships

TEXT 12A

Abraham and Sarah

Mishnah, Bava Kama 8:7

וּמְנַיִן שֶׁלֹּא יְהֵא הַמּוֹחֵל אַכְזָרִי? שֶׁנֶּאֱמַר (בְּרֵאשִׁית כ, יז): "וַיִּתְפַּלֵּל אַבְרָהָם אֶל הָאֱלֹקִים, וַיִּרְפָּא אֱלֹקִים אֶת אֲבִימֶלֶךְ".

Where does the Torah teach us that a victim should not act cruelly by withholding forgiveness? In the verse, "Abraham prayed to G-d and G-d healed Abimelech" (GENESIS 20:17).

TEXT 12B

Moses's Forgiveness

Rashi, Numbers 21:7

"וַיִּתְפַּלֵּל מֹשֶׁה" (בַּמִּדְבָּר כא, ז): מִכָּאן לְמִי שֶׁמְּבַקְשִׁים מִמֶּנּוּ, שֶׁלֹּא יְהֵא אַכְזָרִי מִלִּמְחֹל.

"Moses prayed" (NUMBERS 21:7). This teaches us that when we are asked to forgive, we should not cruelly refuse.

RABBI SHLOMO YITZCHAKI (RASHI) 1040–1105

Most noted biblical and Talmudic commentator. Born in Troyes, France, Rashi studied in the famed *yeshivot* of Mainz and Worms. His commentaries on the Pentateuch and the Talmud, which focus on the straightforward meaning of the text, appear in virtually every edition of the Talmud and Bible.

FIGURE 6.5

The Process of Forgiveness

1. One party chooses to terminate the active quarrel.
2. If the offender fails to initiate reconciliation, the victim conveys his or her feelings to the offender.
3. The offender takes responsibility.
4. The offender engages in an effort to placate the victim, which may include multiple attempts.
5. The victim accepts the overtures and experiences an emotional shift, even if only minimally.
6. The forgiveness matures and deepens with time.

TEXT 13

An Exception

Rabbi Shneur Zalman of Liadi, *Shulchan Aruch HaRav, Orach Chayim* 606:4

שֶׁחוֹשֵׁשׁ שֶׁלֹּא יָבֹא לוֹ לְעַצְמוֹ אֵיזֶה רָעָה עַל יְדֵי שֶׁיִּמְחוֹל לוֹ, דְּאָז אֵינוֹ צָרִיךְ לִמְחוֹל לוֹ, דְּחַיָּיו קוֹדְמִין לְחַיֵּי חֲבֵירוֹ.

There is no need to forgive if you fear that some harm might befall you through granting forgiveness. After all, your own life takes precedence over the life of another.

IV. COURSE CONCLUSION

Our ancient sages urged us to draw inspiration from the pliant reed while navigating the process of reconciliation—and more generally, across all aspects of our relationships.

CIRCLE OF LIFE
Michael Gleizer, oil on canvas,
1999, New York

TEXT 14

Between Cedar and Reed

Talmud, Taanit 20b

לְעוֹלָם יְהֵא אָדָם רַךְ כַּקָּנֶה

וְאַל יְהֵא קָשֶׁה כָּאֶרֶז.

וּלְפִיכָךְ זָכָה קָנֶה לִיטוֹל הֵימֶנָה קוּלְמוֹס

לִכְתּוֹב בּוֹ סֵפֶר תּוֹרָה תְּפִילִין וּמְזוּזוֹת.

Always be pliant, yielding as a reed,

Not firm like a cedar, refusing to cede.

It was therefore the reed that merited the role,

Of scribal quill for *tefilin*, *mezuzah*,
and Torah scroll.

KEY POINTS

1   Modern discussions on forgiveness often highlight its self-help benefits. In this model, forgiveness can mean utter disassociation from the wrongdoer to gain personal peace of mind.

2   The Torah promotes forgiveness as the tool of reconciliation—rooted in the belief that all souls are interconnected, like the limbs of a single body. Consequently, conflicts should be resolved promptly to allow an already-existing unity to express itself in daily life.

3   Accordingly, the more we align with our Divine souls—that naturally pull us toward reconciliation—the more we feel motivated to pursue forgiveness, whether we are the aggrieved or the offender.

4   The initial step in reconciliation involves ceasing hostilities, which often requires silence. Addressing underlying issues should wait until the heat of anger has subsided.

5   Jewish law advises the offender to acknowledge their fault and earnestly seek the victim's forgiveness even multiple times. It instructs the victim to raise the issue with the offender and to be prepared to forgive following genuine remorse.

6   Forgiveness manifests in various degrees—
from simply wishing no harm upon the
offender to fully restoring the relationship.
One might forgive minimally today, yet
progress deeper as time goes on.

7   While offenders are always encouraged to
make amends, the Torah advises the aggrieved
that unilateral forgiveness is a noble act if it
can be granted wholeheartedly. This teaching
is especially useful for minor grievances.

8   Mastering forgiveness encompasses many of the
competencies discussed in previous lessons.

The Process of Forgiveness

Jewish law offers a framework for individuals in strained relationships to openly address their grievances and work toward harmony. In this process, each party bears specific responsibilities, and achieving reconciliation depends on both parties fulfilling their respective roles.

1/ PUTTING OUT THE FIRE

One party chooses to terminate the active quarrel.

" **The world endures only because of those who choose to remain silent during a quarrel.”**

(Talmud, Chulin 89a)

2/ UNILATERAL FORGIVENESS

A victim can choose to unilaterally forgive if they can truly harbor no negative feelings.

" **We may, if we wish, unilaterally forgive an offending party without confronting them.”**

(*Shulchan Aruch HaRav* 156:6)

5/ THE MANDATE TO PLACATE

The offender engages in an effort to placate the victim and asks for forgiveness.

" **One who vexes another . . . needs to placate the victim.”**

(Talmud, Yoma 87a)

" **G-d will not forgive until the offender requests forgiveness from the victim.”**

(Mishnah, Bava Kama 8:7)

6/ ADDITIONAL ATTEMPTS

A wounded heart may lack the strength to provide immediate forgiveness; the transgressor persists in seeking forgiveness a second and even a third time.

" **If the victim is not mollified on the first try, the offender should return and attempt a second time, using a different approach. If the victim is still not placated, the offender should return and attempt a third time, using a third approach.”**

(*Shulchan Aruch HaRav, Orach Chayim* 606:2–3)

3/ STARTING THE PROCESS

If the offender fails to initiate reconciliation and the victim is in pain, the victim conveys their feelings to the offender.

" When someone wrongs us, we should not harbor silent resentment. . . . Rather, it is a mitzvah to inform them."

(*Mishneh Torah*, Laws of Character Development 6:6)

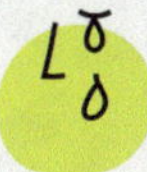

4/ OWNING UP

The offender takes responsibility.

" If we justify ourselves, we feel as though we did no wrong. . . . In that case, we will fail to repent."

(*Sefer Hamaamarim* 5709, pp. 36–37)

7/ THE CALL TO FORGIVE

The victim accepts the overtures and experiences an emotional shift, even if only minimally.

" Once the offender has requested and pleaded for the victim's forgiveness . . . and the victim knows that the offender has indeed repented . . . the victim should forgive."

(*Mishneh Torah*, Laws of Injury and Damage 5:10)

8/ GROWING IN FORGIVENESS

The forgiveness matures and deepens with time.

" There are multiple levels of forgiveness."

(*Likutei Sichot* 28, p. 141)

Unilateral Forgiveness

Numerous Torah sources suggest that unilaterally forgiving an offense is a mark of piety. While it may not always be feasible—which is why the Torah offers a structured approach to addressing grievances to reach reconciliation—it is beneficial to explore these teachings and draw inspiration from them, for they are at minimum relevant to our minor grievances.

Mercy for Mercy

If one is wronged or injured by another party and the offending party fails to request forgiveness, the injured individual should nevertheless pray for mercy on behalf of that offender, as it is stated, "Abraham prayed to G-d [and G-d healed Abimelech]" (Genesis 20:17). . . .

Rabbi Yehudah shared the following teaching of Rabban Gamliel: The Torah states, "He will give you mercy and show mercy to you and multiply you" (Deuteronomy 13:18).

Tosefta, Bava Kama 9:29–30

Secrets of Longevity

When the disciples of Rabbi Nechunia ben Hakanah asked him, "By what virtue have you reached such an old age?" he responded:

» Never in my life did I seek respect through the degradation of my fellow.

» Nor have I ever gone to bed harboring animosity toward another.

» I have been openhanded with my money.

[The Talmud comments on these virtues:]

Never in my life did I seek respect through the degradation of my fellow. This virtue was demonstrated by Rav Huna, who was walking with a spade over his shoulder when he encountered Rav Chana bar Chanilai. The latter sought to honor Rav Huna by carrying his spade for him, but Rav Huna replied, "If you are accustomed to carrying such items in your town, take it. But if you are not, I do not wish to be paid respect through your degradation."

Nor have I ever gone to bed harboring animosity toward another. This virtue was demonstrated by Mar Zutra, who would proclaim as he climbed into bed each night, "I forgive all who have vexed me."

I have been openhanded with my money. This was demonstrated by Job, who used to leave the shopkeeper with a coin [of his change].

Talmud, Megilah 28a

The Cliffside Miracles

Rabbi Abba once sat at the gateway of the city of Lod. He saw a traveler sit down on a pile of rocks at the edge of a cliff overlooking a deep ravine. The traveler was exhausted from his journey and immediately fell asleep.

As Rabbi Abba watched, a deadly snake slithered from between the rocks and headed toward the sleeping man. Suddenly, a giant lizard leaped forward and killed the serpent.

When the man awoke, he stood up and noticed the dead snake lying in front of him. As he stepped away from that spot to continue his journey, the pile of rocks he had been sitting on collapsed and fell into the ravine below.

Rabbi Abba approached him, and exclaimed, "Tell me! What deeds do you do? These miracles were certainly not in vain."

The traveler responded, "Throughout my life, I have never refused to be appeased and to forgive anyone who had wronged me. Moreover, if I were not appeased through the offender's efforts, I would not climb into bed until I would forgive the offender and anyone else who has vexed me. Furthermore, I always do my very best to replace the animosity by performing acts of kindness for the individual who wronged me."

Rabbi Abba burst into tears and declared, "This person's behavior is greater than Joseph's! True, Joseph forgave his brothers—but it is expected that one will have compassion on a sibling. It is indeed proper that G-d performed miracle upon miracle for such a person!"

Zohar 1:201b

Goal: Hate-Free

Someone may have wronged you, but you do not wish to admonish them or even mention the matter to them—for example, if the offender is far from a respectable person or if they are not mentally stable. If you forgive them fully instead, without retaining any feeling of antagonism, then you have behaved piously. For the Torah's directive to raise the matter is merely an insistence against harboring emotional hostility.

Maimonides, *Mishneh Torah*, Laws of Character Development 6:9

The Nightly Prayer of Forgiveness

Master of the universe! I hereby forgive anyone who has angered or vexed me or sinned against me, either physically or financially, against my honor or against anything else that belongs to me, whether accidentally or intentionally, inadvertently or deliberately, by speech or by deed, in this lifetime or a previous lifetime [when my soul was housed in a different body. I hereby forgive] every Jewish person. May no one be punished on my account. . . .

Prayer before Retiring at Night, *Siddur Tehillat Hashem*

Story: I Meant It!

A rabbi who lived in the Land of Israel once traveled to Imperial Russia to visit Rabbi Menachem Mendel of Lubavitch (1789–1866). Due to some undisclosed factor—something he had done or failed to do—he assumed that the Rebbe was upset with him. He therefore approached the Rebbe to work through the matter. He began with the inquiry, "Rebbe! Are you angry with me?"

With a gentle smile, Rabbi Menachem Mendel replied, "Do I not recite *Keri'at Shema* before going to sleep each night? In that prayer, I always say that I forgive!"

Rabbi Shneur Zalman Duchman, *Leshema Ozen* (Brooklyn, N.Y., 1990), p. 249

Psychology References

Aalgaard RA, et al. (2016) A literature review of forgiveness as a beneficial intervention to increase relationship satisfaction in couples therapy. *Journal of Human Behavior in the Social Environment, 26*(1), 46-55. doi.org/10.1080/10911359.2015.1059166.

Lundahl BW, et al. (2008) Process-based forgiveness interventions: A meta-analytic review. *Research on Social Work Practice, 18*(5), 465–478. doi.org/10.1177/1049731507313979.

Luskin FM. (2005) The efficacy of forgiveness intervention in college age adults: Randomized controlled study. *Humboldt Journal of Social Relations, 29*(2), 163–184. http://www.jstor.org/stable/23262800.

Onal AA, Yalçın İ. (2017) Forgiveness of others and self-forgiveness: The predictive role of cognitive distortions, empathy, and rumination. *Eurasian Journal of Educational Research, 17*(68), 99–122. doi.org/10.14689/ejer.2017.68.6.

Toussaint LL, et al. (2016) Forgiveness, stress, and health: a 5-week dynamic parallel process study. *Annals of Behavioral Medicine: A Publication of the Society of Behavioral Medicine, 50*(5):727–735. doi.org/10.1007/s12160-016-9796-6.

Toussaint LL, et al. (2018). Hostility, forgiveness, and cognitive impairment over 10 years in a national sample of American adults. *Health Psychology: Official Journal of the Division of Health Psychology, American Psychological Association, 37*(12), 1102–1106. doi.org/10.1037/hea0000686.

Toussaint L, et al. (2019) Is forgiveness one of the secrets to success? Considering the costs of workplace disharmony and the benefits of teaching employees to forgive. *American Journal of Health Promotion, 33*(7):1090-1093. doi.org/10.1177/0890117119866957e.

Wade NG, et al. (2014). Efficacy of psychotherapeutic interventions to promote forgiveness: a meta-analysis. *Journal of Consulting and Clinical Psychology, 82*(1), 154–170. doi.org/10.1037/a0035268.

Yao S, et al. (2017) Mediator roles of interpersonal forgiveness and self-forgiveness between self-esteem and subjective well-being. *Current Psychology: A Journal for Diverse Perspectives on Diverse Psychological Issues, 36*(3), 585–592. doi.org/10.1007/s12144-016-9447-x.

Acknowledgments

We are grateful to the following individuals for their contributions to this course:

Flagship Director
RABBI SHMULY KARP

Curriculum Coordinator
RIVKI MOCKIN

Flagship Administrator
NAOMI HEBER

Author
RABBI MORDECHAI DINERMAN

Curriculum Development Team
RABBI NAFTALI SILBERBERG
RABBI SHMUEL SUPER

Instructors Advisory Board
RABBI LEVI DUBOV
RABBI MENACHEM FELDMAN
RABBI DOVID FLINKENSTEIN
RABBI LEVI GREENBERG
RABBI SHOLOM NOTIK

Course Consultant
RABBI MICHOEL LIPSKIER

Research
RABBI YAKOV GERSHON

Copywriters
RABBI YONI BROWN
RABBI YAAKOV PALEY

Proofreading
RACHEL MUSICANTE
YA'AKOVAH WEBER

Hebrew Punctuation
RABBI MOSHE WOLFF

Accreditation
MINDY WALLACH

Instructor Support
RABBI LEVI GOLDSHMID
RABBI AVREMI RAPOPORT
RABBI MENDEL WOLFF

Design and Layout Administrator
SARA OSDOBA

Textbook and Marketing Design
CHAYA MUSHKA KANNER
CHAYA KATZ
ESTIE KLEIN
CHANA MARASOW
RABBI LEVI WEINGARTEN

Textbook Layout
RABBI MOTTI KLEIN

Imagery
CHAYA BARNETT
SARA ROSENBLUM

Permissions
SHULAMIS NADLER

Publication and Distribution
RABBI MOSHE RAICHIK
RABBI MENDEL SIROTA

PowerPoint Presentations
CHAYA BARNETT
SARA ROSENBLUM

Course Videos
GETZY RASKIN
MOSHE RASKIN

Key Points Videos
RABBI MOTTI KLEIN

This is the first course that is being launched since the passing of our beloved mentor, friend, and JLI chairman, **Rabbi Moshe Kotlarsky,** *z"l.* Rabbi Kotlarsky was the visionary who saw the potential of JLI from its very inception, supporting and shepherding its growth and expansion wholeheartedly, along with the countless other Chabad programs and services he directed across the globe. May the merit of the Torah study by JLI students worldwide serve to honor Rabbi Kotlarsky's legacy, continuing to be a source of *nachas* to him on High, as it always was during his lifetime.

Thanks to Rabbi Kotlarsky, we are fortunate to have the unwavering support of JLI's principal benefactor, **Mr. George Rohr**, who is fully invested in our work, continues to be instrumental to JLI's monumental growth, and is largely responsible for the Jewish renaissance that is being spearheaded by JLI and its affiliates worldwide.

The commitment and sage direction of JLI's dedicated executive board—**Rabbis Chaim Block, Hesh Epstein, Ronnie Fine, Yosef Gansburg, Shmuel Kaplan, Yisrael Rice**, and **Avrohom Sternberg**—and the countless hours they devote to the development of JLI are what drive the vision, growth, and tremendous success of the organization.

Finally, JLI represents an incredible partnership of more than 1,600 *shluchim* and *shluchot* in more than 1,000 locations across the globe, who contribute their time and talent to furthering Jewish adult education. We thank them for generously sharing feedback and making suggestions that steer JLI's development and growth. They are our most valuable critics and our most cherished contributors.

Inspired by the call of the **Lubavitcher Rebbe**, of righteous memory, it is the mandate of the Rohr JLI to provide a community of learning for all Jews throughout the world where they can participate in their precious heritage of Torah learning and experience its rewards. May this course succeed in fulfilling this sacred charge!

On behalf of the Rohr Jewish Learning Institute,

RABBI EFRAIM MINTZ
Executive Director

RABBI YISRAEL RICE
Chairman, Editorial Board

20 Av, 5784

The Rohr Jewish Learning Institute

AN AFFILIATE OF MERKOS L'INYONEI CHINUCH,
THE EDUCATION ARM OF THE CHABAD-LUBAVITCH MOVEMENT
832 EASTERN PARKWAY, BROOKLYN, NY 11213

CURRICULUM DEVELOPMENT

Rabbi Mordechai Dinerman
Rabbi Naftali Silberberg
EDITORS IN CHIEF

Rabbi Shmuel Klatzkin, PhD
ACADEMIC CONSULTANT

Rabbi Yanki Tauber
SENIOR EDITOR

Rabbi Eli Block
Rabbi Yoni Brown
Rabbi Eliezer Gurkow
Rabbi Meir Kerzner
Rabbi Berel Polityko
Rabbi Yochanan Rivkin
Rabbi Levi Shmotkin
Rabbi Shmuel Super
CURRICULUM AUTHORS

Rabbi Ahrele Loschak
EDITOR, TORAH STUDIES

Rabbi Yaakov Paley
WRITER

Mrs. Rochel Horowitz
Rabbi Moshe Wolff
EDITORIAL SUPPORT

Rabbi Yakov Gershon
RESEARCH

Rabbi Michoel Lipskier
EXPERIENTIAL LEARNING

Mrs. Rivki Mockin
CONTENT COORDINATOR

MARKETING AND BRANDING

Mr. David Kaplan
CHIEF MARKETING OFFICER

Ms. Miriam Posner
MARKETING ADMINISTRATOR

Yonatan Azrielant
Rabbi Mendel Backman
Risa Bursk
Baila Chemel
Lazer Cohen
Yosef Feigelstock
Chana Wrubel
MARKETING AND SOCIAL MEDIA

Ms. Sara Osdoba
DESIGN ADMINISTRATOR

Mrs. Chaya Mushka Kanner
Mrs. Chaya Katz
Mrs. Estie Klein
Mrs. Shifra Tauber
Rabbi Levi Weingarten
GRAPHIC DESIGN

Rabbi Motti Klein
Rabbi Zalman Korf
Rabbi Moshe Wolff
PUBLICATION DESIGN

Rabbi Yaakov Paley
COPYWRITER

Rabbi Yossi Grossbaum
Rabbi Mendel Lifshitz
Rabbi Shraga Sherman
Rabbi Ari Sollish
Rabbi Mendel Teldon
MARKETING COMMITTEE

MARKETING CONSULTANTS

Alan Rosenspan
ALAN ROSENSPAN & ASSOCIATES
Sharon, MA

Gary Wexler
PASSION MARKETING
Los Angeles, CA

JLI CENTRAL

Mrs. Mimi Brawer
Ms. Chanie Chesney
Rabbi Tzali Dubov
Rabbi Levi Goldshmid
Ms. Mushka Majeski
Rabbi Avremi Rapoport
Mrs. Aliza Scheinfeld
Ms. Mushka Silberstein
Rabbi Yosef Vogel
Rabbi Mendel Wolff
ADMINISTRATION

Ms. Liba Leah Gutnick
Rabbi Motti Klein
Mrs. Chana Marasow
Mrs. Rochel Perlstein
Rabbi Shlomie Tenenbaum
PROJECT MANAGERS

Mrs. Mindy Wallach
AFFILIATE ORIENTATION

Ms. Chaya Barnett
Ms. Tova Farro
Rabbi Motti Klein
Getzy Raskin
Moshe Raskin
Mrs. Sara Rosenblum
Mrs. Chana Zajac
MULTIMEDIA DEVELOPMENT

Rabbi Mendel Ashkenazi
Yoni Ben-Oni
Rabbi Mendy Elishevitz
Mendel Grossbaum
Rabbi Aron Liberow
Mrs. Chana Weinbaum
ONLINE DIVISION

Mrs. Ya'akovah Weber
LEAD PROOFREADER

Mrs. Rachel Musicante
Ms. Chaya Barnett
PROOFREADERS

Rabbi Moshe Raichik
Rabbi Mendel Sirota
PRINTING AND DISTRIBUTION

Mrs. Shaina B. Mintz
Mrs. Shulamis Nadler
Ms. Chinkah Zirkind
ACCOUNTING

Mrs. Chaya Katz
Mrs. Shulamis Nadler
Mrs. Mindy Wallach
CONTINUING EDUCATION

JLI FLAGSHIP

Rabbi Yisrael Rice
CHAIRMAN

Rabbi Shmuly Karp
DIRECTOR

Mrs. Naomi Heber
ADMINISTRATOR

PAST FLAGSHIP AUTHORS

Rabbi Yitzchak M. Kagan
of blessed memory

Rabbi Zalman Abraham
Brooklyn, NY

Rabbi Berel Bell
Montreal, QC

E. David Klonsky, PhD
Lisa Miller, PhD
Laura H. Mufson, PhD
Tayyab Rashid, PhD
Sylvia J. Sandler, LMFT
Bella Schanzer, M.D.
Andrew Shatté, PhD
Arielle H. Sheftall, PhD
Jonathan Singer, PhD, LCSW
Casey Skvorc, PhD, JD
Darcy Wallen, LCSW, PC

JLI INTERNATIONAL

Rabbi Avrohom Sternberg
CHAIRMAN

Rabbi Dubi Rabinowitz
DIRECTOR

Rabbi Eli Wolf
ADMINISTRATOR, JLI IN THE CIS

*In Partnership with the Federation
of Jewish Communities of the CIS*

Flor Setton
COORDINATOR,
CHABAD OF ARGENTINA

Rabbi Nochum Schapiro
REGIONAL REPRESENTATIVE, AUSTRALIA

Rabbi Avrohom Steinmetz
REGIONAL REPRESENTATIVE, BRAZIL

Rabbi Shevach Zlatopolsky
EDITOR, JLI IN THE CIS

Rabbi Shlomo Cohen
FRENCH COORDINATOR,
REGIONAL REPRESENTATIVE

Rabbi Avraham Golovacheov
REGIONAL REPRESENTATIVE, GERMANY

Rabbi Shlomo Koves
REGIONAL REPRESENTATIVE, HUNGARY

Rabbi Shmuel Katzman
REGIONAL REPRESENTATIVE,
NETHERLANDS

Rabbi Bentzi Sudak
REGIONAL REPRESENTATIVE,
UNITED KINGDOM

NATIONAL JEWISH RETREAT

Rabbi Hesh Epstein
CHAIRMAN

Mrs. Shaina B. Mintz
DIRECTOR

Bruce Backman
HOTEL LIAISON

Rabbi Shabsy Katz
PROGRAM COORDINATOR

Rabbi Isaac Mintz
SHLUCHIM LIAISON

Rabbi Mendel Rosenfeld
LOGISTICS COORDINATOR

Mrs. Aliza Scheinfeld
Ms. Mushka Silberstein
SERVICE AND SUPPORT

THE LAND & THE SPIRIT
Israel Experience

Rabbi Isaac Mintz
DIRECTOR

Mrs. Shaina B. Mintz
ADMINISTRATOR

Rabbi Yechiel Baitelman
Rabbi Dovid Flinkenstein
Rabbi Chanoch Kaplan
Rabbi Levi Klein
Rabbi Mendy Mangel
Rabbi Sholom Raichik
STEERING COMMITTEE

SHABBAT IN THE HEIGHTS

Rabbi Isaac Mintz
DIRECTOR

Rabbi Avremi Rapoport
SHLUCHIM LIAISON

Mrs. Shulamis Nadler
SERVICE AND SUPPORT

Rabbi Chaim Hanoka
CHAIRMAN

Rabbi Mordechai Dinerman
Rabbi Zalman Marcus
STEERING COMMITTEE

MYSHIUR
Advanced Learning Initiative

Rabbi Shmuel Kaplan
CHAIRMAN

Rabbi Shlomie Tenenbaum
ADMINISTRATOR

TORAHCAFE.COM
Online Learning

Rabbi Mendy Elishevitz
WEBSITE DEVELOPMENT

Moshe Levin
CONTENT MANAGER

Mendel Laine
FILMING

OMEK

Rabbi Mendel Wolff
COORDINATOR

Mrs. Chana Marasow
ADMINISTRATOR

Rabbi Dr. Seth Grauer
Rabbi Zalman Leib Markowitz
ADVISORY BOARD

MACHON SHMUEL
The Sami Rohr Research Institute

Rabbi Zalman Korf
ADMINISTRATOR

Rabbi Moshe Miller, OBM
Rabbi Gedalya Oberlander
Rabbi Chaim Rapoport
Rabbi Levi Yitzchak Raskin
Rabbi Chaim Schapiro
RABBINIC ADVISORY BOARD

Rabbi Yakov Gershon
RESEARCH FELLOW

FOUNDING DEPARTMENT HEADS

Rabbi Mendel Bell
Rabbi Zalman Charytan
Rabbi Mendel Druk
Rabbi Menachem Gansburg
Rabbi Meir Hecht
Rabbi Levi Kaplan
Rabbi Yoni Katz
Rabbi Chaim Zalman Levy
Rabbi Benny Rapoport
Dr. Chana Silberstein
Rabbi Elchonon Tenenbaum
Rabbi Mendy Weg

JLI Chapter Directory

ALABAMA

BIRMINGHAM
Rabbi Yossi Friedman — 205.970.0100

MOBILE
Rabbi Yosef Goldwasser — 251.265.1213

ALASKA

ANCHORAGE
Rabbi Yosef Greenberg
Rabbi Mendy Greenberg — 907.357.8770

ARIZONA

CHANDLER
Rabbi Mendy Deitsch — 480.855.4333

FLAGSTAFF
Rabbi Dovie Shapiro — 928.255.5756

FOUNTAIN HILLS
Rabbi Mendy Lipskier — 480.776.4763

ORO VALLEY
Rabbi Ephraim Zimmerman — 520.477.8672

PARADISE VALLEY
Rabbi Shlomo Levertov — 480.788.9310

PHOENIX
Rabbi Dovber Dechter — 347.410.0785
Rabbi Mendy Levertov — 602.861.1600
Rabbi Yossi Friedman — 602.944.2753

PRESCOTT
Rabbi Elie Filler — 928.362.8924

SCOTTSDALE
Rabbi Yossi Levertov — 480.998.1410
Rabbi Mendel Vaisfiche — 929.309.7811

SEDONA
Rabbi Mendel Kessler — 928.985.0667

TUCSON
Rabbi Yehuda Ceitlin — 520.881.7956

VAIL
Rabbi Yisroel Shemtov — 347.372.3092

ARKANSAS

LITTLE ROCK
Rabbi Pinchus Ciment — 501.217.0053

CALIFORNIA

AGOURA HILLS
Rabbi Moshe Bryski — 818.516.0444

ALAMEDA
Rabbi Meir Shmotkin — 510.640.2590

ARCADIA
Rabbi Sholom Stiefel — 626.539.4578

BAKERSFIELD
Rabbi Shmuli Schlanger — 661.834.1512

BEL AIR
Rabbi Chaim Mentz — 310.475.5311

BEL AIR WEST
Rabbi Mendy Mentz — 310.666.2302

BEVERLY HILLS
Rabbi Dovid Begun — 310.242.7750

BEVERLYWOOD
Rabbi Menachem Mendel Piekarski — 310.597.0967

BURBANK
Rabbi Shmuly Kornfeld — 818.954.0070

CARLSBAD
Rabbi Yeruchem Eilfort
Mrs. Nechama Eilfort — 760.943.8891

CERRITOS
Rabbi Mendel Lehrer — 917.717.8704

CHATSWORTH
Rabbi Yossi Spritzer — 818.307.9907

CHULA VISTA
Rabbi Mendy Begun — 347.587.0979

CONCORD
Rabbi Berel Kesselman — 925.326.1613

CONTRA COSTA
Rabbi Dovber Berkowitz — 925.937.4101

CORONADO
Rabbi Eli Fradkin — 619.365.4728

DANA POINT
Rabbi Eli Goorevitch — 949.290.0628

DANVILLE
Rabbi Shmuli Raitman — 213.447.6694

EMERYVILLE
Rabbi Menachem Blank — 510.859.8808

ENCINO
Rabbi Aryeh Herzog — 818.784.9986
Chapter founded by Rabbi Joshua Gordon, OBM

FOLSOM
Rabbi Yossi Grossbaum — 916.608.9811

FREMONT
Rabbi Eli Landes — 510.300.4090

GLENDALE
Rabbi Simcha Backman — 818.240.2750

HIGHLAND PARK
Rabbi Mendel Korf — 323.872.4876

HOLLYWOOD
Rabbi Zalman Partouche — 818.964.9428

HUNTINGTON BEACH
Rabbi Aron David Berkowitz — 714.846.2285

IRVINE
Rabbi Elly Andrusier — 949.786.5000

LAGUNA NIGUEL
Rabbi Mendy Paltiel — 949.831.7701

LA JOLLA
Rabbi Baruch Shalom Ezagui — 858.455.5433

LAKE BALBOA
Rabbi Eli Gurary — 347.403.6734

LOMITA
Rabbi Sholom Pinson — 310.326.8234

LONG BEACH
Rabbi Abba Perelmuter — 562.773.1350

LOS ANGELES
Rabbi Yossi Elifort — 310.515.5310
Rabbi Leibel Korf — 323.660.5177
Rabbi Zalmy Labkowsky — 213.618.9486
Rabbi Mendel Zajac — 310.770.9051

MALIBU
Rabbi Levi Cunin — 310.456.6588

MAR VISTA
Rabbi Shimon Simpson — 646.401.2354

MARINA DEL REY
Rabbi Danny Yiftach-Hashem
Rabbi Dovid Yiftach — 310.859.0770

MILL VALLEY
Rabbi Hillel Scop — 415.336.3055

MISSION VIEJO
Rabbi Zalman Marcus — 949.689.5159

NEWHALL
Rabbi Choni Marosov — 661.254.3434

NEWPORT BEACH
Rabbi Reuven Mintz — 949.375.3707

NORTHRIDGE
Rabbi Eli Rivkin — 818.368.3937

OJAI
Rabbi Mordechai Nemtzov — 805.613.7181

OXNARD
Rabbi Dov Muchnik — 805.844.9989

PACIFIC PALISADES
Rabbi Zushe Cunin — 310.454.7783

PALO ALTO
Rabbi Menachem Landa — 415.418.4768
Rabbi Yosef Levin
Rabbi Ber Rosenblatt — 650.424.9800

PASADENA
Rabbi Zushe Rivkin — 626.788.3343

PLEASANTON
Rabbi Josh Zebberman — 925.846.0700

PORTOLA VALLEY
Rabbi Mayer Brook — 650.304.2098

POWAY
Rabbi Mendel Goldstein — 858.208.6613

RANCHO CUCAMONGA
Rabbi Sholom Ber Harlig — 909.949.4553

RANCHO MIRAGE
Rabbi Shimon H. Posner — 760.770.7785

RANCHO PALOS VERDES
Rabbi Yitzchok Magalnic — 310.544.5544

RANCHO S. FE
Rabbi Levi Raskin — 858.756.7571

REDONDO BEACH
Rabbi Yossi Mintz
Rabbi Zalman Gordon — 310.214.4999

RESEDA
Rabbi Hershy Spritzer — 818.881.1033

RIVERSIDE
Rabbi Shmuel Fuss — 951.329.2747

S. CLEMENTE
Rabbi Menachem M. Slavin — 949.489.0723

S. CRUZ
Rabbi Yochanan Friedman — 831.454.0101

S. DIEGO
Rabbi Rafi Andrusier — 619.387.8770
Rabbi Yechiel Cagen — 832.216.1534
Rabbi Motte Fradkin — 858.547.0076

S. FRANCISCO
Rabbi Yakov Barber — 424.499.9868
Rebbetzin Mattie Pil — 415.933.4310
Rabbi Gedalia Potash — 415.648.8000
Rabbi Shlomo Zarchi — 415.752.2866

S. LUIS OBISPO
Rabbi Meir Gordon — 347.675.3383

S. MATEO
Rabbi Yossi Marcus — 650.341.4510

S. RAFAEL
Rabbi Yisrael Rice — 415.492.1666

SHERMAN OAKS
Rabbi Nachman Abend — 818.989.9539

SONOMA
Rabbi Mendel Wolvovsky — 707.292.6221

SOUTH LAKE TAHOE
Rabbi Mordechai Richler — 530.539.4363

SOUTH PASADENA
Rabbi Dovid Harlig — 626.921.6256

STOCKHOLM
Rabbi Avremel Brod — 209.952.2081

SUNNYVALE
Rabbi Yisroel Hecht — 408.720.0553

TEMECULA
Rabbi Yonason Abrams — 951.234.4196

TIBURON
Rabbi Levi Mintz — 415.378.9364

TOPANGA
Rabbi Menachem Piekarski — 858.335.7197

TUSTIN
Rabbi Yehoshua Eliezrie — 714.508.2150

VACAVILLE
Rabbi Chaim Zaklos — 707.592.5300

WEST HILLS
Rabbi Avi Rabin — 818.337.4544

WEST HOLLYWOOD
Rabbi Mordechai Kirschenbaum — 310.691.9988

WEST LOS ANGELES
Rabbi Mordechai Zaetz — 424.652.8742

WOODLAND HILLS
Rabbi Menachem M. Gordon — 818.917.8456

YORBA LINDA
Rabbi Dovid Eliezrie — 714.693.0770

COLORADO

ASPEN
Rabbi Mendel Mintz — 970.544.3770

DENVER
Rabbi Mendel Popack — 720.515.4337
Rabbi Yossi Serebryanski — 303.744.9699
Rabbi Mendy Sirota — 720.940.3716

FORT COLLINS
Rabbi Yerachmiel Gorelik — 970.407.1613

HIGHLANDS RANCH
Rabbi Avraham Mintz — 303.694.9119

LONGMONT
Rabbi Yakov Borenstein — 303.678.7595

VAIL
Rabbi Dovid Mintz — 970.476.7887

WESTMINSTER
Rabbi Benjy Brackman — 303.429.5177

CONNECTICUT

FAIRFIELD
Rabbi Shlame Landa — 203.373.7551

GLASTONBURY
Rabbi Yosef Wolvovsky — 860.659.2422

GREENWICH
Rabbi Yossi Deren
Rabbi Menachem Feldman — 203.629.9059

GUILFORD
Rabbi Yossi Yaffe — 203.645.4635

HAMDEN
Rabbi Moshe Hecht — 203.635.7268

MILFORD
Rabbi Schneur Wilhelm — 203.887.7603

NEW HAVEN
Rabbi Mendy Hecht — 203.589.5375
Rabbi Chanoch Wineberg — 203.479.0313

NEW LONDON
Rabbi Avrohom Sternberg — 860.437.8000

ORANGE
Rabbi Hershy Hecht — 203.464.7809

SHELTON
Rabbi Schneur Brook — 203.364.4149

STAMFORD
Rabbi Yisrael Deren
Rabbi Levi Mendelow — 203.3.CHABAD

WEST HARTFORD
Rabbi Shaya Gopin — 860.232.1116

WESTPORT
Rabbi Yehuda Kantor — 561.460.3758

DELAWARE

WILMINGTON
Rabbi Chuni Vogel — 302.529.9900

DISTRICT OF COLUMBIA
Rabbi Levi Shemtov
Rabbi Yitzy Ceitlin — 202.332.5600

FLORIDA

ALTAMONTE SPRINGS
Rabbi Mendy Bronstein — 407.280.0535

AVENTURA
Rabbi Yossi Itkin — 347.300.0439
Rabbi Mendel Rosenblum — 412.807.0584

BOCA RATON
Rabbi Zalman Bukiet — 561.487.2934
Rabbi Moishe Denburg — 561.526.5760
Rabbi Arele Gopin — 561.994.6257
Rabbi Ruvi New — 561.394.9770

BONITA SPRINGS
Rabbi Mendy Greenberg — 239.949.6900

BOYNTON BEACH
Rabbi Sholom Ciment — 561.732.4633
Rabbi Yosef Yitzchok Raichik — 561.740.8738

BRADENTON
Rabbi Menachem Bukiet — 941.388.9656

CAPE CORAL
Rabbi Yossi Labkowski — 239.963.4770

CLERMONT
Rabbi Moshe Dubinsky — 862.812.2174

CORAL GABLES
Rabbi Avraham Stolik — 305.490.7572

CORAL SPRINGS
Rabbi Hershy Bronstein — 954.798.6023
Rabbi Yankie Denburg — 954.471.8646

CUTLER BAY
Rabbi Yossi Wolff — 305.975.6680

DAVIE
Rabbi Aryeh Schwartz — 954.376.9973

DELRAY BEACH
Rabbi Yaakov Perman — 561.666.2770

FISHER ISLAND
Rabbi Efraim Brody — 347.325.1913

FLEMING ISLAND
Rabbi Shmuly Feldman — 904.290.1017

FORT LAUDERDALE
Rabbi Schneur Kaplan — 954.667.8000
Rabbi Yitzchok Naparstek — 954.568.1190

HALLANDALE BEACH
Rabbi Mordy Feiner — 954.458.1877

HOLLYWOOD
Rabbi Leizer Barash — 954.549.5012
Rabbi Leibel Kudan — 954.801.3367

JUPITER
Rabbi Berel Barash — 561.317.0968

KENDALL
Rabbi Yossi Harlig — 305.234.5654

KEY BISCAYNE
Rabbi Avremel Caroline — 305.365.6744

LAUDERHILL
Rabbi Shmuel Heidingsfeld — 323.877.7703

LONGWOOD
Rabbi Yanky Majesky — 407.636.5994

MAITLAND
Rabbi Sholom Dubov
Rabbi Levik Dubov — 470.644.2500
Rabbi Tzviki Dubov — 407.529.8256

MARION COUNTY
Rabbi Yossi Hecht — 352.330.4466

MIAMI

Rabbi Mendy Cheruty — 305.219.3353
Rabbi Yakov Fellig — 305.445.5444
Rabbi Shmuel Gopin — 305.573.9995
Rabbi Chaim Lipskar — 305.373.8303

MIAMI BEACH

Rabbi Yisroel Frankforter — 305.534.3895
Rabbi Sholom Korf — 786.423.6483
Rabbi Shmuel Mann — 305.674.8400

NAPLES

Rabbi Fishel Zaklos — 239.404.6993

N. MIAMI BEACH

Rabbi Leib Ezagui — 561.596.0530
Rabbi Yehoshua Karp — 862.226.2869
Rabbi Eli Laufer — 305.770.4412

ORLANDO

Rabbi Yosef Konikov — 407.354.3660

ORMOND BEACH

Rabbi Asher Farkash — 386.672.9300

OVEIDO

Rabbi Tzviky Dubov — 407.529.8256

PALM BEACH

Rabbi Zalman Levitin — 561.659.3884

PALM BEACH GARDENS

Rabbi Dovid Vigler — 561.624.2223

PALM CITY

Rabbi Shlomo Uminer — 772.485.5501

PALM HARBOR

Rabbi Pinchas Adler — 727.789.0408

PARKLAND

Rabbi Mendy Gutnick — 954.600.6991

PEMBROKE PINES

Rabbi Mordechai Andrusier — 954.874.2280

PENSACOLA

Rabbi Mendel Danow — 850.291.9600

PLANTATION

Rabbi Pinchas Taylor — 954.644.9177

PONTE VEDRA BEACH

Rabbi Nochum Kurinsky — 904.543.9301

PORT ORANGE

Rabbi Mendel Niasoff — 386.679.5756

ROYAL PALM BEACH

Rabbi Nachmen Zeev Schtroks — 561.714.1692

S. AUGUSTINE

Rabbi Levi Vogel — 904.521.8664

S. JOHNS

Rabbi Mendel Sharfstein — 347.461.3765

S. PETERSBURG

Rabbi Alter Korf — 727.344.4900

SARASOTA

Rabbi Chaim Shaul Steinmetz — 941.925.0770
Rabbi Levi Steinmetz — 941.928.9267

SATELLITE BEACH

Rabbi Zvi Konikov — 321.777.2770

SINGER ISLAND

Rabbi Berel Namdar — 347.276.6985

SOUTH PALM BEACH

Rabbi Leibel Stolik — 561.889.3499

SOUTH TAMPA

Rabbi Mendy Dubrowski — 813.922.1723

SOUTHWEST BROWARD COUNTY

Rabbi Aryeh Schwartz — 954.252.1770

SUNNY ISLES BEACH

Rabbi Alexander Kaller — 305.803.5315

SURFSIDE

Rabbi Dov Schochet — 305.790.8294

TAMARAC

Rabbi Kopel Silberberg — 954.882.7434

TAMPA

Rabbi Chaim Lipszyc — 954.882.7434

VENICE

Rabbi Sholom Ber Schmerling — 845.238.0770

VERO BEACH

Rabbi Motty Rosenfeld — 772.245.6712

WATERWAYS

Rabbi Yisroel Brusowankin — 786.663.8731

WESLEY CHAPEL

Rabbi Mendy Yarmush
Rabbi Mendel Friedman — 813.731.2977

WEST DELRAY BEACH

Rabbi Yossi Schapiro — 561.221.1618

WEST PALM BEACH

Rabbi Yoel Gancz — 561.659.7770

WESTON

Rabbi Yisroel Spalter — 954.349.6565

GEORGIA

ALPHARETTA

Rabbi Hirshy Minkowicz — 770.410.9000

ATLANTA

Rabbi Yossi New
Rabbi Isser New — 404.843.2464
Rabbi Alexander Piekarski — 678.267.6418
Rabbi Ari Sollish — 404.898.0434

ATLANTA: INTOWN

Rabbi Eliyahu Schusterman
Rabbi Chanan Rose — 415.370.1333

AUGUSTA

Rabbi Zalman Fischer — 706.836.1576

CUMMING

Rabbi Levi Mentz — 310.666.2218

DUNWOODY

Rabbi Mendy Wineberg — 347.770.2414

GAINESVILLE

Rabbi Nechemia Gurevitz — 770.906.4970

GWINNETT

Rabbi Yossi Lerman — 678.595.0196

MARIETTA

Rabbi Ephraim Silverman — 770.565.4412

ROSWELL

Rabbi Chaim Schwartz — 770.363.4644

HAWAII

KAILUA-KONA
Rabbi Levi Gerlitzky — 917.853.2787

KAPA'A
Rabbi Michoel Goldman — 808.647.4293

IDAHO

BOISE
Rabbi Mendel Lifshitz — 208.853.9200

ILLINOIS

ARLINGTON HEIGHTS
Rabbi Yaakov Kotlarsky — 224.357.7002

CHAMPAIGN
Rabbi Dovid Tiechtel — 217.355.8672

CHICAGO
Rabbi Mendy Benhiyoun — 312.498.7704
Rabbi Mordechai Gershon — 773.412.5189
Rabbi Dovid Kotlarsky — 773.495.7127
Rabbi Yosef Moscowitz — 773.772.3770
Rabbi Levi Notik — 773.274.5123

ELGIN
Rabbi Mendel Shemtov — 847.440.4486

GLENVIEW
Rabbi Yishaya Benjaminson — 847.910.1738

GURNEE
Rabbi Sholom Tenenbaum — 847.782.1800

HIGHLAND PARK
Mrs. Michla Schanowitz — 847.266.0770

NAPERVILLE
Rabbi Mendy Goldstein — 630.957.8122

NORTHBROOK
Rabbi Meir Moscowitz — 847.564.8770

NORWOOD PARK
Rabbi Mendel Perlstein — 312.752.8894

OAK PARK
Rabbi Yitzchok Bergstein — 708.524.1530

PARK RIDGE
Rabbi Lazer Hershkovich — 224.392.4442

PEORIA
Rabbi Eli Langsam — 309.370.7701

RIVERWOODS
Rabbi Sholom Notik — 847.208.8794

SKOKIE
Rabbi Yochanan Posner — 847.677.1770

VERNON HILLS
Rabbi Shimmy Susskind — 718.755.5356

WILMETTE
Rabbi Dovid Flinkenstein — 847.251.7707

INDIANA

INDIANAPOLIS
Rabbi Avraham Grossbaum
Rabbi Dr. Shmuel Klatzkin — 317.251.5573

IOWA

BETTENDORF
Rabbi Shneur Cadaner — 563.355.1065

KANSAS

OVERLAND PARK
Rabbi Mendy Wineberg — 913.649.4852

KENTUCKY

LOUISVILLE
Rabbi Avrohom Litvin — 502.459.1770

LOUISIANA

BATON ROUGE
Rabbi Peretz Kazen — 225.267.7047

METAIRIE
Rabbi Yossie Nemes
Rabbi Mendel Ceitlin — 504.454.2910

NEW ORLEANS
Rabbi Mendel Rivkin — 504.302.1830

MAINE

BANGOR
Rabbi Chaim Wilansky — 207.650.7223

PORTLAND
Rabbi Levi Wilansky — 207.650.1783

MARYLAND

BALTIMORE
Rabbi Velvel Belinsky — 410.764.5000
Classes in Russian

Rabbi Dovid Reyder — 781.796.4204

BEL AIR
Rabbi Kushi Schusterman — 443.353.9718

BETHESDA
Rabbi Sender Geisinsky — 301.913.9777

CHEVY CHASE
Rabbi Zalman Minkowitz — 301.260.5000

COLUMBIA
Rabbi Hillel Baron
Rabbi Yosef Chaim Sufrin — 410.740.2424

FREDERICK
Rabbi Boruch Labkowski — 301.996.3659

GAITHERSBURG
Rabbi Sholom Raichik — 301.926.3632

OLNEY
Rabbi Bentzy Stolik — 301.660.6770

OWINGS MILLS
Rabbi Nochum Katsenelenbogen — 410.356.5156

POTOMAC
Rabbi Mendel Bluming — 301.983.4200
Rabbi Mendel Kaplan — 301.983.1485

ROCKVILLE
Rabbi Shlomo Beitsh — 646.773.2675
Rabbi Moishe Kavka — 301.836.1242

MASSACHUSETTS

ANDOVER
Rabbi Asher Bronstein — 978.470.2288

ARLINGTON
Rabbi Avi Bukiet — 617.909.8653

BOSTON
Rabbi Yosef Zaklos — 617.297.7282

BRIGHTON
Rabbi Dan Rodkin — 617.787.2200

CAPE COD
Rabbi Yekusiel Alperowitz — 508.775.2324

CHESTNUT HILL
Rabbi Mendy Uminer — 617.738.9770

LEXINGTON
Rabbi Yisroel New — 646.248.9053

LONGMEADOW
Rabbi Yakov Wolff — 413.567.8665

NEWTON
Rabbi Shalom Ber Prus — 617.244.1200

PEABODY
Rabbi Nechemia Schusterman — 978.977.9111

SOUTH SHORE
Rabbi Levi Lezell — 617.862.2770

SUDBURY
Rabbi Yisroel Freeman — 978.443.0110

SWAMPSCOTT
Rabbi Yossi Lipsker — 781.581.3833

VINEYARD HAVEN
Rabbi Tzvi Alperowitz — 508.560.8650

MICHIGAN

ANN ARBOR
Rabbi Aharon Goldstein — 734.995.3276

BLOOMFIELD HILLS
Rabbi Levi Dubov — 248.949.6210

GRAND RAPIDS
Rabbi Mordechai Haller — 616.957.0770

TROY
Rabbi Menachem Caytak — 248.873.5851

WEST BLOOMFIELD
Rabbi Zelig Shemtov — 248.788.4000
Rabbi Elimelech Silberberg — 248.855.6170
Rabbi Schneur Silberberg — 248.207.5513

MINNESOTA

MINNETONKA
Rabbi Mordechai Grossbaum
Rabbi Shmuel Silberstein — 952.929.9922

PLYMOUTH
Rabbi Nissan Naparstek — 310.430.0960

S. PAUL
Rabbi Shneur Zalman Bendet — 651.998.9298

MISSOURI

CHESTERFIELD
Rabbi Avi Rubenfeld — 314.258.3401

S. LOUIS
Rabbi Yosef Abenson — 314.448.0927
Rabbi Yosef Landa — 314.725.0400

MONTANA

BOZEMAN
Rabbi Chaim Shaul Bruk — 406.600.4934

KALISPELL
Rabbi Shneur Wolf — 406.885.2541

NEVADA

LAS VEGAS
Rabbi Yosef Rivkin — 702.217.2170

RENO
Rabbi Levi Sputz — 347.262.4531

SUMMERLIN
Rabbi Yisroel Schanowitz
Rabbi Tzvi Bronchtain — 702.855.0770

NEW JERSEY

BASKING RIDGE
Rabbi Mendy Herson
Rabbi Mendel Shemtov — 908.604.8844

CHERRY HILL
Rabbi Mendel Mangel — 856.874.1500

CLINTON
Rabbi Eli Kornfeld — 908.623.7000

ENGLEWOOD
Rabbi Shmuel Konikov — 201.519.7343

FAIR LAWN
Rabbi Avrohom Bergstein — 201.794.3770

FANWOOD
Rabbi Avrohom Blesofsky — 908.790.0008

FLANDERS
Rabbi Yaacov Shusterman — 973.723.6868

FORT LEE
Rabbi Meir Konikov — 201.886.1238

GREATER MERCER COUNTY
Rabbi Dovid Dubov
Rabbi Yaakov Chaiton — 609.213.4136

HASKELL
Rabbi Mendy Gurkov — 201.696.7609

HOLMDEL
Rabbi Shmaya Galperin — 732.772.1998

JACKSON
Rabbi Shmuel Naparstek — 732.668.7702

JERICHO
Rabbi Mendy Brownstein — 516.850.4486

MADISON
Rabbi Shalom Lubin — 973.377.0707

MANALAPAN
Rabbi Boruch Chazanow
Rabbi Levi Wolosow — 732.972.3687

MEDFORD
Rabbi Yitzchok Kahan — 609.451.3522

MONTCLAIR
Rabbi Yaacov Leaf — 862.252.5666

MORRISTOWN
Rabbi Moishe Gurevitz   973.216.8077

MOUNTAIN LAKES
Rabbi Levi Dubinsky   973.551.1898

MULLICA HILL
Rabbi Avrohom Richler   856.733.0770

OLD TAPPAN
Rabbi Mendy Lewis   201.767.4008

RANDOLPH
Rabbi Avraham Bekhor   973.723.0933

RED BANK
Rabbi Dovid Harrison   973.895.3070

ROCKAWAY
Rabbi Asher Herson
Rabbi Mordechai Baumgarten   973.625.1525

RUTHERFORD
Rabbi Yitzchok Lerman   347.834.7500

SCOTCH PLAINS
Rabbi Avrohom Blesofsky   908.790.0008

SHORT HILLS
Rabbi Mendel Solomon
Rabbi Avrohom Levin   973.725.7008

SOUTH BRUNSWICK
Rabbi Levi Azimov   732.398.9492

TENAFLY
Rabbi Mordechai Shain   201.871.1152

TOMS RIVER
Rabbi Moshe Gourarie   732.349.4199

VENTNOR
Rabbi Avrohom Rapoport   609.822.8500

WEST ORANGE
Rabbi Mendy Kasowitz   973.325.6311

WOODCLIFF LAKE
Rabbi Dov Drizin   201.476.0157

NEW MEXICO

LAS CRUCES
Rabbi Bery Schmukler   575.524.1330

S. FE
Rabbi Berel Levertov   505.920.4324

NEW YORK

ALBANY
Rabbi Mordechai Rubin   518.368.7886

BEDFORD
Rabbi Arik Wolf   914.666.6065

BENSONHURST
Rabbi Avrohom Hertz   718.753.7768

BINGHAMTON
Mrs. Rivkah Slonim   607.797.0015

BRIGHTON BEACH
Rabbi Dovid Okonov   718.368.4490

BRONXVILLE
Rabbi Sruli Deitsch   917.755.0078

BROOKVILLE
Rabbi Mendy Heber   516.626.0600

CEDARHURST
Rabbi Zalman Wolowik   516.295.2478

CLIFTON PARK
Rabbi Yossi Rubin   518.495.0772

COMMACK
Rabbi Mendel Teldon   631.543.3343

DELMAR
Rabbi Zalman Simon   518.866.7658

DOBBS FERRY
Rabbi Benjy Silverman   914.693.6100

EAST HAMPTON
Rabbi Leibel Baumgarten
Rabbi Mendy Goldberg   631.329.5800

ELLENVILLE
Rabbi Shlomie Deren   845.647.4450

FOREST HILLS
Rabbi Yossi Mendelson   917.861.9726

GLEN OAKS
Rabbi Shmuel Nadler   347.388.7064

GREAT NECK
Rabbi Yoseph Geisinsky   516.487.4554

HOWARD BEACH
Rabbi Avrohom Richler   917.541.7374

ISLIP
Rabbi Shimon Stillerman   631.913.8770

KINGSTON
Rabbi Yitzchok Hecht   845.334.9044

LARCHMONT
Rabbi Mendel Silberstein   914.834.4321

LITTLE NECK
Rabbi Eli Shifrin   718.423.1235

LONG BEACH
Rabbi Eli Goodman   516.574.3905

LONG ISLAND CITY
Rabbi Zev Wineberg   347.218.2927

MANHASSET
Rabbi Mendel Paltiel   516.984.0701

MELVILLE
Rabbi Yosef Raskin   631.276.4453

MINEOLA
Rabbi Anchelle Perl   516.739.3636

NEW HARTFORD
Rabbi Levi Charitonow   716.322.8692

NEW YORK
Rabbi Yakov Bankhalter   917.613.1678
Rabbi Nissi Eber   347.677.2276
Rabbi Berel Gurevitch   212.518.3122
Rabbi Daniel Kraus   917.294.5567
Rabbi Shmuel Metzger   212.758.3770

NYC TRIBECA
Rabbi Zalman Paris   212.566.6764

NYC UPPER EAST SIDE
Rabbi Uriel Vigler   212.369.7310

NYC WEST SIDE
Rabbi Shlomo Kugel   212.864.5010

OCEANSIDE
Rabbi Levi Gurkow   516.764.7385

OSSINING
Rabbi Dovid Labkowski — 914.923.2522

OYSTER BAY
Rabbi Shmuel Lipszyc
Rabbi Shalom Lipszyc — 347.853.9992

PARK SLOPE
Rabbi Menashe Wolf — 347.957.1291

PORT WASHINGTON
Rabbi Shalom Paltiel — 516.767.8672

PROSPECT HEIGHTS
Rabbi Mendy Hecht — 347.622.3599

ROCHESTER
Rabbi Nechemia Vogel — 585.271.0330

ROSLYN
Rabbi Yaakov Reiter — 516.484.3500

ROSLYN HEIGHTS
Rabbi Aaron Konikov — 516.484.3500

SEA GATE
Rabbi Chaim Brikman — 347.524.3214

SOUTHAMPTON
Rabbi Chaim Pape — 917.627.4865

STATEN ISLAND
Rabbi Mendy Katzman — 718.370.8953

STONY BROOK
Rabbi Shalom Ber Cohen — 631.585.0521

SUFFERN
Rabbi Shmuel Gancz — 845.368.1889

WEST BRIGHTON BEACH
Rabbi Moshe Winner — 718.946.9833

YORKTOWN HEIGHTS
Rabbi Yehuda Heber — 914.962.1111

NORTH CAROLINA

ASHEVILLE
Rabbi Shaya Susskind — 828.335.4604

CARY
Rabbi Yisroel Cotlar — 919.651.9710

CHAPEL HILL
Rabbi Zalman Bluming — 919.357.5904

CHARLOTTE
Rabbi Yossi Groner
Rabbi Shlomo Cohen — 704.366.3984

GREENSBORO
Rabbi Yosef Plotkin — 336.617.8120

RALEIGH
Rabbi Pinchas Herman
Rabbi Mendy Wilschanski — 919.847.8986

WILMINGTON
Rabbi Moshe Lieblich — 910.763.4770

WINSTON-SALEM
Rabbi Levi Gurevitz — 336.756.9069

OHIO

BEACHWOOD
Rabbi Moshe Gancz — 216.647.4884

CINCINNATI
Rabbi Yisroel Mangel — 513.793.5200

COLUMBUS
Rabbi Shea Kaltmann — 614.935.2804
Rabbi Yitzi Kaltmann — 614.294.3296

DAYTON
Rabbi Nochum Mangel — 937.643.0770

TWINSBURG
Rabbi Mendy Greenberg — 440.465.2063

OKLAHOMA

OKLAHOMA CITY
Rabbi Ovadia Goldman — 405.524.4800

TULSA
Rabbi Yehuda Weg — 918.492.4499

OREGON

PORTLAND
Rabbi Mordechai Wilhelm — 503.977.9947

SALEM
Rabbi Avrohom Y. Perlstein — 503.383.9569

TIGARD
Rabbi Menachem Orenstein — 971.329.6661

WEST LINN
Rabbi Shimon Wilhelm — 503.753.4744

PENNSYLVANIA

AMBLER
Rabbi Shaya Deitsch — 215.591.9310

BALA CYNWYD
Rabbi Shraga Sherman — 610.660.9192

CLARKS SUMMIT
Rabbi Benny Rapoport — 570.587.3300

DOYLESTOWN
Rabbi Mendel Prus — 215.340.1303

FREEDOM
Rabbi Yosef Feller — 612.275.6438

GLEN MILLS
Rabbi Yehuda Gerber — 484.620.4162

LAFAYETTE HILL
Rabbi Yisroel Kotlarsky — 484.533.7009

LANCASTER
Rabbi Elazar Green — 717.723.8783

LEWISBURG
Rabbi Yisroel Baumgarten — 631.880.2801

MECHANICSBURG
Rabbi Nissen Pewzner — 717.798.0053

MONROEVILLE
Rabbi Mendy Schapiro — 412.372.1000

NEWTOWN
Rabbi Aryeh Weinstein — 215.497.9925

PHILADELPHIA
Rabbi Berel Paltiel — 718.288.8574

PHILADELPHIA: CENTER CITY
Rabbi Yochonon Goldman — 215.238.2100

PITTSBURGH
Rabbi Yisroel Altein — 412.422.7300 #269

PITTSBURGH: SOUTH HILLS
Rabbi Mendy Rosenblum 412.278.3693

READING
Rabbi Yosef Lipsker 610.334.3218

RYDAL
Rabbi Zushe Gurevitz 267.536.5757

UNIVERSITY PARK
Rabbi Nosson Meretsky 814.863.4929

WYNNEWOOD
Rabbi Moishe Brennan 610.529.9011

PUERTO RICO

CAROLINA
Rabbi Mendel Zarchi 787.253.0894

RHODE ISLAND

WARWICK
Rabbi Yossi Laufer 401.884.7888

SOUTH CAROLINA

BLUFFTON
Rabbi Menachem Hertz 843.301.1819

COLUMBIA
Rabbi Hesh Epstein
Rabbi Levi Marrus 803.782.1831

GREENVILLE
Rabbi Leibel Kesselman 864.534.7739

MYRTLE BEACH
Rabbi Doron Aizenman 843.448.0035

TENNESSEE

CHATTANOOGA
Rabbi Shaul Perlstein 423.910.9770

KNOXVILLE
Rabbi Yossi Wilhelm 865.588.8584

MEMPHIS
Rabbi Levi Klein 901.754.0404

NASHVILLE
Rabbi Yitzchok Tiechtel 615.646.5750

TEXAS

AUSTIN
Rabbi Mendy Levertov 512.905.2778

BELLAIRE
Rabbi Yossi Zaklikofsky 713.839.8887

CYPRESS
Rabbi Levi Marinovsky 832.651.6964

DALLAS
Rabbi Zvi Drizin 214.632.2633
Rabbi Mendel Dubrawsky 214.215.1540
Rabbi Boruch Hecht 310.704.5403
Rabbi Moshe Naparstek 972.818.0770

EL PASO
Rabbi Levi Greenberg 347.678.9762

FORT WORTH
Rabbi Dov Mandel 817.263.7701

FRISCO
Rabbi Mendy Kesselman 214.460.7773

HOUSTON
Rabbi Dovid Goldstein
Rabbi Zally Lazarus 281.589.7188
Rabbi Moishe Traxler 713.774.0300

HOUSTON: RICE UNIVERSITY AREA
Rabbi Eliezer Lazaroff 713.522.2004

LEAGUE CITY
Rabbi Yitzchok Schmukler 281.724.1554

PLANO
Rabbi Eli Block 214.620.4083
Rabbi Mendel Block 972.596.8270

ROCKWALL
Rabbi Moshe Kalmenson 469.350.5735

ROUND ROCK
Rabbi Mendel Marasow 512.387.3171

S. ANTONIO
Rabbi Chaim Block
Rabbi Levi Teldon 210.492.1085
Rabbi Tal Shaul 210.877.4218

SOUTHLAKE
Rabbi Levi Gurevitch 817.451.1171

SUGAR LAND
Rabbi Ari Feigenson
Rabbi Mendel Feigenson 832.758.0685

THE WOODLANDS
Rabbi Mendel Blecher 281.865.7242

UTAH

LEHI
Rabbi Chaim Zippel 801.674.4566

PARK CITY
Rabbi Yehuda Steiger 435.714.8590

S. GEORGE
Rabbi Mendy Cohen 862.812.6224

SALT LAKE CITY
Rabbi Benny Zippel 801.467.7777

VERMONT

BURLINGTON
Rabbi Yitzchok Raskin 802.658.5770

MANCHESTER
Rabbi Menachem Andrusier 518.506.8678

WATERBURY CENTER
Rabbi Boruch Simon 518.360.7337

VIRGINIA

ALEXANDRIA/ARLINGTON
Rabbi Mordechai Newman 703.370.2774

FAIRFAX
Rabbi Leibel Fajnland 703.426.1980

GAINESVILLE
Rabbi Shmuel Perlstein 571.445.0342

Column 1

LOUDOUN COUNTY
Rabbi Chaim Cohen — 248.298.9279

NORFOLK
Rabbi Aaron Margolin
Rabbi Levi Brashevitzky — 757.616.0770

RICHMOND
Rabbi Shlomo Pereira — 804.740.2000

WILLIAMSBURG
Rabbi Mendy Heber — 234.770.0306

WINCHESTER
Rabbi Yishai Dinerman — 540.324.9879

WASHINGTON

BAINBRIDGE ISLAND
Rabbi Mendy Goldshmid — 206.397.7679

BELLINGHAM
Rabbi Yosef Truxton — 360.224.9919

KIRKLAND
Rabbi Chaim S. Rivkin — 425.749.8512

LYNNWOOD
Rabbi Berel Paltiel — 425.286.7465

MERCER ISLAND
Rabbi Elazar Bogomilsky — 206.527.1411
Rabbi Nissan Kornfeld — 206.851.2324

NORMANDY PARK
Rabbi Moshe Wolff — 206.946.2477

OLYMPIA
Rabbi Yosef Schtroks — 360.867.8804

SEATTLE
Rabbi Yoni Levitin — 206.851.9831
Rabbi Shmuel Levitin — 347.415.2271
Rabbi Shnai Levitin — 347.342.2259

SPOKANE COUNTY
Rabbi Yisroel Hahn — 509.443.0770

WISCONSIN

BAYSIDE
Rabbi Cheski Edelman — 414.439.5041

Column 2

BROOKFIELD
Rabbi Levi Brook — 925.708.4203

KENOSHA
Rabbi Tzali Wilschanski — 262.359.0770

MADISON
Rabbi Avremel Matusof — 608.335.3777

MEQUON
Rabbi Doobie Lisker — 323.216.6139
Rabbi Menachem Rapoport — 262.242.2235

MILWAUKEE
Rabbi Levi Emmer — 414.277.8839
Rabbi Mendel Shmotkin — 414.961.6100

WYOMING

LARAMIE
Rabbi Yaakov Raskin — 307.920.2613

ARGENTINA

BAHIA BLANCA
Rabbi Shmuel Freedman — 347.300.2779

BUENOS AIRES
Rabbi Abraham Benchimol — 54.11.6048.5333
Rabbi Yossi Birman — 54.11.5334.6606
Mrs. Chani Gorowitz — 54.11.4865.0445
Rabbi M. M. Grunblatt — 54.911.3574.0037
Rabbi Mendy Gurevitch — 55.11.4545.7771
Rabbi Mendel Levy — 54.11.3687.8258
Rabbi Shlomo Levy — 54.11.4807.2223
Rabbi Yosef Levy — 54.11.4504.1908
Rabbi Yosef Yitzjok Levy — 54.11.6292.4125
Rabbi Tzvi Lipinsky — 54.11.5249.2693
Rabbi Yossi Ludman — 54.11.3935.0214
Rabbi Yoel Migdal — 54.11.4963.1221
Rabbi Mendi Mizrahi — 54.11.4963.1221
Rabbi Shiele Plotka — 54.11.4634.3111
Rabbi Itzjak Safranchik — 54.11.3699.3977
Rabbi Shniur Z. Schvetz — 54.11.3552.5208
Rabbi Shloimi Setton — 54.11.4982.8637
Rabbi Pinhas Sudry — 54.1.4822.2285

CORDOBA
Rabbi Menajem Turk — 54.351.233.8250

Column 3

ROSARIO
Rabbi Shlomo Tawil — 54.93.4152.0039

S. MIGUEL DE TUCUMÁN
Rabbi Ariel Levy — 54.381.473.6944

SALTA
Rabbi Rafael Tawil — 54.387.421.4947

AUSTRALIA

NEW SOUTH WALES

BELLEVUE HILL
Mrs. Chaya Kaye — 614.3342.2755

DOUBLE BAY
Rabbi Yanky Berger — 612.9327.1644

DOVER HEIGHTS
Rabbi Motti Feldman — 614.0400.8572

MAROUBRA
Rabbi Schneur Goldstein — 614.3476.0722

NEWTOWN
Rabbi Eli Feldman — 614.0077.0613

NORTH SHORE
Rabbi Nochum Schapiro
Rebbetzin Fruma Schapiro — 612.9488.9548

SYDNEY
Rabbi Levi Wolff — 614.2162.2622

THE HILL
Rabbi Yossi Rodal — 614.2573.0412

QUEENSLAND

BOKARINA
Rabbi Asher Goodman — 898.6763.0334

BRISBANE
Rabbi Levi Jaffe — 617.3843.6770

TASMANIA

SOUTH LAUNCESTON
Mrs. Rochel Gordon — 614.2055.0405

VICTORIA

EAST S. KILDA
Rabbi Sholem Gorelik — 614.5244.8770

MOORABBIN
Rabbi Elisha Greenbaum — 614.0349.0434

WESTERN AUSTRALIA

PERTH
Rabbi Shalom White — 618.9275.2106

AZERBAIJAN

BAKU
Mrs. Chavi Segal — 994.12.597.91.90

BELARUS

BOBRUISK
Mrs. Mina Hababo — 375.29.104.3230

MINSK
Rabbi Shneur Deitsch
Mrs. Bassie Deitsch — 375.29.330.6675

BELGIUM

ANTWERP
Rabbi Mendel Gurary — 32.48.656.9878

BRUSSELS
Rabbi Shmuel Pinson — 375.29.330.6675

BRAZIL

CURITIBA
Rabbi Mendy Labkowski — 55.41.3079.1338

S. PAULO
Rabbi Avraham Steinmetz — 55.11.3081.3081

CANADA

ALBERTA

CALGARY
Rabbi Mordechai Groner — 403.281.3770

EDMONTON
Rabbi Ari Drelich
Rabbi Mendy Blachman — 780.200.5770

BRITISH COLUMBIA

COQUITLAM
Rabbi Mordechai Gurevitz — 604.787.5667

NANAIMO
Rabbi Benzti Shemtov — 250.797.7877

RICHMOND
Rabbi Yechiel Baitelman — 604.277.6427

VANCOUVER
Rabbi Dovid Rosenfeld — 604.266.1313
Rabbi Shmuel Yeshayahu — 604.738.7060

VICTORIA
Rabbi Meir Kaplan — 250.595.7656

MANITOBA

WINNIPEG
Rabbi Menachem Altein — 204.869.7631
Rabbi Shmuel Altein — 204.339.8737

ONTARIO

BAYVIEW
Rabbi Levi Gansburg — 416.551.9391

EAST THORNHILL
Rabbi Mendel Zaltzman — 647.998.7105

GREATER TORONTO REGIONAL OFFICE & THORNHILL
Rabbi Yossi Gansburg — 905.731.7000

INNISFIL
Rabbi Zevi Kaplan — 705.970.7074

KINGSTON
Rabbi Yisroel Simon — 613.770.1884

MAPLE
Rabbi Yechezkel Deren — 647.883.6372

MISSISSAUGA
Rabbi Yitzchok Slavin — 905.820.4432

NORTH YORK
Rabbi Sruli Steiner — 647.501.5618

OTTAWA
Rabbi Menachem M. Blum — 613.843.7770
Rabbi Moshe Caytak — 613.902.4394

RICHMOND HILL
Rabbi Mendel Bernstein — 905.303.1880

TORONTO
Rabbi Menachem Gansburg — 647.409.6480
Rabbi Sholom Lezell — 416.809.1365
Rabbi Shmuel Neft — 647.966.7105
Rabbi Moshe Steiner — 416.635.9606

WATERLOO
Rabbi Moshe Goldman — 226.338.7770

WHITBY
Rabbi Tzali Borenstein — 905.447.8215

QUEBEC

CÔTE S.-LUC
Rabbi Levi Naparstek — 438.409.6770

DOLLARD-DES ORMEAUX
Rabbi Leibel Fine — 514.777.4675

HAMPSTEAD
Rabbi Moshe New
Rabbi Berel Bell
Mrs. Chanie Teitlebaum — 514.739.0770

MONTREAL
Rabbi Ronnie Fine
Pesach Nussbaum — 514.738.3434

MONTREAL WEST
Rabbi Mendy Marlow — 514.632.9649

OLD MONTREAL/GRIFFINTOWN
Rabbi Nissan Gansbourg
Rabbi Berel Bell — 514.800.6966

S. LAURENT
Rabbi Schneur Z. Silberstein — 514.747.1199

S. LAZARE
Rabbi Nochum Labkowski — 514.436.7426

TOWN OF MOUNT ROYAL
Rabbi Moshe Krasnanski
Rabbi Shneur Zalman Rader — 514.342.1770

SASKATCHEWAN

SASKATOON
Rabbi Raphael Kats　　306.384.4370

CAYMAN ISLANDS

GEORGE TOWN
Rabbi Berel Pewzner　　717.798.1040

COLOMBIA

BOGOTA
Rabbi Chanoch Piekarski　　57.1.635.8251

COSTA RICA

S. JOSÉ
Rabbi Hershel Spalter
Rabbi Moshe Bitton　　506.4010.1515

CROATIA

ZAGREB
Rabbi Pinchas Zaklas　　385.1.481.2227

DENMARK

COPENHAGEN
Rabbi Yitzchok Loewenthal　　45.3316.1850

DOMINICAN REPUBLIC

S. DOMINGO
Rabbi Shimon Pelman　　829.341.2770

ESTONIA

TALLINN
Rabbi Shmuel Kot　　372.662.30.50

FRANCE

BOULOGNE
Rabbi Michael Sojcher　　33.1.46.99.87.85

DIJON
Rabbi Chaim Slonim　　33.6.52.05.26.65

LA VARENNE-S.-HILAIRE
Rabbi Mena'hem Mendel
Benelbaz　　33.6.17.81.57.47

MARSEILLE
Rabbi Eliahou Altabe　　33.6.11.60.03.05
Rabbi Mena'hem Mendel
Assouline　　33.6.64.88.25.04
Rabbi Emmanuel
Taubenblatt　　33.4.88.00.94.85

PARIS
Rabbi Yona Hasky　　33.1.53.75.36.01
Rabbi Acher Marciano　　33.6.15.15.01.02
Rabbi Avraham Barou'h
Pevzner　　33.6.99.64.07.70

PONTAULT-COMBAULT
Rabbi Yossi Amar　　33.6.61.36.07.70

VILLIERS-SUR-MARNE
Rabbi Mena'hem M. Mergui　　33.1.49.30.89.66

GEORGIA

TBILISI
Rabbi Meir Kozlovsky　　995.32.2429770

GERMANY

BERLIN
Rabbi Yehuda Tiechtel　　49.30.2128.0830

DUSSELDORF
Rabbi Chaim Barkahn　　49.173.2871.770

HAMBURG
Rabbi Shlomo Bistritzky　　49.40.4142.4190

HANNOVER
　　49.511.811.2822
Chapter founded by Rabbi Binyamin Wolff, OBM

GREECE

ATHENS
Rabbi Mendel Hendel　　30.210.323.3825

GUATEMALA

GUATEMALA CITY
Rabbi Shalom Pelman　　502.2485.0770

HUNGARY

BUDAPEST
Rabbi Shlomo Kovesh　　361.268.0183

IRELAND

DUBLIN
Rabbi Zalman Lent　　3538.7419.5354

ISRAEL

ASHKELON
Rabbi Shneor Lieberman　　054.977.0512

BALFURYA
Rabbi Noam Bar-Tov　　054.580.4770

CAESAREA
Rabbi Chaim Meir Lieberman　　054.621.2586

EVEN YEHUDA
Rabbi Menachem Noyman　　054.777.0707

GANEI TIKVA
Rabbi Gershon Shnur　　054.524.2358

GIV'ATAYIM
Rabbi Pinchus Bitton　　052.643.8770

JERUSALEM
Rabbi Levi Diamond　　055.665.7702
Rabbi Avraham Hendel　　054.830.5799

KARMIEL
Rabbi Mendy Elishevitz　　054.521.3073

KFAR SABA
Rabbi Yossi Baitch　　054.445.5020

KIRYAT BIALIK
Rabbi Pinny Marton　　050.661.1768

KIRYAT MOTZKIN
Rabbi Shimon Eizenbach　　050.902.0770

KOCHAV YAIR
Rabbi Dovi Greenberg　　054.332.6244

MACCABIM-RE'UT
Rabbi Yosef Yitzchak Noiman 054.977.0549

NESS ZIONA
Rabbi Menachem Feldman 054.497.7092

NETANYA
Rabbi Schneur Brod 054.579.7572

RAMAT GAN-KRINITZI
Rabbi Yisroel Gurevitz 052.743.2814

RAMAT GAN-MAROM NAVE
Rabbi Binyamin Meir Kali 050.476.0770

RAMAT YISHAI
Rabbi Shneor Z. Wolosow 052.324.5475

RISHON LEZION
Rabbi Uri Keshet 050.722.4593

ROSH PINA
Rabbi Sholom Ber Hertzel 052.458.7600

TEL AVIV
Rabbi Shneur Piekarski 054.971.5568

JAMAICA

MONTEGO BAY
Rabbi Yaakov Raskin 876.452.3223

JAPAN

TOKYO
Rabbi Mendi Sudakevich 81.3.5789.2846

KAZAKHSTAN

ALMATY
Rabbi Shevach Zlatopolsky 7.7272.77.59.49

KYRGYZSTAN

BISHKEK
Rabbi Arye Raichman 996.312.68.19.66

LATVIA

RIGA
Rabbi Shneur Zalman Kot
Mrs. Rivka Glazman 371.6720.40.22

LITHUANIA

VILNIUS
Rabbi Sholom Ber Krinsky 370.6817.1367

LUXEMBOURG

LUXEMBOURG
Rabbi Mendel Edelman 352.2877.7079

MEXICO

PUERTO VALLARTA
Rabbi Shneur Hecht 52.32.2141.7279

S. MIGUEL DE ALLENDE
Rabbi Daniel Huebner 52.41.5181.8092

NETHERLANDS

ALMERE
Rabbi Moshe Stiefel 31.36.744.0509

AMSTERDAM
Rabbi Yanki Jacobs 31.644.988.627
Rabbi Jaacov Zwi Spiero 31.652.328.065

EINDHOVEN
Rabbi Simcha Steinberg 31.63.635.7593

HAGUE
Rabbi Shmuel Katzman 31.70.347.0222

HEEMSTEDE-HAARLEM
Rabbi Shmuel Spiero 31.23.532.0707

MAASTRICHT
Rabbi Avrohom Cohen 32.48.549.6766

NIJMEGEN
Rabbi Menachem M. Levine 31.621.586.575

ROTTERDAM
Rabbi Yehuda Vorst 31.10.265.5530

PANAMA

PANAMA CITY
Rabbi Ari Laine
Rabbi Gabriel Benayon 507.223.3383

RUSSIA

ASTRAKHAN
Rabbi Yisroel Melamed 7.851.239.28.24

BRYANSK
Rabbi Menachem M. Zaklas 7.483.264.55.15

CHELYABINSK
Rabbi Meir Kirsh 7.351.263.24.68

MOSCOW
Rabbi Aizik Rosenfeld 7.906.762.88.81
Rabbi Mordechai Weisberg 7.495.645.50.00

NIZHNY NOVGOROD
Rabbi Shimon Bergman 7.920.253.47.70

NOVOSIBIRSK
Rabbi Shneur Z. Zaklos 7.903.900.43.22

OMSK
Rabbi Osher Krichevsky 7.381.231.33.07

PERM
Rabbi Zalman Deutch 7.342.212.47.32

ROSTOV
Rabbi Chaim Danzinger 7.8632.99.02.68

S. PETERSBURG
Rabbi Shalom Pewzner 7.911.726.21.19
Rabbi Zvi Pinsky 7.812.713.62.09

SAMARA
Rabbi Shlomo Deutch 7.846.333.40.64

SARATOV
Rabbi Yaakov Kubitshek 7.8452.21.58.00

TOGLIATTI
Rabbi Meier Fischer 7.848.273.02.84

UFA
Rabbi Dan Krichevsky 7.347.244.55.33

VORONEZH
Rabbi Levi Stiefel 7.473.252.96.99

SINGAPORE

SINGAPORE
Rabbi Mordechai Abergel   656.337.2189
Rabbi Netanel Rivni   656.336.2127
Classes in Hebrew

SOUTH AFRICA

JOHANNESBURG
Rabbi Dovid Masinter
Rabbi Ari Kievman   27.11.440.6600

SWEDEN

STOCKHOLM
Rabbi Chaim Greisman   46.70.790.8994

SWITZERLAND

LUZERN
Rabbi Chaim Drukman   41.41.361.1770

ZURICH
Rabbi Mendel Rosenfeld   41.44.289.7050

THAILAND

BANGKOK
Rabbi Yosef C. Kantor   6681.837.7618

UKRAINE

BERDITCHEV
Mrs. Chana Thaler   380.637.70.37.70

DNEPROPETROVSK
Rabbi Dan Makagon   380.504.51.13.18

NIKOLAYEV
Rabbi Sholom Gotlieb   380.512.37.37.71

ODESSA
Rabbi Avraham Wolf
Rabbi Yaakov Neiman 38.048.728.0770 #280

ZAPOROZHYE
Mrs. Nechama Dina
Ehrentreu   380.957.19.96.08

ZHITOMIR
Rabbi Shlomo Wilhelm   380.504.63.01.32

UNITED KINGDOM

BOURNEMOUTH
Rabbi Bentzion Alperowitz   44.749.456.7177

CHEADLE
Rabbi Peretz Chein   44.161.428.1818

EPPING
Rabbi Yossi Posen   44.749.650.4345

LEEDS
Rabbi Eli Pink   44.113.266.3311

LONDON
Rabbi Moshe Adler   44.771.052.4460
Rabbi Boruch Altein   44.749.612.3342
Rabbi Mendel Cohen   44.736.640.8244
Rabbi Mechel Gancz   44.758.332.3074
Rabbi Chaim Hoch   44.753.879.9524
Rabbi Mendel Kalmenson   44.758.592.0195
Rabbi Dovid Katz   44.207.625.2682
Mrs. Esther Kesselman   44.794.432.4829
Rabbi Mendy Korer   44.794.632.5444
Rabbi Baruch Levin   44.208.905.4141
Rabbi Eli Levin   44.754.046.1568
Rabbi Yisroel Lew   44.787.987.1571
Mrs. Chanie Simon   44.208.458.0416
Rabbi Bentzi Sudak   44.781.211.1890
Rabbi Yisroel Weisz   44.797.652.2807
Rabbi Shneur Wineberg   44.745.628.6538

MANCHESTER
Rabbi Levi Cohen   44.161.792.6335
Rabbi Shmuli Jaffe   44.161.766.1812

NOTTINGHAM
Rabbi Mendy Lent   44.759.005.1261

RADLETT, HERTFORDSHIRE
Rabbi Alexander Sender
Dubrawsky   44.794.380.8965

The Jewish Learning Multiplex

Brought to you by the Rohr Jewish Learning Institute

In fulfillment of the mandate of the Lubavitcher Rebbe, of blessed memory, whose leadership guides every step of our work, the mission of the Rohr Jewish Learning Institute is to transform Jewish life and the greater community through the study of Torah, connecting each Jew to our shared heritage of Jewish learning.

While our flagship program remains the cornerstone of our organization, JLI is proud to feature additional divisions catering to specific populations, in order to meet a wide array of educational needs.

THE ROHR JEWISH LEARNING INSTITUTE

A subsidiary of Merkos L'Inyonei Chinuch,
the adult education arm of the Chabad-Lubavitch movement

Made in the USA
Columbia, SC
20 January 2025

Torah Studies provides a rich and nuanced encounter with the weekly Torah reading.

Jewish teens forge their identity as they engage in Torah study, social interaction, and serious fun.

The Rosh Chodesh Society gathers Jewish women together once a month for intensive textual study.

TorahCafe.com provides an exclusive selection of top-rated Jewish educational videos.

Participants delve into our nation's past while exploring the Holy Land's relevance and meaning today.

This yearly event rejuvenates mind, body, and spirit with a powerful synthesis of Jewish learning and community.

Equips youths facing adulthood with education and resources to address youth mental health

Select affiliates are invited to partner with peers and noted professionals, as leaders of innovation and excellence.

MyShiur courses are designed to assist students in developing the skills needed to study Talmud independently.

This rigorous fellowship program invites select college students to explore the fundamentals of Judaism.

A crash course that teaches adults to read Hebrew in just five sessions

Machon Shmuel is an institute providing Torah research in the service of educators worldwide.